Multimedia Security Using Chaos Theory and Secret Sharing Schemes

With the quick advancement of web technology and network applications, protecting digitized information from unwanted access and modification has become a critical problem in today's digital world. The security issue in electronic media has presented a complex challenge, initiating the development of cryptographic algorithms incorporating Chaos theory and secret sharing schemes. Chaos theory and secret sharing have been used to develop various multimedia application encryption strategies. Encryption converts multimedia data, i.e., images, audio, and videos, into noise-like data. The chaotic map characteristics, such as nonlinearity and sensitivity to the initial conditions, make it suitable for use in cryptography. At the same time, secret schemes can protect essential information against loss, modification, or destruction. Numerous techniques based on Chaos theory and secret sharing have been created to overcome these issues. These security techniques have become very popular for developing image and video cryptosystems. Also, the authors have developed chaotic map-based cryptosystems for other forms of multimedia data and other research fields such as IoT, cloud computing, smart grid, etc. Moreover, the authors have proposed different secret-sharing schemes to recognize and secure multimedia data based on their characteristics. Furthermore, some books have been edited by the authors, concentrating only on different methodologies proposed by the researchers. However, no authored book that discusses this important research topic from the viewpoint of chaotic map-based multimedia encryption is available in the market. To this end, the book aims to review and highlight the challenges of intelligent multimedia security and present the recent developments to address those challenges.

Multimedia Security Using Chaos Theory and Secret Sharing Schemes

Mohit Dua, Krishan Berwal, Ankit Kumar Jain,
Shelza Dua, and Deepti Dhingra

CRC Press
Taylor & Francis Group
Boca Raton London New York

CRC Press is an imprint of the
Taylor & Francis Group, an **informa** business

First edition published 2027
by CRC Press

2385 NW Executive Center Drive, Suite 320, Boca Raton FL 33431

and by CRC Press
4 Park Square, Milton Park, Abingdon, Oxon, OX14 4RN

CRC Press is an imprint of Taylor & Francis Group, LLC

ISBN: 9781032802442 (hbk)
ISBN: 9781032816722 (pbk)
ISBN: 9781003500841 (ebk)

DOI: 10.1201/9781003500841

Typeset in Caslon
by Deanta Global Publishing Services, Chennai, India

Contents

About the Authors		vii
Foreword		x
Preface		xii
Chapter 1	Introduction	1
	1.1 Background	1
	1.2 Definition	2
	1.3 History	4
	1.4 Classification	5
	1.5 Book Organization	13
	References	15
Chapter 2	Chaos Theory	17
	2.1 Overview of Chaos Theory	17
	2.2 Properties and Applications of Chaos	18
	2.3 Chaos and Cryptography	21
	2.4 Application of Chaos Theory in Cryptography	22
	2.5 Chaos Map and Types	24
	2.6 Chaos System Analysis	38
	2.7 Conclusion	44
	References	45
Chapter 3	Secret Sharing Schemes	47
	3.1 Introduction to Secret Sharing Scheme	47
	3.2 Challenges of Secret Sharing Scheme	54
	3.3 Mathematics Background of Secret Schemes	55
	3.5 Characteristics of Secret Sharing Schemes	64
	References	65
Chapter 4	Text Encryption	69
	4.1 Introduction to Text Encryption	69
	4.2 Traditional Cryptographic-Based Text Encryption Methods	71
	4.3 Secret Sharing Scheme-Based Text Encryption Algorithms	75
	4.4 Chaotic Maps-Based Text Encryption Algorithms	87
	References	87
Chapter 5	Image Encryption	90
	5.1 Introduction	90
	5.2 Need for Image Encryption	92
	5.3 Image Encryption Using Chaos Theory	94

5.4 Secret Sharing Schemes-Based Encryption of an Image 98
5.5 Performance Analysis 100
Decryption Parameters 105
References 107

Chapter 6 Audio Encryption Strategy 109
6.1 Introduction to the Audio and Its Encryption 109
6.2 Need for Audio Encryption 113
6.3 Role of Audio Encryption in the Digital Era 121
6.4 Audio Encryption Using Chaos Theory 124
6.5 Audio Encryption Performance Metrics 127
6.6 Audio Decryption Performance Metrics 132
6.7 Applications of Audio Encryption 135
References 137

Chapter 7 Video Encryption Strategy 139
7.1 Introduction to Video and Video Summarization 139
7.2 Video Encryption Using Chaos Theory 145
7.3 Use Secret Sharing Schemes to Protect Video 147
7.4 Evaluation of the Video Encryption Methods' Performance 153
References 164

Chapter 8 Recent Trends, Challenges, and Open Issues 167
8.1 Recent Trends in Audio, Video, and Image Security 167
8.2 Open Issues and Challenges 175
References 178

Chapter 9 Implementation and Adoptability of the Multimedia Encryption Strategies Using Python 180
9.1 Platforms Supporting Implementation 180
9.2 Python Libraries for Chaotic Map-Based Encryption 181
9.3 Installation of Libraries 181
9.4 Python Implementation Code 182
References 193

About the Authors

Mohit Dua: He received a PhD in the area of Automatic Speech Recognition from the National Institute of Technology, Kurukshetra, India, in 2018. He is presently working as Assistant Professor in the Department of Computer Engineering at NIT Kurukshetra, India. He has more than 20 years of teaching and research experience. He is a member of the Institute of Electrical and Electronics Engineers (IEEE) and a life member of the Computer Society of India (CSI) and the Indian Society for Technical Education (ISTE). His research interests include speech processing, chaos-based cryptography, information security, theory of formal languages, statistical modeling, and natural language processing. He has published approximately 150 research papers, including presentations at international conferences in the USA, Canada, Australia, Singapore, Mauritius, and Dubai.

Krishan Berwal: He is Associate Professor at the Military College of Telecommunication Engineering, Ministry of Defence, GoI, where he serves as Associate Dean (Synergy & Outreach), spearheading strategic collaborations with national agencies including MeitY, C-DAC, SAMEER, IITs, IIITs, NITs, and NIELIT. Prior to this assignment, he served for over a decade at National Institutes of Technology under the Ministry of Education, holding key leadership roles such as Head of Department, Placement Coordinator, and Chairman of the Institute Perception Committee, among other academic and administrative responsibilities. He is a member of the National Cyber Security Division Working Group and Program Review & Steering Group (PRSG) for multiple R&D initiatives under MeitY, contributing to the national research strategy in cybersecurity, AI, and secure communications. Dr Berwal has led and executed several high-value defense and government-funded projects, including an iDEX-supported ₹13 crore innovation program for the Indian Army, and has submitted multidisciplinary proposals exceeding ₹100 crore in collaboration with premier institutions. With over 130 research publications, 2,500+ citations, and recognition among the world's Top 2% Scientists by Stanford University, he combines academic excellence with translational defense research, making significant contributions to secure systems, cyber forensics, video processing, multimedia security, and intelligent technologies.

Ankit Kumar Jain: He is working as Assistant Professor at the National Institute of Technology, Kurukshetra, India, where he has been serving since 2013. Dr Jain earned his PhD from the National Institute of Technology, Kurukshetra, with a specialization in Information and Cyber Security. He has published more than 100 research papers in reputed international journals and conferences, including those published by Elsevier, Springer, Taylor & Francis, Inderscience, and IEEE. His research interests include Information and Cyber Security, Phishing Website Detection, Web Security, Mobile Security, IoT Security, Online Social Networks, and Machine Learning. His research work has received over 5,000 citations, with an h-index of 34 and an i10-index of 50. Currently, he is serving as the Coordinator of the M.Tech. program in Cyber Security at NIT Kurukshetra.

Shelza Dua: She received a PhD in the area of Image Encryption from Banasthali Vidyapith, Banasthali, Rajasthan, India, in 2019. She is presently working as a Research Associate in the Department of Electrical Engineering at NIT Kurukshetra, India. She has more than 20 years of Teaching and Research experience. She is a life member of IETE. Her research interests include chaos-based Cryptography and Image Encryption. She has published approximately 30 research papers in various reputed journals and international conferences.

Deepti Dhingra: She received a PhD in the area of Multimedia Encryption from the National Institute of Technology Kurukshetra,

India, in 2025. She is presently working as Assistant Professor in Computer Science and Engineering at the Panipat Institute of Engineering and Technology, Samalkha, Haryana. She has more than 12 years of Teaching and Research experience. Her research interests include chaos-based cryptography and image encryption. She has published approximately 20 research papers in various reputed journals and international conferences.

Foreword

With the rapid growth of digital communication, multimedia content such as images, audio, and videos has become an integral part of modern information exchange. However, this widespread use of multimedia content poses security threats such as unauthorized access, piracy, data tampering, and privacy breaches. Research in multimedia security revolved around traditional cryptographic methods for many years. However, over the last few decades, with advancements in attack technologies, the use of traditional cryptographic practices to secure multimedia data is no longer advisable. Asdevice sizes are shrinking and communication between devices is growing, advanced and lightweight cryptosystems are the need of the hour.

Chaotic map-based cryptography and secret sharing scheme methodsin the last few decades, have shown great potential and developed interest among researchers to handle the security of multimedia data. A book on this important topic has arrived at the opportune time. To date, the literature on the topic has been fragmented and distributed among articles, reviews, and conference proceedings. Hence, there was an urgent requirement for one such book that can help upcoming researchers to work in this crucial field. I hope the book's distinctive features, such as coverage of the latest concepts in intelligent multimedia for securing image data, presentation of the applications of intelligent multimedia for the security of textual data, and review of the latest research topics in the field of chaotic map-based video encryption, will not only make this book an academic contribution but also make it a tool to enable future research.

Professor Mahesh Chandra Govil

Director, National Institute of Technology, Sikkim, India

Preface

Traditional cryptographic techniques, while effective for textual data, often struggle to meet the requirements of multimedia content due to their large size, high redundancy, and strong pixel-level correlation. This has created an urgent need for advanced and adaptive multimedia security solutions.

Multimedia Security Using Chaos Theory and Secret Sharing Schemes provides a comprehensive and systematic exploration of two powerful and complementary security paradigms. Chaos theory, with its properties of sensitivity to initial conditions, randomness, and ergodicity, offers an excellent foundation for designing robust encryption algorithms. Secret sharing schemes, on the other hand, enable the secure distribution and storage of sensitive multimedia content by dividing it into multiple shares, ensuring that the original data can be reconstructed only when authorized participants collaborate.

This book bridges theoretical foundations and practical implementations by explaining chaotic maps, hybrid chaotic systems, and permutation–diffusion architectures. It also explores various secret sharing models, including threshold schemes and visual secret sharing. Evaluation parameters such as NPCR, UACI, entropy, correlation analysis, PSNR, and computational complexity are discussed to assess security strength and performance. By combining chaos-based encryption with secret sharing strategies, it presents modern, resilient, and scalable approaches to multimedia security. The book also discusses current challenges, emerging trends, and open research issues, making it a valuable resource for those working in cryptography, information security, and multimedia systems.

This book is written in a comprehensive and simple manner and is designed for researchers, postgraduate students, academicians, and professionals. The text is accompanied by tables and illustrative figures for a better understanding of the topic. We hope this book will serve as both a reference and a learning guide.

1
Introduction

1.1 Background

The advancement in digital technologies and communication networks has led to an increase in the creation, storage, and transmission of multimedia data. The multimedia data (image, audio, or video) is widely shared and posted on social platforms, YouTube, surveillance, OTT platforms, virtual meetings, video calls, and conferences, among many others. Multimedia data takes a lot of time and space to be securely communicated and processed, decreasing the system's performance. Multimedia analysis covers many disciplines, including multimedia summarization, annotation, retrieval, security, event detection, object tracking, etc. This has generated new challenges related to the creation, transmission, processing, computation, or protection of multimedia data services, digital content, and applications. The security and secrecy of multimedia information is a natural concern in the current digital scenario. Ensuring multimedia security signifies the safeguarding of multimedia services and content. Unauthorized access and privacy breaches have made multimedia security a critical area of research in the field of information security and cryptography.

Traditional security mechanisms are not suitable for multimedia data. Huge size and correlation of multimedia data demand security approaches that can provide confidentiality, integrity, and robustness. Cryptography protects the confidentiality of multimedia content by transforming it into a noise-like form that is unrecognizable. Cryptographic algorithms ensure that only authorized users with the correct secret keys can access the original data. Although traditional cryptographic methods provide strong security, they may be computationally intensive for large multimedia files. This limitation has

DOI: 10.1201/9781003500841-1

motivated researchers to develop encryption schemes that are highly secure, such as chaos-based cryptographic approaches. Advanced Encryption Standard (AES) and (RSA (Rivest-Shamir-Adleman) are highly secure for text data but may not be optimal for multimedia applications [1]. To address these limitations, researchers have explored alternative approaches such as chaos theory and secret sharing schemes due to their intrinsic properties.

Digital watermarking is another famous technique to protect multimedia data. It focuses on protecting the ownership and authenticity of multimedia content rather than concealing its content. Additional information, such as copyright details or authentication codes, is embedded into the multimedia data that plays a crucial role in copyright protection and digital rights management [2]. Steganography means hiding confidential information inside another normal-looking file. Instead of locking the message (like cryptography), steganography hides its existence [3].

Chaos theory, a branch of nonlinear dynamics, is highly unpredictable and sensitive to initial conditions [4]. These properties closely resemble the fundamental requirements of cryptographic systems. Confusion and diffusion add randomness to the multimedia data [5, 6]. Therefore, chaotic map-based techniques have been widely adopted in multimedia encryption [7]. These maps are frequently used to generate encryption keys, permutation sequences, and diffusion mechanisms to enhance security while maintaining computational efficiency.

In addition to chaos-based approaches, secret sharing schemes protect sensitive information by dividing a secret (the confidential information) into multiple parts (called shares) to prevent unauthorized access. These shares individually can't reveal any information and thereby ensure confidentiality. The integration of chaos theory with secret sharing schemes offers a promising framework for advanced multimedia security systems. Chaos-based mechanisms enhance the randomness and unpredictability, while secret sharing provides robustness against partial data loss.

1.2 Definition

With the quick advancement of information and communication technology (ICT), the generation and transmission of digital data have increased exponentially. This expansion has increased the chances of security threats. Therefore, the protection of data to maintain confidentiality and integrity is crucial. Multimedia security is defined as the protection of multimedia data such as images, audio, and video from unauthorized access. Advanced computational and mathematical techniques are used to prevent data manipulation and misuse by eavesdroppers. Preserving data quality and maintaining system efficiency are also among the key responsibilities of security mechanisms.

Multimedia security using chaos theory integrates properties of chaotic systems to develop robust security mechanisms. Chaotic maps are the functions that contribute strong randomness, sensitivity to initial conditions, and complex dynamic behavior. They produce values that can be exploited to design efficient encryption algorithms. Permutation and diffusion are the fundamental operations of chaos-based encryption mechanisms. The permutation operation, also known as scrambling, rearranges the positions of multimedia data elements. In the case of images, permutation changes the spatial positions of pixels; for audio and video data, it reorders samples or frames. The primary objective of permutation is to destroy the strong correlation among neighboring pixels or samples in the data. Permutation is typically controlled by sequences generated from chaotic maps. These chaotic sequences produce pseudorandom index values that determine the new positions of pixels or samples. Even a minute change in the control parameters or initial values results in a completely different permutation pattern. The permutation process provides the first layer of security for multimedia data by disrupting the spatial correlation among data elements, thereby resisting statistical and visual attacks. Subsequently, the diffusion operation alters the actual values of multimedia data elements, ensuring that slight changes in the input produce significant changes in the encrypted output, thereby further enhancing the overall security of the encryption scheme. In images, diffusion alters pixel intensity values; in audio and video, it changes sample amplitudes or signal values. The goal of diffusion is to spread the influence of a single data element over many others. In chaos-based systems, diffusion is achieved by combining multimedia data with chaotic sequences using mathematical operations such as addition, subtraction, exclusive-OR (XOR), or modular arithmetic. An effective diffusion mechanism ensures that even a one-bit change in the plaintext multimedia data results in a drastically different ciphertext. This property is crucial for achieving high security levels and preventing attackers from exploiting statistical similarities between the original and encrypted data. Permutation and diffusion are typically applied in successive or iterative rounds to maximize security.

Secret sharing schemes (SSS) provide security by dividing the confidential information, also referred to as secret, into multiple parts called shares [8]. Individual shares can't reveal any information about the secret [9].

SSS are valuable in distributed and cloud-based environments. These are decentralized environments where security depends on collaboration among multiple entities. By ensuring that no single share discloses sensitive information, secret sharing schemes provide robustness and protection of multimedia data against unauthorized access and partial disclosure attacks.

1.3 History

The development of multimedia security has evolved gradually as a response to changes in communication methods and the growing need for information protection. The earliest roots of multimedia security can be traced back to the history of cryptography. In 1990 BCE, scribes of the kings in Egypt transmitted secret messages using hieroglyphs. Ancient Greeks used the Caesar cipher, which is a substitution technique that replaces each character by a fixed number of positions. The Vigenère cipher was designed in the 16th century, in which the encryption key is repeated to encrypt the entire message using modulo 26 operators. The Data Encryption Standard (DES) is a symmetric key algorithm having a key size of 56 bits. It was discontinued as it had a small key size and was broken by attacks. In 1997, the Advanced Encryption Standard (AES) encryption technique was designed. Its key sizes are 128 bits, 192 bits, and 256 bits [10, 11]. IDEA is the famous cryptographic algorithm introduced in 1990, which uses algebraic operations for data encryption. Mostly, it is used for the encryption of text or binary data. It has a 128-bit secret key, and it can encrypt a 64-bit data block size. IDEA encryption is secure but slower than DES.

RSA is used for public-key encryption and digital signatures. It was first described in 1977. It uses key length (usually of 512 bits) and plaintext block size, which are variable in nature.

The growing demand for copyright protection, in 1993, Tirkel et al. [9] focused on embedding information into digital images. In 1995, Cox et al. introduced a robust watermarking technique in the frequency domain to provide resistance against common signal processing attacks. In 1996, Johnson and Jajodia formalized digital steganography techniques that were primarily focused on Least Significant Bit (LSB) embedding.

Chaos theory was introduced by Edward N. Lorenz in 1963 through his discovery of deterministic chaos while studying weather systems. In 1998, Fridrich proposed one of the earliest chaos-based image encryption schemes using chaotic maps for permutation and diffusion. Secret sharing schemes were first formally introduced by Adi Shamir in 1979, known as Shamir's (t, n) threshold secret sharing scheme.

1.4 Classification

Figure 1.1 illustrates the classification of multimedia security based on its operations. Multimedia security is classified as traditional cryptographic-based methods, watermarking-based techniques, steganography-based techniques, advanced security techniques, and hybrid technologies. Advanced security techniques are further categorized as chaotic map-based encryption methods and secret sharing schemes.

1.4.1 Traditional Cryptography-Based Techniques

Classical cryptography, such as the Caesar cipher and Vigenère cipher methods, is based on substitution and transposition. Substitution means replacing the data, and transposition means rearranging their

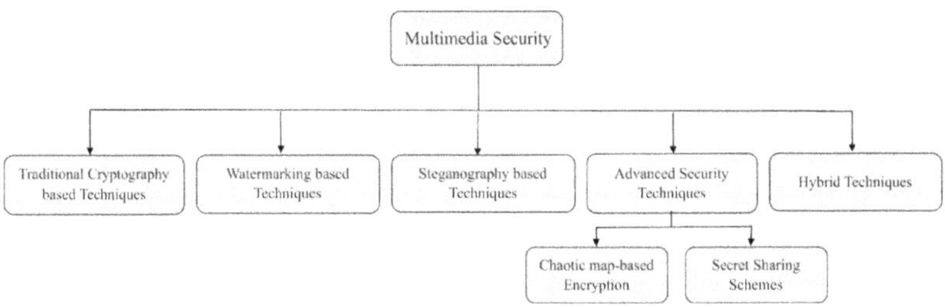

Figure 1.1 Categorization of multimedia security.

order. These are the foundations of modern cryptography but are vulnerable to cryptanalysis. A large volume of multimedia data is shared over the internet due to the advancement of technology. Malicious individuals have found a way to intercept the important information that is being transmitted across the network. Therefore, the encryption method of cryptography that changes the data into an unrecognizable format is very important. The original data, either in the form of audio, video, or image, is converted into a noise-like structure using the key at the sender's side. And at the receiver's side, the same noise-like structure is decoded using the key. The original data is called the plain text (plain image/video), and the encrypted data is called the cipher text (cipher image/video). Figure 1.2 represents encryption and decryption of an image. Only the authorized individuals possessing the secret key can decrypt and thereafter access the contents.

There are two categories of traditional encryption methods: symmetric key encryption algorithms (that use the same key for encryption and decryption) and asymmetric key encryption [11] (that uses different keys for encryption and decryption). Block ciphers and stream ciphers are types of symmetric key encryption algorithms. One bit or one byte of the input data is encrypted at a time by a stream cipher. These are some examples of stream cipher algorithms: RC4, ISAAC, FISH, and SEAL. One block of plain text can be converted into another block of ciphertext using a block cipher. A block has a size of either 64 or 128 bits. Some examples of block ciphers are DES, AES, RC6, and IDEA. In asymmetric encryption, the data is encrypted and decrypted using two distinct keys, referred to as the public key and private key. To encrypt data, the sender uses the recipient's public key; to decode data, the recipient uses its private key. Asymmetric key encryption algorithms include Diffie-Hellman,

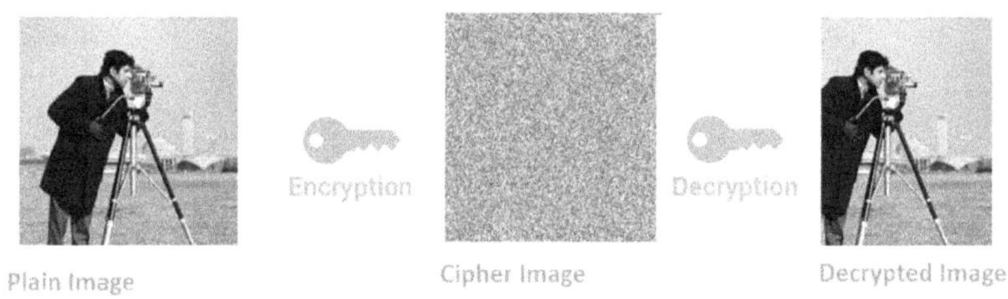

Figure 1.2 Encryption and decryption of an image.

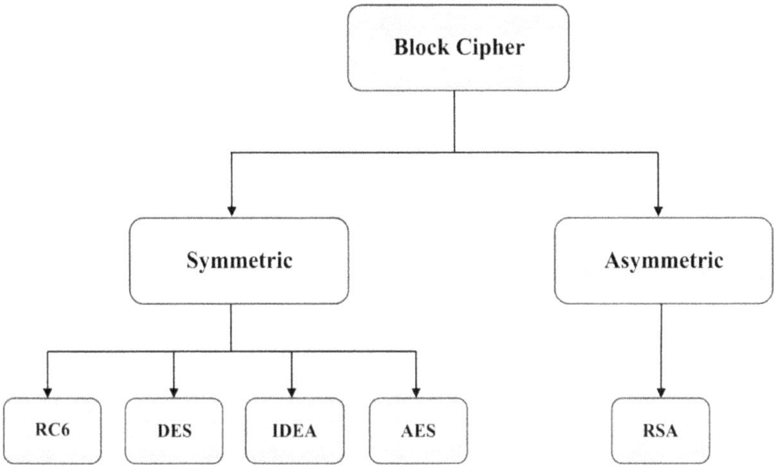

Figure 1.3 Block cipher encryption algorithms.

RSA, and Elliptic Curve Cryptography (ECC). Figure 1.3 represents the block cipher algorithms.

1.4.2 Watermarking-Based Techniques

Digital watermarking is a process of embedding information about the data into multimedia data, such as audio, video, or image, to identify the ownership. The embedded data do not make any changes to the host data. Watermarking is defined by its embedding function, extraction function, and confidence level [12]. The embedding function determines the information to be embedded; the extraction function is responsible for retrieving the watermark. Digital watermarking is of two types: visible and invisible. Visible watermarking is the method in which embedded watermarks in the form of text or images can be clearly seen to identify the ownership. On the other hand, in invisible watermarking, embedded information can be seen by the human visual system. Digital watermarking techniques can be categorized as Spatial Domain, Frequency Domain, and Spread Spectrum, as shown in Figure 1.4. In the Spatial domain, the value of the pixels in the original image/video is altered; for example, changing the least significant bit. These methods are simple and fast, but they lack robustness. The watermarks are embedded in transform coefficients of an image, such as discrete cosine coefficients, wavelet

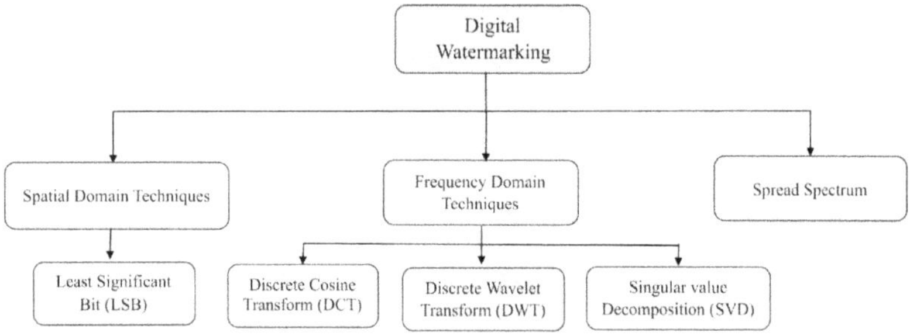

Figure 1.4 Categorization of digital watermarking techniques.

coefficients, and singular values in frequency domain watermarking techniques. These methods provide better robustness than the spatial domain watermarking techniques. Another approach to embed the watermark is to spread it across the entire frequency domain, which is more robust than all the methods.

1.4.3 Steganography-Based Techniques

The process of hiding or embedding confidential information inside a predefined cover file of any type (image/video/audio). Except for the receiver and sender, no one can guess the hidden secret information. The steganography process is described in Figure 1.5. The secret message and a cover image are fed into a steganography encoder, which hides the secret message in the cover image by embedding it. The

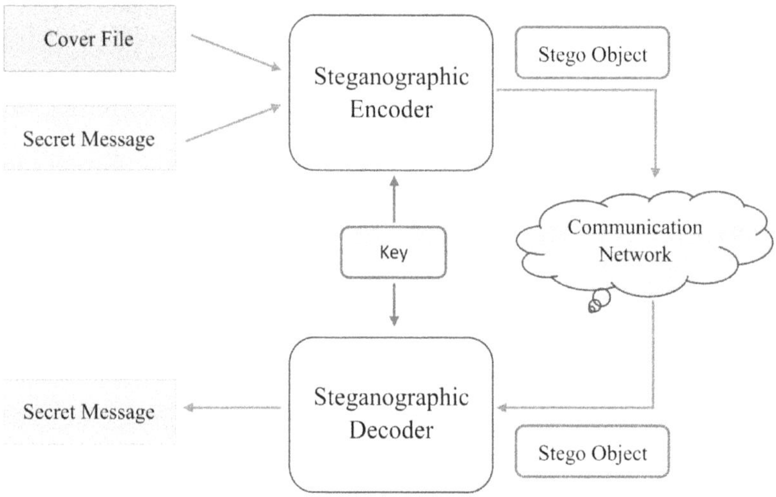

Figure 1.5 Steganography process.

output of the steganography encoder is referred to as the stego object. The stego object is the embedded hidden message in the cover image. The stego object is transmitted across the network. Therefore, the secret message is kept hidden and is not visible to intruders. At the receiver end, the steganography decoder extracts the secret message from the stego object using the appropriate key.

1.4.4 Chaotic Map-Based Encryption

Chaos theory also finds its applications in cryptography research as it has the ability to produce the deterministic pseudo-haphazardness required in cryptography. The main idea behind every encryption system is pseudorandom sequence generation and random mixing. A chaotic function is similar in behavior to a noise function; however, unlike noise, it is deterministic in nature, i.e., initial values and necessary parameters can reproduce it.

Commonly, all chaotic map-based encryption schemes have a common architecture as shown in Figure 1.6. The input to the algorithm

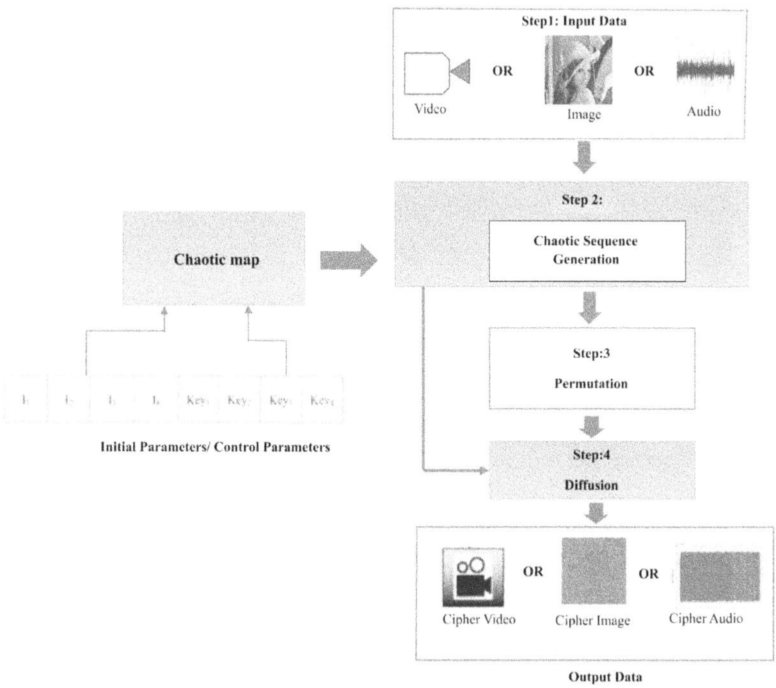

Figure 1.6 Architecture of chaotic map-based encryption.

may be any type of data, such as video, image, or audio, depending upon the requirements. The algorithm will process the data accordingly. The chaotic map function is responsible for generating some random chaotic values that can be used as a pseudorandom sequence or key. The pseudorandom sequence or key will be used to change the position of pixels in the permutation stage [13]. In the next stage referred to as the diffusion phase, the value of pixels is modified by applying various operations using the same chaotic sequence. Depending upon the type of data, we can categorize chaotic map-based encryption algorithms into chaotic map-based video encryption, chaotic map-based image encryption, and chaotic map-based audio encryption, as shown in Figure 1.7. Video encryption algorithms can be broadly divided into two types depending upon the way of encrypting the data: full encryption and selective encryption. In full encryption, the complete video stream is encrypted directly by the encryption algorithm. Full encryption algorithms offer robust security but take high processing time. They find application in critical areas like the military and medical fields. Selective encryption is the method to encrypt only a subset of video streams [14]. The main goal of selective encryption is to reduce the computational complexity and select a significant part of the video to encrypt.

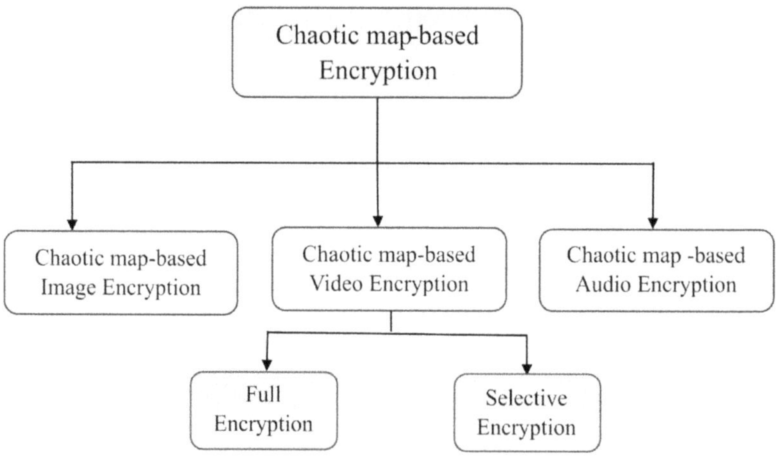

Figure 1.7 Chaotic map-based encryption classification.

1.4.5 Secret Sharing Schemes

Secret sharing schemes are cryptographic strategies utilized to spread a secret among multiple participants so that only a predefined number of them can reconstruct it. These schemes play a crucial role in secure data storage, secure multiparty computation, and access control systems. Secret sharing schemes are classified into different threshold structures, where the total number of participants is the lowest number required to reconstruct the secret. Figure 1.8 shows the classification of a secret sharing scheme.

(n, n)—All-or-Nothing Secret Sharing: In this scheme, all n participants are required to reconstruct the secret. No subset with fewer than **n** participants can gain any information about the secret, ensuring perfect secrecy. This approach is highly secure, as even $\mathbf{n}-1$ participants cannot retrieve any partial information about the secret. One of the earliest examples of such a scheme is Blakley's secret sharing scheme [5], which is a geometric-based approach. In Blakley's scheme, the secret is represented as a point in an n-dimensional space, and each participant receives a hyperplane that intersects at the secret point. The secret can only be reconstructed when all participants combine their shares to determine the unique intersection point. Unlike Shamir's polynomial-based scheme, Blakley's method relies on linear algebra principles, making it an alternative approach to secret sharing with strong security guarantees.

(2, n)—Two-out-of-N Secret Sharing: In this scheme, any two participants out of the n total participants can reconstruct the secret. This is a special case of (t,n) threshold secret sharing schemes, where the threshold value is set to $t=2$. The scheme ensures that any single

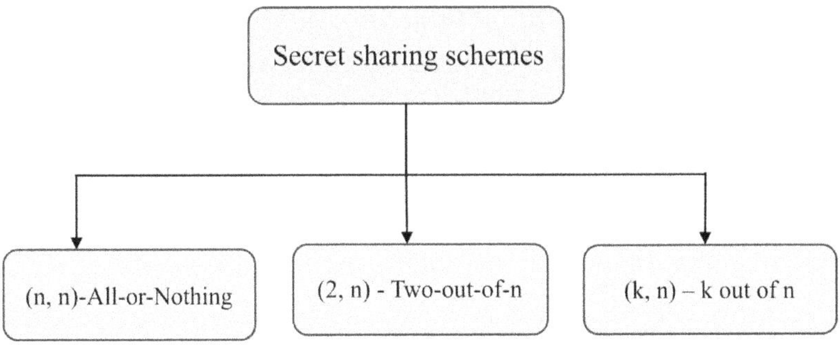

Figure 1.8 Secret sharing schemes classification.

participant alone cannot obtain any information about the secret, preserving its confidentiality. A well-known example of this approach is Shamir's secret sharing scheme [4] with $t = 2$. In Shamir's scheme, the secret is encoded using a polynomial of degree $t - 1$, meaning that for $t = 2$, a linear polynomial of the form: $\left(x\right) = a$ is used, where $a + a$ represents the secret and ax is a randomly chosen coefficient. Each participant receives a share of the secret based on their assigned value of x. Since two points uniquely determine a line, any two participants can reconstruct the polynomial and retrieve the secret. However, any single participant alone has no way to determine without another share, ensuring the scheme's security.

(k, n)—Threshold Secret Sharing: Any k number of n participants can reconstruct the secret. If fewer than k shares are available, the secret remains completely hidden, ensuring perfect security against partial knowledge. Threshold secret sharing is widely used in cryptographic protocols, secure multiparty computation, and distributed key management.

1.4.6 Hybrid Techniques

Due to the explosive growth of data, it is essential to develop a strong protection mechanism. Hybrid techniques combine two or more security approaches to provide robustness in security systems. These hybrid methods overcome the limitations of individual approaches. Many researchers have worked on integrating one or more approaches together to design security approaches, such as in [15], where the author combined the logistic map with the watermarking method to develop a security solution. The approach of alpha blending was used in which the watermark image was embedded in the Y component of YCbCr color space. The scheme also achieves a high value of evaluation parameters. Mohamed et al. [2] proposed a method by combining a chaotic map-based approach with watermarking to design a hybrid cryptosystem. The method used PN-codes embedding strategy to embed the watermark, and four different dimensions of chaotic maps (1D, 2D, 3D logistic map, and 2D Henon map) were used to implement permutation and diffusion steps. The method achieves a high value of peak-signal-to-noise ratio (PSNR). Razzaq et al. [16] blended the three technologies: encryption, steganography, and watermarking. Firstly, an XOR operation was applied to the input image, and then a stego image was obtained by changing the least significant bit of the encrypted image. The stego image was finally watermarked in the time and frequency domains. The scheme was highly secure against various attacks. Zainal et al. [17] combined the steganography and watermarking methods. The approach used two images; the first image was used as a cover image and the second image was the hidden image. During the embedding, discrete cosine transform (DCT) components of the cover image were transformed to Discrete Wavelet Transform (DWT) components. The hidden image was encoded using One-Time Pad (OTP) followed by the Playfair algorithm. The security of the approach was also evaluated by the authors using various parameters.

1.5 Book Organization

The book *Multimedia Security Using Chaos Theory and Secret Sharing Schemes* provides structured and comprehensive details of multimedia security approaches. All the pieces of information on theoretical foundations, implementation, mathematical models, and conceptual details related to multimedia security techniques are provided in the book.

The book is structured in nine chapters, and a brief description of all the chapters is as follows:

- **Chapter 1**: The "Introduction" chapter highlights the need for multimedia security, followed by introducing the key concepts related to security. It defines all the terms related to multimedia security, cryptography, chaos theory, and secret sharing schemes. The evolution of various multimedia security techniques is also provided in the chapter. Multimedia security approaches are classified into various categories in this chapter to provide a deeper understanding of the different types of security techniques.
- **Chapter 2**: The second chapter, "Chaos Theory," introduces chaotic systems and their applications in cryptography. It provides details about all types of chaotic maps by classifying

them into transformed, multidimensional, and hybrid chaotic maps. Additionally, parameters to evaluate the sensitivity, randomness, and unpredictability, such as bifurcation diagrams, Lyapunov exponents, and entropy measures (Shannon entropy, sample entropy), are also explained in the chapter.

- **Chapter 3**: The third chapter, "Secret Sharing Scheme," introduces the principles of secret sharing schemes and explores their mathematical background. The chapter categorizes secret sharing techniques into various types, such as multilayered secret sharing scheme and threshold cryptography to provide deep insight about them. The advantages and challenges of secret sharing schemes are also explored in the chapter.
- **Chapter 4**: The fourth chapter, "Text Encryption," discusses the importance of text encryption. The chapter explains various text encryption techniques based on secret sharing schemes. The performance analysis of all the text encryption approaches is also provided in the chapter.
- **Chapter 5**: The fifth chapter, "Image Encryption," provides the basic concepts, needs, and details of various image encryption techniques. It explores the architecture of chaotic map-based image encryption schemes. The chapter also classifies chaotic map-based image encryption schemes into four types: only chaos-based confusion-diffusion, Chaos combined with AES, Chaos integrated with DNA computing approach, and Chaos integrated with cellular automata. A description of image encryption evaluation parameters is also provided in the chapter.
- **Chapter 6**: The sixth chapter, "Audio Encryption Strategy," introduces audio and audio encryption. The chapter highlights the need for audio encryption. The chapter covers all types of audio encryption strategies. Chaotic map-based audio encryption is explored in detail by classifying it into various types. Audio encryption evaluation parameters are also provided in the chapter.
- **Chapter 7**: The seventh chapter, "Video Encryption Strategy," explains the key concepts involved in video encryption and video summarization. The architecture and types of video encryption are provided in the chapter. Video summarization

techniques, along with the applications of chaos theory in video encryption, are provided in the chapter. Details about video security using various secret sharing schemes are also provided in the chapter. Various video encryption performance metrics are also provided in the chapter.

- **Chapter 8**: The eighth chapter is "Recent Trends, Challenges, and Open Issues." This chapter provides insight into the latest advancements in multimedia security. The chapter also discusses challenges in the field of multimedia security to encourage researchers to explore the area.
- **Chapter 9**: The last chapter, "Implementation and Adoptability of Multimedia Encryption Strategies using Python," presents various details required to implement multimedia security such as supported platforms, libraries, and installation process of various packages. The chapter also provides the pseudocode to implement chaotic maps, chaotic sequence evaluation parameters, image, and video encryption using Python. This will benefit the researchers to innovate new advancements in the field.

The book aims to benefit researchers, academicians, cybersecurity professionals, and students interested in the field of multimedia security. It not only provides theoretical insights but also emphasizes real-world applications and practical implementations. The readers will get a deep understanding of multimedia security using chaos theory and secret sharing schemes.

References

1. Sahari, M. L., & Boukemara, I. (2018). A pseudo-random numbers generator based on a novel 3D chaotic map with an application to color image encryption. *Nonlinear Dynamics*, *94*, 723–744. https://doi.org/10.1007/s11071-018-4390-z.
2. Mohamed, M. A., Abdel-Atty, H. M., & Abdel-Fattah, M. G. (2015). Hybrid watermarking scheme for copyright protection using chaotic maps cryptography. *International Journal of Computer Applications, 126*, 0975–8887.
3. Xiang, X., Tan, Y., Qin, J., & Tan, Y. (2025). Advancements and challenges in coverless image steganography: A survey. *Signal Processing, 228*, 109761. https://doi.org/10.1016/j.sigpro.2024.109761.

4. Patro, K., Acharya, B., & Nath, V. (2019). Secure multilevel permutation-diffusion based image encryption using chaotic and hyper-chaotic maps. *Microsystem Technologies, 25*, 4593–4607.
5. Gao, X. (2021). Image encryption algorithm based on 2D hyperchaotic map. *Optics and Laser Technology, 142*, 107252. https://doi.org/10.1016/j.optlastec.2021.107252.
6. Dhingra, D., & Dua, M. (2023). *A Chaos-based Novel Approach to Video Encryption Using Dynamic S-box*. Springer. https://doi.org/10.1007/s11042-023-15593-6.
7. Dhingra, D., & Dua, M. (2023). A novel Sine–Tangent–Sine chaotic map and dynamic S-box-based video encryption scheme. *Imaging Science Journal*, 1–24. https://doi.org/10.1080/13682199.2023.2187513.
8. Schemes, D. S., & Chaudhury, S. S. (2025). Construction of quantum anamorphic evolving. *IEEE Transactions on Communications, 73*, 11753–11768. https://doi.org/10.1109/TCOMM.2025.3587045.
9. Tirkel, A., Rankin, G., van Schyndel, R., & Mee, N. (1993). Electronic watermark. In *The Proceedings of Digital Image Computing Technology and Applications* (pp. 666–673). Sydney, Australia.
10. Kadam, K. S., & Deshmukh, A. (2016). Video frame encryption algorithm using AES. *International Journal of Engineering Research, 5*, 588–591. https://doi.org/10.17577/ijertv5is060670.
11. Deshmukh, P., & Kolhe, V. (2014). Modified AES based algorithm for MPEG video encryption. In *IEEE Conference on Information Communication Embedded Systems* (pp. 1–5).
12. Hu, X., & Zhang, X. I. (2026). A survey of text watermarking in the era of large language models. *ACM Computing Surveys, 57*. https://doi.org/10.1145/3691626.
13. Maolood, A. T., Gbashi, E. K., & Mahmood, E. S. (2022). Novel lightweight video encryption method based on ChaCha20 stream cipher and hybrid chaotic map. *International Journal of Electrical and Computer Engineering, 12*, 4988–5000.
14. Kumari, S., Dua, M., Dua, S., & Dhingra, D. (2024). A novel Cosine-Cosine chaotic map-based video encryption scheme. *Journal of Engineering and Applied Science, 71*, 36.
15. Dong, Y., Yan, R., & Yin, C. (2024). An adaptive robust watermarking scheme based on chaotic mapping. *Scientific Reports, 14*, 24735. https://doi.org/10.1038/s41598-024-76101-w.
16. Razzaq, M. A., Shaikh, R. A., Baig, M. A., & Memon, A. A. (2017). Digital image security: Fusion of encryption, steganography and watermarking. *International Journal of Advanced Computer Science and Applications, 8*, 224–228.
17. Zainal, N., Hoshi, A. R., Ismail, M., Rahem, A. A. T., & Muhsin, S. (2024). A hybrid steganography and watermark algorithm for copyright protection by using multiple embedding approaches. *Bulletin of Electrical Engineering and Informatics, 13*, 1877–1896. https://doi.org/10.11591/eei.v13i3.6337.

2
Chaos Theory

2.1 Overview of Chaos Theory

Chaotic systems are also sensitive to initial conditions, indicating the random numbers needed to create secure encryption keys, which makes chaos theory a suitable basis for the design of solid cryptographic algorithms [1]. Chaotic maps are mathematical functions that describe the evolution of chaotic systems, and they are essential for studying chaotic dynamics and its applications. It began with Henri Poincaré's contributions [2] to the three-body problem of celestial mechanics. Due to its sensitivity to initial conditions, the paths taken by three mutually interacting bodies under gravitational attraction can never fully be predicted, and even slight perturbations in initial conditions lead to course outcomes that can gravely differ from one another; this was demonstrated by Henri Poincaré in 1890. In 1963, Edward N. Lorenz took this idea a step further by showing that tiny changes in initial conditions within a system could lead to totally different outcomes, a phenomenon famously called the "butterfly effect [3].

Chaos theory is a natural science and mathematics of complex systems that have high sensitivity to initial conditions [4, 5]. These systems are deterministic in nature. The complex and random behavior of chaotic systems is long-term analysis that can be expressed by a strange attractor in the phase space. The behavior of chaotic systems is nonlinear and unpredictable, which makes it suitable for various real-world applications such as cryptography [6].

DOI: 10.1201/9781003500841-2

2.2 Properties and Applications of Chaos

Chaos is defined by sensitive dependence on initial conditions, so that small differences in initial parameters produce widely different results. The behavior is highly variable, even though it follows a certain set path, such that minor changes can cascade and cause very different outcomes given enough time. Such features are immensely useful in different domains, owing to which many well-established engineering applications have exploited them, such as quasi-random sequence generation, chaotic communication channel modeling, secure chaotic cryptography, and digital image encoding.

2.2.1 Properties of the Chaos

Chaotic behavior is an interesting phenomenon that is observed in many systems we see in our daily lives. Unlike simple random noise, chaotic systems contain a complex mixture of order and chaos. To understand chaos theory, we must know what makes chaos, chaos, and what separates it from other types of systems. This emphasizes the important aspect of chaotic systems being unpredictable in the long time limit, but does not give the same probability to each level of detail [6, 7]. Here are the main features:

- **Deterministics**: At the same time, though completely unpredictable to us, chaotic systems are deterministic—their future behavior is entirely determined by their initial conditions, and they involve no random elements. But they seem random and chaotic due to their sensitivity to initial conditions.
- **Sensitivity to Initial Conditions**: Small discrepancies in the initial values of variables in chaotic systems increase exponentially with time, generating drastically different and completely inconclusive, confusing, or horrible sequential values. This phenomenon, known as sensitivity to initial conditions, means that the tiniest variations at the start can produce vastly varying results. While the trajectory of the system may be anticipated for the initial rolling stages, it will soon deviate from its expected path as the system continues to evolve, making it extremely unreliable to thoroughly predict the system over time.

- **Nonlinearity and Aperiodicity**: Chaotic systems are nonlinear (not directly proportional output and input); this leads to unpredictable and complex behavior. This nonlinearity leads to aperiodicity; the system never falls into a repeating pattern, unlike periodic systems like a pendulum or planetary orbit. Instead, such systems develop irregular, non-repeating behavior, which is one of the crucial signatures of chaos.
- **Attractors**: An attractor in dynamical systems is a set of numerical values toward which a system tends to evolve for an unattainable series of time, despite the shifts and boundary values. These describe the system's asymptotic behavior. In chaotic systems, however, the attractors are more complex and are known as "strange attractors." Simple attractors can be a point or a looping motion, but strange attractors have fractal-like forms. The system never quite drifts into these attractors and instead wanders around them in an unpredictable yet bounded manner. These are the attractors that influence the system over long timescales, drawing it into certain zones of its phase space even if the precise route is unknown.
- **Ergodicity**: Put simply, ergodicity describes the situation in which a system will eventually, over enough time, sample all available states in its phase space. Chaotic systems are typically ergodic; that is, their time-averaged behavior equals their space-averaged behavior. The system, in the long term, visits all those states widely and uniformly.
- **Bifurcation and Period Doubling**: When the parameters of a chaotic system vary, it can enter bifurcations, in which a slight change in the value of a parameter results in significant qualitative changes in the behavior of the system. Period doubling is a common route to chaos, where the period of oscillations doubles.

2.2.2 Applications of Chaos

Simulation and real-time implementation of chaotic systems have many applications in various fields, including but not limited to aerospace, electrical and mechanical engineering, robotics, and cryptography [8–10]. General approaches and techniques for chaos control can have practical implications in engineering applications.

- **Meteorology**: It is one of the most classic and well-known applications of chaos theory. It is not surprising since the behavior of the atmosphere is that of a chaotic system. Chaos theory states that small variations at the start can lead to large variations down the road, a phenomenon colloquially referred to as the "butterfly effect." And this means that although short-term forecasts have reasonable accuracy, forecasting over the long-term becomes very difficult. The atmosphere is very sensitive to minor differences in temperature, pressure, moisture, and so on. A slight, practically negligible difference in any of these factors can multiply through time, resulting in dramatically divergent weather systems. A tiny change in wind speed or temperature in one region can produce dramatically different conditions in another region days later. So, chaos theory shows how small differences in initial conditions make weather systems sensitive to change, teaching meteorologists to love predictability's limits.
- **Biology and Medicine**: Chaos theory is applied in biological systems to study population dynamics, the spread of diseases, and the functioning of the human brain. Chaos-based image encryption is predominantly utilized in protecting medical images, which contain sensitive information and are vital to remote surgery and diagnostics. This area consists of methods such as integration with chaotic systems and ciphers. It utilizes chaotic maps for secure transmission of images in the online environment, combining DNA technology, hash functions, and chaotic systems to provide better protection. For instance, chaotic models can explain the disordered rhythms of heartbeat patterns and neural mechanisms.
- **IoT and Microcontroller**: Image encryption based on chaos is highly beneficial for Internet of Things (IoT) and microcontroller applications that require quick and safe data transportation. Algorithms such as Cat maps, Logistic maps, and hyperchaotic systems are highly chaotic, which means that an attacker is not able to reverse the parameters at all; thus, they cannot decode the image without exact keys. These encryption algorithms can be efficiently implemented even on constrained devices, as is often the case with IoT, because here,

computational overhead and memory usage are at a minimum. In addition, they are very microcontroller-friendly, being small and efficient, and keeping sensitive data such as passwords and customer information secure. Technologies such as 6G and M2M communication require high-speed real-time secure data exchange that can be achieved using chaos-based encryption that would help fulfill those demands.

2.3 Chaos and Cryptography

There are beneficial aspects of chaos that prove to be useful in cryptography. The chaos-based cryptosystems utilize chaotic behavior to increase the security of cryptographic algorithms, sensitive to initial conditions and nonlinear dynamics. Chaos theory is significantly valuable in cryptography in the sense that its systems possess intrinsic unpredictability and complexity, which are critical components for securing data in different databases [11]. The nature of the characteristics of chaos, sensitive dependence on initial conditions and determinism, or randomness, closely resonates with cryptographic needs.

Cryptography is the process of converting information into a code to protect it from unauthorized access. Three pillars of data security are shown in Figure 2.1. Encryption involves the use of algorithms

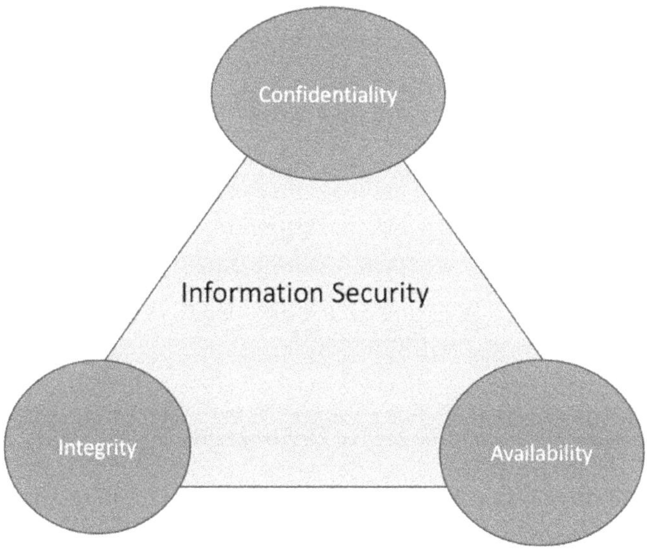

Figure 2.1 Three pillars of data security.

and encryption keys to convert original data (for example, text, image, audio, video, etc.) into encrypted data that can only be returned to its original form by decryption using the right keys.

By using the key elements of chaos theory, cryptography can improve the security of encryption algorithms. These elements introduce more randomness and therefore less predictable patterns into the system, making it much harder for attackers to access the systems using the encryption. This randomness fortifies the following key features of cryptography:

- **Confidentiality**: Confidentiality means protection of sensitive data from unauthorized access. Authentication is the process of confirming that a user, system, or entity is who they claim to be before providing access to resources or services [12]. It prevents unauthorized users or devices from accessing sensitive data or systems. It is an important piece here also because it provides a layer of security, preventing unauthorized access and ensuring information integrity and confidentiality.
- **Data Integrity**: It guarantees that the information is not altered, corrupted, or deleted in an unauthorized or accidental way.
- **Availability**: Availability is about ensuring authorized users have consistent access to the information and resources they require when needed. Availability improvement is possible through chaotic systems with efficient decentralized cryptographic schemes. Other possible uses include supporting the distributed system to reduce single points of failure dependence and improving system resilience at high service volume or in the event of an attack. Chaotic properties also contribute to fast encryption and decryption of these images and enable legal users to access them quickly.

2.4 Application of Chaos Theory in Cryptography

In various fields, cryptography that integrates chaos theory is used where encryption must be secure, unpredictable, and complex. Some main fields are like this:

- **Healthcare and Medical Records**: Patient data protection has become a necessity in healthcare these days, and most healthcare providers are using Electronic Health Records (EHR) for data management and storage digitally. In EHR systems, medical images such as X-ray, MRI, CT scan, and ultrasound are also typically shared as they are crucial for diagnosing and treating diseases. Since these images contain sensitive patient data, it is critical that exchanges between healthcare professionals maintain the privacy, security, and integrity of these images. Such a high degree of data security is of utmost importance for accurate diagnosis and treatment plans since it conserves patients' personal health information confidentiality and integrity [13]. The chaotic patterns can also be utilized in devising stronger encryption techniques in order to secure medical data and improve its privacy.
- **Multimedia Security**: In multimedia security, special measures in the form of encryption are implemented for images, videos, and audio files to keep the information secure while transmitted over networks. Chaos-based cryptographic approaches are particularly suitable for multimedia encryption, as they can efficiently deal with high-dimensional and complicated data. Real-time and recorded footage of video surveillance systems are protected from interception through chaotic encryption. The provided techniques are extensively utilized in confidential communications, especially in sensitive audio and video calls in both governmental and military capacities, among others. Chaos-based methods have also become important in the area of digital media distribution using chaos mapping to prevent illegal copying, as well as in VR/AR applications to secure virtualized digital assets. During the R&D phase, chaos encryption is used to encrypt proprietary multimedia files shared among teams to keep intellectual property confidential.
- **Security and Defense**: Protecting the confidentiality and integrity of sensitive communications, data storage, and transmission in the security and defense sector is critical to national security. Some of the most critical applications in this industry include secure radio and satellite communications, which allow security forces to coordinate operations and exchange

real-time data between ground units, command centers, and airborne and other remote assets. In chaos-based cryptography, intercepted messages are useless unless the right key is applied, making it difficult for unauthorized persons to eavesdrop on communication. For instance, chaotic algorithms protect defense networks, databases, and Internet of Things (IoT) devices like surveillance cameras, autonomous vehicles, and sensor networks used for intelligence and surveillance.

- **Cloud Computing and Cybersecurity**: To secure cloud-stored data and ensure secure data transmission across networks, chaos-based encryption improves data privacy while limiting access to cloud-stored data only to those users with the correct key and protecting sensitive information from interception. Also, chaos-based techniques are lightweight, allowing good scalability in clouds due to the fact that they do not require huge resources, which extend computing and cybersecurity needs in cloud computing.
- **Blockchain and Cryptocurrency**: Leveraging chaos theory principles can provide greater integrity to the cryptographic operations behind transactions, consensus algorithms, and wallets in blockchain and cryptocurrency. Fundamentally, security in blockchain arises from a mathematical principle known as the hash function, which takes information of any size and distills it into a fixed-size string of characters. In the process, it generates a hash that acts as the digital fingerprint of that block, maintaining data integrity, authenticity, and immutability on the blockchain. This principle can be applied to make the avalanche effect of blockchain hash functions stronger, which ensures that even when one bit of the input data is modified, it results in a completely different hash. When chaotic maps are integrated into primitive hash functions to produce unpredictable hash functions, they cannot be reverse-engineered or tampered with in blockchain transactions.

2.5 Chaos Map and Types

The concept of chaos maps comes from the field of mathematics and physics, when scientists wanted to study dynamical systems and how simple, deterministic systems can give rise to complexity and unpredictability. This quest emerged in the early 20th century when scientists began to observe that certain natural phenomena—planetary orbits, fluid dynamics, population growth, or even pattern formation in the weather—were especially difficult to predict, principally because they are sensitive to initial conditions.

2.5.1 Chaos Map

A chaos map is a mathematical function that describes chaotic behavior in a dynamical system. It shows how small changes in initial conditions can lead to wildly different and unexpected results. Most chaos maps, in a general way, are in the form of Equation (2.1).

$$xn+1 = f\left(xn\right) \tag{2.1}$$

The chaos map is applied iteratively, and it generates a sequence of values. The future state $xn+1$ is uniquely determined by the current state xn. The purpose of a chaos function is to exhibit random behavior and introduce nonlinearity over a specific time interval [11–13]. To exhibit deterministic chaos for specified parameter values, a nonlinear dynamical system must demonstrate three key characteristics:

- **Sensitivity to Initial Conditions**: Small differences in starting points cause trajectories to move apart rapidly over time. This makes it impossible to predict long-term outcomes, even though the system follows fixed rules.
- **Chaotic Motion in Phase Space**: The unique volume of phase space desirable for harmony but which activates when chaos takes over, becoming deliberately bifurcated into volumes that do not intersect. In these areas, chaotic behavior produces complex, oscillating patterns that can resemble random noise, although they emerge from deterministic rules.
- **Structural Shifts in Solution Behavior**: over the course of the evolution within the system, the system alternates periodically between significant changes in the inferred functional landscapes (solution behavior). These changes are characterized by bifurcations—points at which the system divides into new patterns or paths in phase space, resulting in progressively more complex behavior.

The Logistic Map (LM), Sine Map, and Tent Map are among the commonly used chaotic maps that researchers use to study complex and unpredictable behavior in simple mathematical systems. These maps are iterative maps. Their mathematical equations are as follows:

- **Logistic Map**: The logistic map is mathematically defined as follows:

$$x_{i+1} = r^* x_i^* \left(1 - x_i\right) \tag{2.2}$$

where, $r \in \left[0,4\right]$ and $x0$ is defined as the initial value for generating the map [14].

- **Sine Map**: The Sine map is another one-dimensional chaotic map that makes use of the sine trigonometric function where, $r \in \left[0,1\right]$ [15] and is mathematically defined in Equation (2.3).

$$x_{i+1} = r^* \sin\left(\pi x_i\right) \tag{2.3}$$

- **Tent Map**: The Tent Map is defined by Equation (2.4), which breaks into two parts. If the value of x_i is less than 0.5, then x_{i+1} is calculated as $r^* x_i$. Conversely, if x_i is greater than or equal to 0.5, x_{i+1} is computed using $r^* x_i$. The Tent Map has a control parameter r, which takes values within the range $r \in \left[0,1\right]$.

$$x_{i+1} = \begin{Bmatrix} r^* x_i, x_i < 0.5 \\ r^* \left(1 - x_i\right),\ x_i \geq 0.5 \end{Bmatrix} \tag{2.4}$$

2.5.2 Types of Chaos Map

This part will categorize chaotic systems. Figure 2.2 categorizes chaos maps based on three main criteria: time evolution, dimensionality, and modification type.

1. Based on Time Evolution

Chaotic systems exhibit two primary types of behaviors—**discrete** and **continuous**:

- **Discrete Chaos Maps**: In discrete chaotic systems, changes happen in distinct steps or intervals, rather than continuously.

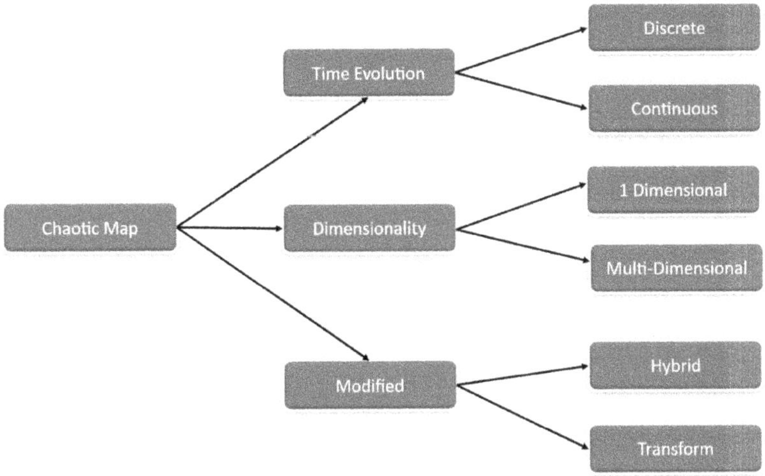

Figure 2.2 Classification of chaotic map.

This type of chaos is seen in systems like population models or economic cycles, and the dynamics are governed by recursive relationships or iterated functions. These systems are typically described by differential equations, where the state of the system at time t+1 depends on the state at time t. The system progresses from one state to another in distinct, often equal, time intervals. Examples of Discrete Chaos Maps are the Logistic map and the Tent Map.

Bifurcation and period doubling are some of the key characteristics of a discrete chaos maps; as the parameter (e.g., r) is varied, the system undergoes bifurcations where periodic behavior transitions to chaos.

- **Continuous Chaos Map**: Continuous chaotic maps evolve continuously with time. They are represented by differential equations. Continuous chaotic systems are highly sensitive to initial conditions and small perturbations. The solution to continuous map differential equations is called a strange attractors. The strange attractor describes long-term behavior that is chaotic and unpredictable. It never reaches a stationary point or periodic cycle. For example:
- **Lorenz System**: A type of nonlinear differential equations that describe atmospheric convection. Its structure is like a "butterfly."

Table 2.1 Key Differences between Discrete and Continuous Chaos Maps

FEATURE	DISCRETE CHAOS MAPS	CONTINUOUS CHAOS MAPS
Time representation	Evolve in discrete time steps	Evolve continuously over time
Mathematical formulation	Difference equations (iterative)	Differential equations (rate of change)
State update	State updated in fixed intervals	State evolves smoothly over time
Examples	Logistic map, Tent map	Lorenz system, Rossler attractor
Typical applications	Population dynamics, economics	Weather modeling, fluid dynamics, electrical circuits

- **Rössler Attractor**: The Rossler attractor is a combination of three nonlinear differential equations. It has a loop-like structure in its phase space.

2. **Based on Dimensionality**

Generally, chaos maps are categorized into **one-dimensional** and **multidimensional**.

- **One-Dimensional Chaos Map**: A one-dimensional chaos map is a simple chaotic system in which the state is represented by a single variable that evolves over time, according to a nonlinear iterative function. Despite being governed by just one state variable, such maps can still exhibit complex, unpredictable behavior. In a one-dimensional chaos map where tiny perturbations grow exponentially, leading to vastly different outcomes, which makes long-term prediction extremely difficult.

Examples of One-Dimensional Chaos Maps

Logistic Map: The logistic map is a one-dimensional chaos map, and mathematically it is represented by the given Equation (2.5)

$$x_{i+1} = r^* x_i {}^*(1 - x_i) \tag{2.5}$$

where, $r \in [0,4]$ and $x0$ is defined as the initial value for generating map [14].

Sine Map: The Sine map is also a one-dimensional chaotic map that uses the sine trigonometric function where, $r \in [0,1]$ [15] and is mathematically defined in equation (2.6).

$$x_{i+1} = r^{*}\sin(\pi x_i) \tag{2.6}$$

Chebyshev Map: The Chebyshev map is a one-dimensional chaos map based on the Chebyshev polynomial.

$$x_{i+1} = cos\left(k\ arc\ cos\left(x_n\right)\right) \tag{2.7}$$

The map shows chaotic behavior for $k > 2$ and $x_n \in (-1,1)$,

Tent Map: The Tent Map, as described in Equation (2.8), is divided into two segments. If the value of x_i is less than 0.5, then x_{i+1} is calculated as $r^{*} x_i$. Conversely, if x_i is greater than or equal to 0.5, x_{i+1} is computed using $r^{*}x_i$.

$$x_{i+1} = \begin{cases} r^{*} x_i, x_i < 0.5 \\ r^{*}\left(1 - x_i\right), x_i \geq 0.5 \end{cases} \tag{2.8}$$

The Tent Map utilizes a control parameter r, which takes values within the range $r \in [0,1]$.

Some of the key benefits of one-dimensional chaos maps are the following:

- **Simple Structure**: One-dimensional (1D) chaotic maps are single variable functions which are described by simple equations. The implementation of 1D chaotic maps becomes very easy. The study of behaviors using bifurcation and trajectory is also very simple in the case of 1D chaotic maps.
- **Computational Efficiency**: The single variable associated with 1D chaotic maps reduces the complexity and makes it computationally efficient. The amount of data to be processed is also low for each iteration and therefore makes the execution of 1D chaotic maps faster.
- **Applications in Cryptography**: The use of 1D chaotic maps in cryptography involves the generation of pseudorandom sequences and using them in the encryption phases. These generated sequences are sensitive to initial conditions and can

be generated in less time due to their simple structure. The random behavior of sequences prevents them from reverse engineering and brute-force attacks.

Some key challenges associated with using a one-dimensional chaotic map are the following:

- **Limited Complexity**: In some cryptosystems, there is a requirement for more than one chaotic sequence. In such systems, high-dimensional chaotic maps are preferred as compared to 1D chaotic maps. Also, due to the involvement of only one variable, some 1D chaotic maps exhibit less complexity. The development of new 1D chaotic maps that are highly complex is still an area of research in this domain.
- **Finite Precision**: In a real-world scenario, 1D chaotic maps are usually implemented with finite precision on digital systems, forcing the initial conditions and parameters through rounding or truncation. This does play havoc with the sensitive dependence on initial conditions, as over time the rounding errors accumulate and lead to unexpected behavior compared to the theoretically chaotic model.
- **Parameter Sensitivity**: In many 1D maps, the behavior of these functions is only chaotic in certain narrow ranges of their parameters. Outside of these ranges, only small deviations from them lead the map to produce non-chaotic, predictable outputs. Thus, keeping genuine chaotic motions accurately is rather difficult work; the system needs to be tuned and monitored to keep it well within the appropriate values for each parameter. An area where the system does not retain its random, sensitive-to-initial-conditions behavior is when the system is periodic or quasiperiodic rather than chaotic, a so-called blank-windows problem. The blank window problem is a major issue in applications that use chaos maps to generate pseudorandom sequences or encryption keys.
- **Short Periodic Cycles**: In finite precision, many 1D chaotic maps may produce periodic sequences after a certain number of iterations, particularly when the map is implemented in digital systems. This short-period cycling can reduce the

effectiveness of 1D maps in applications that require long, non-repeating sequences, like random number generation.

- **Vulnerability to Reverse Engineering**: Due to their simpler structure, some 1D chaotic maps can be more vulnerable to reverse engineering, especially when used in isolation for secure applications. The simplicity that makes them computationally efficient also makes it easier for attackers to analyze and potentially predict future values or reconstruct the initial conditions.

Multidimensional Chaos Map: Multidimensional chaotic maps refer to mathematical models that exhibit chaotic behavior in more than one dimension. In chaotic maps, the state of the system is described by multiple variables, and the evolution of these variables is governed by a set of equations. Multiple chaotic maps exhibit highly random behavior, high dependency on initial conditions, and a larger chaotic range. Arnold's Cat map, the Henon map, and the Baker map are two-dimensional chaotic maps.

Examples of Multidimensional Chaos Maps

Henon Map: The Henon map is a simple 2-D map and is mathematically defined as Equation (2.9).

$$x_{n+1} = 1 - ax_n^2 + y_n$$

$$y_{n+1} = bx_n \tag{2.9}$$

This map uses two control parameters x and y. For $a = 1.4$ and $b = 0.3$, this map is chaotic in nature.

- **Baker's Map**

The 2-D Baker chaos map is mathematically defined as Equation (2.10)

$$x_{n+1} = \begin{cases} 2x_n, \ if \ y_n < \frac{1}{2} \\ 2x_n - 1, \ if \ y_n \geq \frac{1}{2} \end{cases}$$

$$y_{n+1} = \begin{Bmatrix} \frac{y_n}{2} \;\; if \;\; y_n < \frac{1}{2} \\ \frac{y_n}{2} + \frac{1}{2}, \;\; if \;\; y_n \geq \frac{1}{2} \end{Bmatrix} \tag{2.10}$$

- **Rossler Attractor**

Rossler Attractor is a 3-D chaotic system and is described by three ordinary differential equations. The mathematical definition of Rossler Attractor is as follows.

$$\frac{dx}{dt} = -y - z$$

$$\frac{dy}{dt} = x + ay$$

$$\frac{dz}{dt} = b + z(x - c) \tag{2.11}$$

- **Lorenz Chaotic System**

The Lorenz Chaotic system is a very popular 3-D chaotic system, and it is defined by ordinary differential equations. This chaotic map was developed by Edward Lorenz. The equation of the Lorenz Chaotic system is mathematically defined as Equation (2.12).

$$\frac{dx}{dt} = \sigma(y - x)$$

$$\frac{dy}{dt} = x(\rho - z) - y$$

$$\frac{dz}{dt} = xy - \beta z \tag{2.12}$$

- **4D Chen's System**

Chen's chaotic system is a 4D chaotic system defined by four differential equations.

$$\frac{dx}{dt} = a(y - x)$$

$$\frac{dy}{dt} = cx - y - xz$$

$$\frac{dz}{dt} - b + z\left(x - d\right)$$

$$\frac{dw}{dt} = \alpha\left(x - w\right) \tag{2.13}$$

This chaos map uses four system variables x, y, z, w and a, b, c, d and α as control parameters.

- **4-Dimensional Hyperchaotic System**

Hui proposed a four-dimensional chaotic map known as a hyperchaotic system. This system is characterized by four state variables—x, y, z, and w—each of which evolves over time based on the interactions among the others. It also relies on four control parameters—a, b, c, and d—that define the behavior and stability of the system [17]. This hyperchaotic map is represented by four interdependent equations:

$$x_{k+1} = a^* \, x_k{}^*\left(1 - x_k\right)$$

$$y_{k+1} = b^* \, y_k{}^* z_k - c^* w_k$$

$$z_{k+1} = x_k + y_k$$

$$u_{k+1} = y_k + d^* w_k \tag{2.14}$$

Some of the key benefits of Multidimensional chaos maps are the following:

- **Larger Key Space:** Multidimensional Chaos Maps (MDCMs) offer a significantly larger key space than one-dimensional maps. Each additional dimension introduces new variables and control parameters, exponentially increasing the number of possible keys and making brute-force attacks more difficult.
- **Complex Systems:** Multidimensional Chaos Maps are maps that have more than one state variable. Their trajectories diverge in more than one state space, and hence, they are capable of generating more than one chaotic system. Therefore,

they are highly complex and are capable of developing strong cryptosystems.

- **Applications in Secure Communication and Cryptography**: Multidimensional chaotic systems are more complex, and they can generate more than one chaotic sequence depending upon their dimensionality. Therefore, the cryptosystems designed using multidimensional chaotic maps are highly robust as compared to cryptosystems that use 1D chaotic maps.

Some key challenges associated with using multidimensional chaotic map are the following:

- **Computational Complexity**: Due to the presence of more than one variable in the definition of multidimensional chaotic maps, their implementation becomes complex. The complexity also depends upon the dimensionality, or we can say, the number of equations. Therefore, multidimensional chaos maps require much more computational resources compared to the one-dimensional chaos maps.
- **Difficult Analysis**: Analyzing multidimensional chaotic maps becomes difficult due to their complex structure. While one-dimensional chaotic maps can be effectively represented and studied using tools such as bifurcation diagrams and state-space trajectories, higher-dimensional systems are significantly more complex and abstract. As the dimensionality increases, understanding the system dynamics becomes increasingly difficult. In particular, for systems beyond three dimensions, it is not feasible to directly visualize important dynamical features such as strange attractors, basin boundaries, and periodic orbits.
- **Implementation Challenges**: The practical implementation of multidimensional chaotic maps is very challenging due to the dimensions. Debugging and preventing errors are very challenging.
- **Control Problems**: Single-dimensional maps may be controlled using quite simple feedback strategies, but on the other hand, high-dimensional systems require more sophisticated control methods. With each extra dimension, the task of stabilizing periodic orbits or handling control parameters becomes challenging.

3. Modified Chaos Map

Some traditional chaotic maps like Sine or Logistic maps lack complex and random structure. Therefore, developing new chaotic maps using the existing traditional chaotic maps is an open area of research nowadays. Modified chaotic maps are special chaotic systems that have been designed by applying some modifications to the existing traditional chaotic maps. Modified chaotic maps can be generated by various methods such as coupling more than one chaotic map, changing the dimension, cosine transformation, and many more. The performance of modified chaotic maps is greater than that of their existing versions. They are highly unpredictable; their range is much larger than that of the constituted map. Modified chaotic maps are categorized as: **Hybrid Chaos Maps** and **Transformed Chaos Maps**.

- **Hybrid Chaos Maps**: Hybrid chaotic maps are designed by merging more than one chaotic map. The combination of various chaotic maps yields improved performance characteristics. Hybrid chaos maps are based on the synthesis of different chaotic behaviors. Researchers can combine different maps to produce systems with richer dynamics, greater randomness, enhanced security properties, or superior application-specific behavior. A systematic methodology is followed for designing hybrid chaos maps. The cross property of both chaotic maps is profiled to determine the compatibility of both the maps and the stability of the hybrid system. Furthermore, suitable coupling structures are designed to embed these maps.

Examples of Hybrid Chaos Maps are the following:

- **3-Dimensional Lorenz Logistic map (LLM)**

A three-dimensional **Lorenz Logistic map** (LLM), defined by the following Equations (2.15).

$$x_i = a * \left\{ \left[dy_{i-1} * \left(1 - y_{i-1}\right) \right] - \left[dx_{i-1} * \left(1 - x_{i-1}\right) \right] \right\}$$

$$y_i = b * \{ \left[dx_{i-1} * \left(1 - x_{i-1}\right) \right] - \left[dx_{i-1} * \left(1 - x_{i-1}\right) \right]$$
$$\left[dz_{i-1} \left(1 - z_{i-1}\right) \right] - \left[dy_{i-1} (1 - y_{i-1} \right] \}$$

$$z_i = \left\{\left[dx_{i-1} * \left(1 - x_{i-1}\right)\right]\left[dy_{i-1} * \left(1 - y_{i-1}\right)\right] - c * \left[dz_{i-1} * \left(1 - z_{i-1}\right)\right]\right\} \tag{2.15}$$

The LLM represents a highly sensitive chaotic system where small changes in initial values of $x_i - 1$, $y_i - 1$, $z_i - 1$ or in parameters a, b, c, and d significantly affect system dynamics [16]. The parameters fall within the ranges $a \in [8,10]$, $b \in [15,30]$, $c \in [1,3]$, $d \in [0,4]$.

- **2D Sine Logistic Modulation Map (2D-SLMM):**

The 2D-SLMM is a complex hybrid chaotic map that integrates the one-dimensional Sine map with the Logistic map to produce a more intricate and dynamic chaotic system [18]. It has two major control parameters: alpha $(0 \le \alpha \le 1)$ and beta $(0 \le \beta \le 30)$. The alternating between these two maps produces an unusual chaotic behavior that shows both sine periodicities and the logistic map diagram.

The system's dynamics exhibit high sensitivity to the two control parameters, in which α is tuned to increase the amplitude of oscillations while β is tuned to increase the frequency and complexity of chaotic behavior.

$$x_{i+1} = \alpha * \left(Sin\left(\pi y_i\right) + \beta\right) * x_i * \left(1 - x_i\right)$$

$$y_{i+1} = \alpha * \left(Sin\left(\pi x_{i+1}\right) + \beta\right) * y_i * \left(1 - y_i\right) \tag{2.16}$$

- **Two-dimensional Logistic Tent Modular map (2D-LTMM):**

The 2D-LTMM chaotic map is created by coupling the Logistic map with the Tent maps [19]. The control parameter values are in the range of 0 to 1. The map for the 2D-LTMM is mathematically expressed by Equation (2.17).

$$\left\{\begin{array}{l} x_{i+1} = \left\{\begin{array}{l} \left(4ax_i\left(1 - x_i\right) + 2by_i\right) mod\, 1, \, for\ y_i < 0.5 \\ 4ax_i\left(1 - x_i\right) + 2b\left(1 - y_i\right) mod\, 1, \, for\ y_i \ge 0.5 \end{array}\right\} \\ y_{i+1} = \left\{\begin{array}{l} \left(4ay_i\left(1 - y_i\right) + 2bx_i\right) mod\, 1, \, for\ x_i < 0.5 \\ \left(4ay_i\left(1 - y_i\right) + 2b\left(1 - x_i\right)\right) mod\, 1, \, for\ x_i \ge 0.5 \end{array}\right\} \end{array}\right\} \tag{2.17}$$

- **Transformed Chaos Maps**: Mathematical transformations can be applied to transform mathematical regular chaos maps into transformed chaos maps, producing modified maps with unique and stronger chaotic features. These transformations add functions of the new ones, such as sine and cosine, and so on. These changes can be consistent and significantly change the original map statistics like threshold and periodicity entropies to be more fully-là-state and faceless.

Examples of Transformed Chaos Maps are the following:

- **2-Dimensional Logistic Map**

A 2D logistic map extends the one-dimensional logistic map by incorporating two variables *x* and *y*, which evolve based on a set of coupled equations. It is defined by the following Equation (2.18)

$$\left\{ \begin{array}{l} x_{i+1} = r * (3y_i + 1) * x_i * (1 - x_i) \\ y_{i+1} = r * (3x_{i+1} + 1) * y_i * (1 - y_i) \end{array} \right\} \tag{2.18}$$

The above-mentioned equation illustrates that even a simple system can display chaotic dynamics when its variables interact through non-linear relationships.

- **Cosine-Transform-based Chaotic System (CTBCS)**

It combines the output of multiple chaotic maps using a cosine transformation, resulting in the Cosine-Transform-Based Chaotic System (CTBCS). CTBCS is an advanced chaotic system, a combination of two chaotic maps $F(a, x_i)$ and $G(b, x_i)$ [20]. Mathematically, CTBCS can be represented by Equation (2.19):

$$x_{i+1} = cos\left(\pi\left(F(a, x_i) + G(b, x_i) + \beta\right)\right) \tag{2.19}$$

Using several existing maps as seeds, such as the Logistic, Sine, and Tent maps, CTBCS generates new chaotic maps with a rich chaotic universe.

- **Cosine-Transformed Intertwining Logistic Map (CTILM)**

CTILM refers to Cosine-Transformed Intertwining Logistic Map, being the modification of the structure of Intertwining Logistic Map

(ILM), which is a further improved version of the structure of the logistic map. Introduced by Dua et al. [21], the CTILM utilizes cosine transformations and mixes the results from multiple logistic maps in order to obtain complex chaotic dynamics.

$$l_{k+1} = cos\left(\left[\lambda \times l \times m_k \times \left(1 - l_k\right) + n_k\right] mod 1 + \beta\right)$$

$$m_{k+1} = cos\left(\left[\lambda \times \beta \times m_k + n_k \times \left(1 + l_{k+1}^2\right)\right] mod 1 + \beta\right)$$

$$n_{k+1} = cos\left(\left[\lambda \times \left(m_{k+1} + l_{k+1} + \lambda\right) \times sin\left(n_k\right)\right] mod 1 + \beta\right) \quad (2.20)$$

2.6 Chaos System Analysis

Chaos System Analysis is the study of chaos in dynamic systems, where apparent chaos comes from deterministic rules. Understanding chaotic systems helps us to control and direct processes in areas such as weather forecasting, engineering, and economics. It also gives new perspectives on natural processes, uncovering basic structures in apparently random actions. In chaos system analysis, we use tools such as the bifurcation diagram (BF), Lyapunov exponent (LE), Sample, and Shannon entropy to study and characterize chaotic maps, so we can identify their characteristics and behaviors, revealing their patterns ahead of time.

2.6.1 Bifurcation Diagram Analysis

The bifurcation diagram of a chaotic equation is a visualization of how the behavior of a dynamical system changes when the control parameter of the system moves. It indicates the crossing points of fixed, periodic, and chaotic states [22]. The bifurcation diagram allows one to detect a set of parameter values where the system experiences qualitative changes that can take the form of period doubling and the emergence of chaos. It is an essential tool for figuring out the map to chaos and the zones of stability in a dynamic system. A good chaos function is distributed uniformly over the entire range. The chaos function is effective when no blank window emerges in the bifurcation diagram. For example, the logistic map equation is:

$$X_{t+1} = r * X_t * (1 - X_t) where 0 <= X < 1 and 1 < r < 4$$

The bifurcation diagram is a visual map of the way small changes in the growth rate parameter *r* change the dynamics of the population. The trajectory demonstrates a transition from stable (behaving the same) to complex, chaotic behavior as *r* increases.

For $1 < r \leq 3$: instance when $r = 2.6$, the system converges to a single fixed point, often around $x = 0.5$, No oscillation; the population reaches a stable value after several iterations.

For $3 < r \leq 3.45$: In this range, the population oscillates between two distinct values of *x*, meaning the system alternates between two states in successive iterations. As *r* increases further, around $r = 3.45$, another bifurcation occurs, and the system now oscillates between four values of *x*, meaning it takes four iterations to return to the same state.

For $3.54 < r \leq 3.57$: The rapid bifurcations are observed in chaotic systems in this period.

Figure 2.3 represents the bifurcation diagram of the logistic map. The horizontal axis denotes system parameters, while the vertical axis represents the system state. The diagram helps us to visualize the evolution of the system. We can check from the diagram that it is stable for $1 < r \leq 3$, it oscillates in range $3 < r \leq 3.45$ and shows chaotic behavior in range $3.54 < r \leq 3.57$. In the diagram, stable behavior appears as flat segments, and points where the system begins to

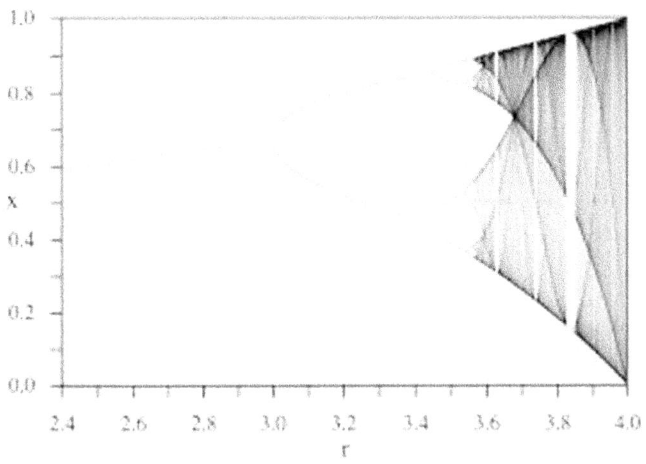

Figure 2.3 Bifurcation diagram of logistic chaos map.

oscillate or repeat in cycles show up as splits or branches. At certain thresholds, abrupt changes in the system's response create discontinuities. As parameters increase further, chaotic behavior appears as fragmented, intertwined structures.

In the logistic bifurcation diagram, as the growth rate r increases, the system transitions from a stable state (single line) to periodic oscillations (branching) and eventually to chaos, where population values become unpredictable and form complex, fragmented patterns. Other examples of bifurcation diagrams of the sine map and the Tent Map are shown in Figure 2.4.

2.6.2 Lyapunav Exponent

In a chaotic map, the Lyapunov exponent (LE) is used to measure the sensitivity of a system to slight changes in input. It quantifies the rate at which nearby trajectories of a system diverge or converge over time [22]. By measuring the sensitivity of a system to initial conditions, the Lyapunov exponent can reveal whether a system is chaotic, stable, or somewhere in between. For a chaotic system $f(y_i)$, the LE is defined by:

$$LE = \lim_{N \to \infty} \frac{1}{N} \sum_{i=0}^{N} \ln | f'(y_i) | \tag{2.21}$$

Where, $f'(y_i)$ is the differentiation of the function $f(y_i)$. For a chaotic system, the LE value should be greater than zero. For example, in

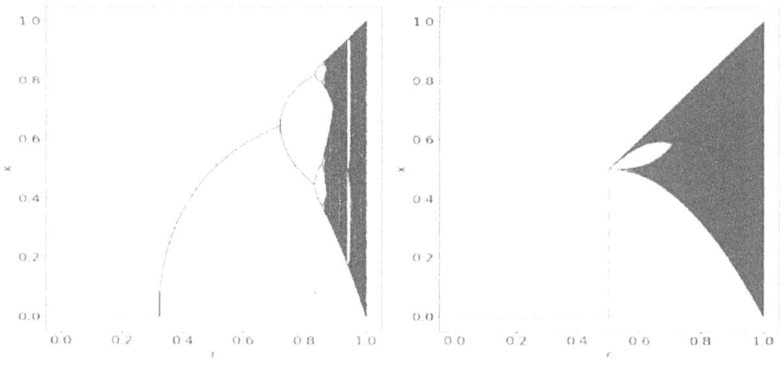

Figure 2.4 Bifurcation diagram of: (a) sine map, (b) tent map.

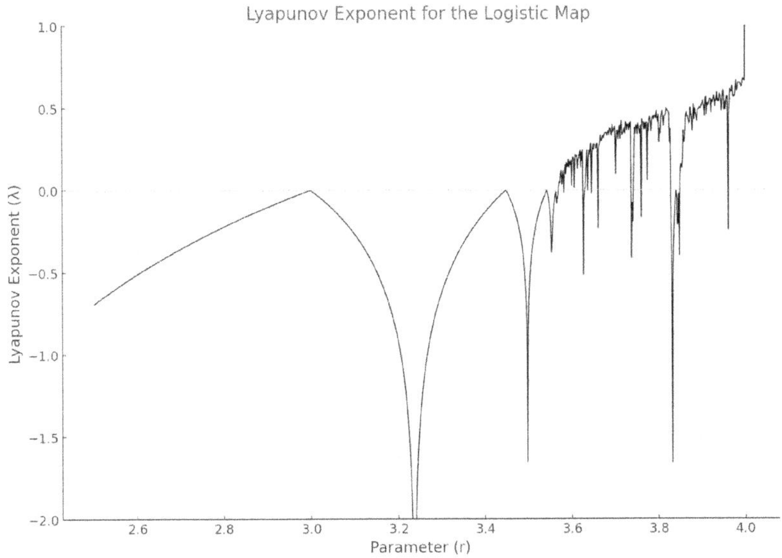

Figure 2.5 Lyapunov exponent of logistic map.

Figure 2.5, the Lyapunov exponent of the logistic chaotic map is positive for values of r in the range approximately from 3.57 to 4, which indicates chaotic behavior. When $1 < r < 3.571$ Lyapunov exponent is negative, the system shows predictable behavior where trajectories converge, either toward fixed points.

- **Positive Lyapunov Exponent (LE>0)**: When the LE is positive, the system exhibits chaotic behavior. Small differences in initial conditions lead to exponentially increasing divergence between trajectories, making long-term predictions impossible. An example of a chaotic system is the weather: tiny variations in measurements (like temperature or pressure) can lead to large differences in predictions.
- **Negative Lyapunov Exponent (LE<0)**: A negative LE indicates stability. Small perturbations decay over time and trajectories converge. Such systems are resilient to initial disturbances, and differences in starting conditions tend to vanish, leading to predictable, steady-state behavior.

Lyapunov exponents of the Sine map and the Tent map are shown in Figure 2.6.

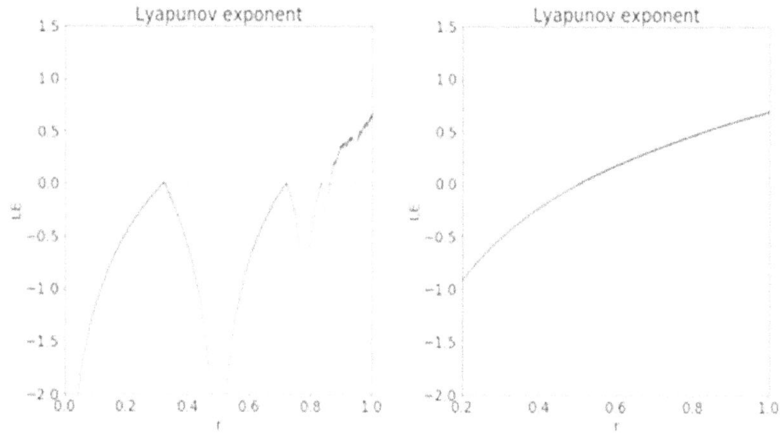

Figure 2.6 Lyapunov exponents of: (a) sine map, (b) tent map

2.6.3 Sample Entropy

In its basic form, sample entropy (SE) is a measure of the regularity or predictability of a time series. It is usually used for time series data to analyze systems that change over time, such as heart rate or financial markets. The logic starts by setting some fundamental things: the pattern length m, determining how many consecutive data points to consider as a unique plot. So, for $m = 2$, it will create a shape of two data points in one pattern. For higher values of m, the algorithm looks back longer patterns (thus can capture more complex structures) and r, which is the tolerance level for comparing each pattern. When two patterns have differences smaller than r, they are considered "matching." The choice of r is crucial, as a very small r will make pattern matching too strict, potentially missing broader patterns, while a larger r will relax the criteria, possibly treating unrelated patterns as similar [23].

To calculate sample entropy (SE), each possible sequence of m points in the dataset is compared to others to find matching patterns within a threshold r. Matches are counted when differences fall within r. Lower SE values imply that patterns of length m often extend into similar patterns of length $m+1$, indicating regularity. Higher SE values indicate that extending patterns to length $m+1$ results in fewer matches, pointing to increased complexity and less predictability in the data. The sample entropy is defined as:

$$SE(m,r,N) = -\log \frac{A}{B} \tag{2.22}$$

Where A represents the number of matching patterns of length $m+1$, B represents the number of matching patterns of length m, and N is the length of the time series.

Sample entropy (SE) offers a quantifiable method for assessing system complexity by examining the predictability of patterns in time series data. The SE has been used in understanding heart rate variability in physiology, relating a high SE value to a good condition mechanism of adaptation. In financial markets, SE assists in understanding the predictability of price fluctuations, indicating periods of stability or volatility. In engineering, SE is important as it is used in monitoring signals in evolving systems; if SE is increased, it might signal faults or irregularities.

2.6.4 Shannon Entropy (SE)

One of the pioneering metrics in information theory from Claude Shannon, SE, is a way to quantify the level of uncertainty or unpredictability of the potential results of a given system. It measures how random the information output by a system is, measuring how much "surprise" would occur if one were to see that outcome. Equation (2.14) defines Shannon entropy.

$$H(X) = -\sum_i P(x_i) \log P(x_i) \tag{2.23}$$

Shannon entropy, denoted by $H(X)$, as it is dependent on the probability distribution of the possible states or outcomes of the system. If the distribution is very uneven, the resulting entropy is small partly because the system becomes more predictable. Conversely, higher uncertainty or unpredictability occurs when there is a more uniform distribution (all outcomes equally likely), which is a high entropy scenario. Maximum uncertainty occurs when all possible outcomes are equally likely and is referred to as the Shannon entropy. The maximum entropy of a random variable with n possible outcomes is log n, corresponding to the case when the probabilities of all outcomes are equal. If the system has only one possible outcome or the system is fully deterministic, then the entropy is zero. There is no uncertainty at all, since there is always the same outcome. This method is used in many domains to evaluate uncertainty. It quantifies the amount of information produced by a source in communication systems and directs the construction of efficient coding and transmission methods; more entropy means more data or bandwidth needed to communicate the information. In cryptography, Shannon entropy is vital for evaluating how strong or random an encryption key is; the more entropy, the stronger and less susceptible to prediction the key. Entropy also plays a role in other fields such as machine learning and data science, where it is used for feature selection and analysis of the data distribution, since features that exhibit greater entropy usually also exhibit complex and informative patterns. In natural sciences, entropy gives us a glimpse into the disorder or complexity in biological, physical, and ecological systems. In general, Shannon entropy is a more universal measure for judging the equilibrium and is discussed through various systems.

2.7 Conclusion

Finally, this chapter has covered all the foundational principles and practical applications of chaos theory. Chaos theory: deterministic but sensitive to initial conditions, nonlinear, filled with strange attractors, ergodic at some scales, and bifurcating. From economics to meteorology, chaos theory can be applied to many different disciplines. In meteorology, it highlights the fundamental limits on longer-range predictions of the weather, a product of the atmosphere's sensitivity. In the fields of biology and medicine, chaotic models also contribute to complex biological processes, assist in disease modeling, and ensure the security of private medical data. On the other side, in the world of IoT and microcontrollers, chaos-based encryption takes a significant role because of its low resource consumption that we need for lightweight devices with a guarantee of secure data transmission. It is helpful for robotics and AI to use chaos theory to find their way through dynamic environments and their ability to adapt to new challenges, helping flexibility in their behavior. Chaos theory, in the domain of economics and finance, provides a way to model observed market behaviors that consider the nonlinear and complex systems that actual financial systems are. We demonstrated how chaos maps were modeled as well as introduced the various types of chaos maps useful in studying chaotic systems. We discussed some popular chaotic maps like logistic, tent, and sine maps, along with more sophisticated chaotic maps, including transformed, multidimensional, and hybrid chaotic maps, combining or altering existing maps for greater flexibility and complexity. In the end, we also discussed all the chaos analysis parameters such as bifurcation diagrams, Lyapunov exponents, Shannon entropy, and sample entropy.

References

1. Hasselblatt, B., & Katok, A. (2003). *A First Course in Dynamics: With a Panorama of Recent Developments*. Cambridge University Press.
2. Poincaré, H. (2017). *The Three-body Problem and the Equations of Dynamics: Poincaré's Foundational Work on Dynamical Systems Theory* (Vol. 443). Springer.
3. Ghys, É. (2015). The butterfly effect. In *The Proceedings of the 12th International Congress on Mathematical Education* (pp. 19–39). Cham: Springer.
4. Kocarev, L., Jakimoski, G., Stojanovski, T., & Parlitz, U. (1998). From chaotic maps to encryption schemes. ISCAS'98. In *Proceedings of the 1998 IEEE International Symposium on Circuits and Systems (Cat. No. 98CH36187)* (Vol. 4, pp. 514–517).
5. Letellier, C., Abraham, R., Shepelyansky, D. L., Rössler, O. E., Holmes, P., Lozi, R., ... Tsuda, I. (2021). Some elements for a history of the dynamical systems theory. *Chaos: An Interdisciplinary Journal of Nonlinear Science*, *31*(5), 53110.
6. Levy, D. (1994). Chaos theory and strategy: Theory, application, and managerial implications. *Strategic Management Journal*, *15*(S2), 167–178.
7. Palmer, T. N., Döring, A., & Seregin, G. (2014). The real butterfly effect. *Nonlinearity*, *27*(9), R123.
8. Boccaletti, S., Grebogi, C., Lai, Y. C., Mancini, H., & Maza, D. (2000). The control of chaos: Theory and applications. *Physics Reports*, 329(3), 103–197.
9. Samonas, S., & Coss, D. (2014). The CIA strikes back: Redefining confidentiality, integrity and availability in security. *Journal of Information System Security*, 10(3), 21–45.
10. Kocarev, L., & Lian, S. (2011). *Chaos-based Cryptography: Theory, Algorithms and Applications. Springer Science & Business Media* (Vol. 354). Springer.
11. Praveenkumar, P., Hemalatha, R., Uma, R., Madhunisha, K., Thenmozhi, K., & Amirtharajan, R. (2014). Image Zoning encryption. *Research Journal of Information Technology*, *6*. https://doi.org/10.3923/rjit.2014.368.378

12. Özkaynak, F. (2018). Brief review on application of nonlinear dynamics in image encryption. *Nonlinear Dynamics*, *92*(2), 305–313.
13. Skinner, J. E., Molnar, M., Vybiral, T., & Mitra, M. (1992). Application of chaos theory to biology and medicine. *Integrative Physiological and Behavioral Science*, *27*, 39–53.
14. Praveenkumar, P., Hemalatha, R., Uma, R., Madhunisha, K., Thenmozhi, K., & Amirtharajan, R. (2014). Image Zoning encryption. *Research Journal of Information Technology*, *6*. https://doi.org/10.3923/rjit.2014.368.378
15. Lu, H., Wang, X., Fei, Z., & Qiu, M. (2014). The effects of using chaotic map on improving the performance of multiobjective evolutionary algorithms. *Mathematical Problems in Engineering*, *2014*, 1–16.
16 Sathiyamurthi, P., & Ramakrishnan, S. (2020). Speech encryption algorithm using FFT and 3DLorenz–logistic chaotic map. *Multimedia Tools and Applications*, *79*(25–26), 17817–17835.
17 Hui, Y., Liu, H., & Fang, P. (2021). A DNA image encryption based on a new hyperchaotic system. *Multimedia Tools and Applications*, *82*, 21983–22007.
18 Hua, Z., Zhou, Y., Pun, C. M., & Chen, C. L. P. (2015). 2D Sine Logistic modulation map for image encryption. *Information Sciences*, *297*, 80–94. https://doi.org/10.1016/j.ins.2014.11.018
19 Hua, Z., Zhu, Z., Yi, S., Zhang, Z., & Huang, H. (2021). Cross-plane colour image encryption using a two-dimensional logistic tent modular map. *Information Sciences*, *546*, 1063–1083. https://doi.org/10.1016/j.ins.2020.09.032
20 Hua, Z., Zhou, Y., & Huang, H. (2019). Cosine-transform-based chaotic system for image encryption. *Information Sciences*, *480*, 403–419. https://doi.org/10.1016/j.ins.2018.12.048
21 Dua, M., Suthar, A., Garg, A., & Garg, V. (2020). An ILM-cosine transform-based improved approach to image encryption. *Complex & Intelligent Systems*, 1–17. https://doi.org/10.1007/s40747-020-00201z
22 Roy, M., Chakraborty, S., & Mali, K. (2021). A chaotic framework and its application in image encryption. *Multimedia Tools and Applications*, *80*, 24069–24110.
23 Mansouri, A., & Wang, X. (2021). A novel block-based image encryption scheme using a new Sine powered chaotic map generator. *Multimedia Tools and Applications*, *80*, 21955–21978.

3
SECRET SHARING SCHEMES

3.1 Introduction to Secret Sharing Scheme

In today's digital era, sharing huge amounts of multimedia data over unreliable communication networks has increased the chances of risks and vulnerabilities. Multimedia security plays an important role in this scenario to safeguard important multimedia content such as audio, video, and images from unauthorized access [1–3]. Secret sharing schemes are cryptographic methods that help to protect sensitive information by dividing the sensitive information (known as the secret) into several groups. Only these groups can reconstruct the secret. Any attacker who possesses only partial information will not be able to access the secret. The following are the steps involved in secret sharing schemes:

Step 1: Secret Information: The sensitive information that is to be shared and needs protection against unauthorized access is called secret. In the case of multimedia data, it may be audio, video, or image.

Step 2: Share Creation: During the share creation phase, the secret can be partitioned into n segments and allocated to participants. Figure 3.1 illustrates that n represents the number of participants and "Share" denotes the distribution of the secret (Share 1, Share 2, Share 3, Share n) [5, 6]. A threshold value K is established to govern the decryption process. The threshold K is set such that fewer than K shares cannot reveal or recover the original secret. To retrieve the secret S, at least K shares from the total N shares are required. This method is commonly referred to as a (K, N) SSS. Importantly, each generated share is designed to disclose no information about the original secret independently.

DOI: 10.1201/9781003500841-3

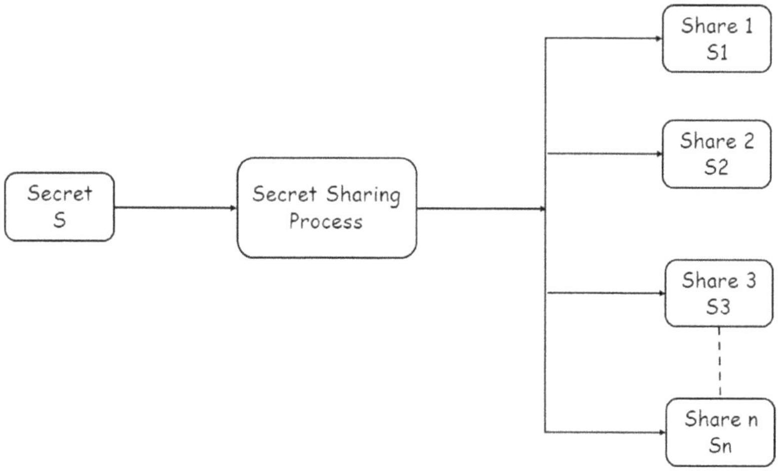

Figure 3.1 Share creation process.

Step 3: Sharing Process: The generated shares are securely distributed in several groups. The authorized groups can only reconstruct the original secret.

Step 4: Reconstruction Process: The recovery of the secret is carried out using the specified SSS encryption technique. To successfully compute and recover the secret SSS, at least *K* or more shares from S1, S2, S3, …, Sn are required.

Step 5: Secret Reconstruction: During this final step, the required shares are combined to regenerate the original secret data. The successful recovery process ensures that the sensitive information is restored accurately and securely using the steps outlined above.

As multimedia technology advances, digital data distribution and access become more straightforward. So, the keyframes extracted from the VS process are the secret images that must be secured in this technological advancement. Researchers have focused a lot of emphasis on secret sharing because of the benefits listed below.

- SSS provides a way of authentication.
- It increases the dependability of transmitting confidential information without raising the risk.

These schemes are constructed utilizing many methods, including steganography [7], visual encryption [8], watermarking [9], discrete wavelet transformation [10], discrete cosine transformation [11], threshold schemes [12], DNA encoding [13], and chaotic mapping [14]. Table 3.1 shows an overview of SSS developed by researchers, focusing on their basic models and contributions to secure information sharing. Secret sharing, a crucial cryptographic technique, was first introduced to ensure that a secret could be split into multiple shares, only reconstructable when a sufficient number of participants collaborate. Table 3.1 lists key researchers and their pioneering schemes, which have significantly influenced the evolution of secret sharing techniques.

Adi Shamir's scheme [4], introduced in 1979, is the most widely recognized secret sharing method. It is based on polynomial interpolation, where a secret is divided into shares using a randomly chosen polynomial, and reconstruction requires a threshold number of shares. Around the same time, Blakley [12] proposed a vector space-based SSS, using geometric principles where the secret is represented as a point in space, and each share corresponds to a hyperplane. McEliece and Sarwate later helped by creating a strong SSS that can handle errors and attacks from opponents. Another fundamental approach was introduced by Asmuth and Bloom [28], who utilized the Chinese Remainder Theorem to construct a modular, arithmetic-based secret sharing system. This method improved security by leveraging number theory principles. Kafri and Keren [16] proposed a novel visual cryptographic technique known as Random Grids-based Visual Secret Sharing (VSS), allowing secrets to be reconstructed through human visual perception. Beutelspacher [32] introduced a veto-capability-based SSS, enabling participants to enforce access control mechanisms in secret reconstruction. In 1995, Herzberg et al. [22] introduced the concept of proactive secret sharing, a scheme that periodically updates

Table 3.1 Primarily Secret Sharing Scheme Techniques

MODEL	SECRET SHARING SCHEME
Blakley [12]	Vector space-based SSS
McEliece and Sarwate [31]	Robust SSS
Adi Shamir [4]	Polynomial-based SSS
Asmuth and Bloom [28]	CRT-based SSS
Kafri and Keren [16]	Random-Grids-based VSS
Naor and Shamir [8]	Visual SSS
Ateniese et al. [29]	Extended visual SS
Gutub et al. [30]	Counting based SSS

secret shares to counteract long-term security threats. Another major advancement in visual cryptography was made by Naor and Shamir [8], who introduced the Visual Secret Sharing (VSS) scheme, where images are split into multiple transparencies that reveal the secret only when stacked together.

A deterministic and lossless (n, n) VSS system was proposed in [15]. The algorithm's secret image S serves as its input, producing n shared images—S1, S2, …, and Sn as its output. The first step is to use the rand function to create $n-1$ random matrices labeled R1, R2, and $Rn-1$. The Boolean XOR method is used to calculate n shares. The final percentage is computed using the $(n-1)$th random matrix, S-secret image, and the Boolean XOR function. The XOR operation recurses the secret image (S) across all shares. Kafri and Keren [16] were the first to define a random grid (RG). Black color pixels are represented by one, whereas white color pixels are denoted by zero. Binary images can be divided into two grids (RGs), with some parts being randomly chosen and others having information. The correlated areas will be restored when the two RGs are stacked together. Kafri and Keren [16] expanded the approach [17] to create an (n, n) VSS scheme based on RG. An encrypted binary image referred to as secret is divided into n RGs (R1, R2…, Rn), and the decryption process involves stacking all the RGs. The human visual system quickly recognizes the decoded image. YOLO-Based Secret Shares [18] is an approach for generating shares of an image by recognizing and encrypting the objects in the image, as shown in Figure 3.2. The YOLO algorithm [19] is used to recognize the objects in the image, and then shares are produced utilizing the found objects. Rather than encoding the whole image, only the objects are encoded.

The outcomes show that the suggested algorithm is more efficient for forming shares than existing secret sharing algorithms. With an increase in the number of objects in the picture, the size of the objects, and the number of shares, the method becomes more complex. An image encryption method utilizing confusion and diffusion

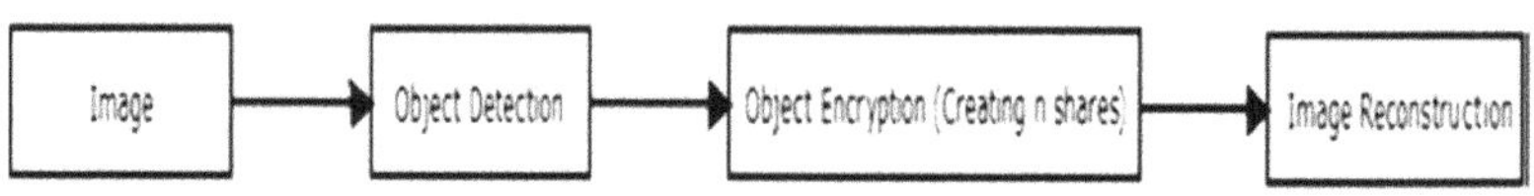

Figure 3.2 Yolo-based model [18].

is introduced, wherein picture pixels are initially rearranged to create a scrambled image. The Visual Secret Share technique [21] is illustrated in Figure 3.3, whereby each RGB pixel is shared independently, and the RSA (Rivest-Shamir-Adleman) algorithm is employed for the encryption and decryption.

It's also possible to share multiple secrets at once. Multi-secret sharing (MSS) schemes can share more than one secret. Many algorithms were proposed in the literature based on XOR operation, modular arithmetic operations, the Chinese Remainder Theorem (CRT), and many more based on hybrid approaches for share generation and reconstruction. To generate *n* shares from *n* secret images, the XOR algorithm was utilized to streamline the scheme's temporal complexity. It possesses two aspects that could be enhanced. Initially, the scheme has a limited sharing capacity, potentially disseminating $(n-1)/n$ hidden images instead of *n* secret ones. The second aspect has a low level of security. The proposed symmetric sharing-recovery function (SSRF) is used in a symmetric (n,n) multi-secret image-sharing method for sharing and retrieving images.

The author suggested CRT-based Multi-secret Sharing (MSS) [22]. Due to the greater degree of sharing randomization, this scheme does not disclose all secret information [23]. The study provides an arithmetic-based universal share-based multi-secret image sharing system. To convert *n* secret images into n shares, the Master uses this randomly generated common share known as a universal share. The proposed approach uses a function that chooses a unique value representation for the individual location of shares. It meets threshold

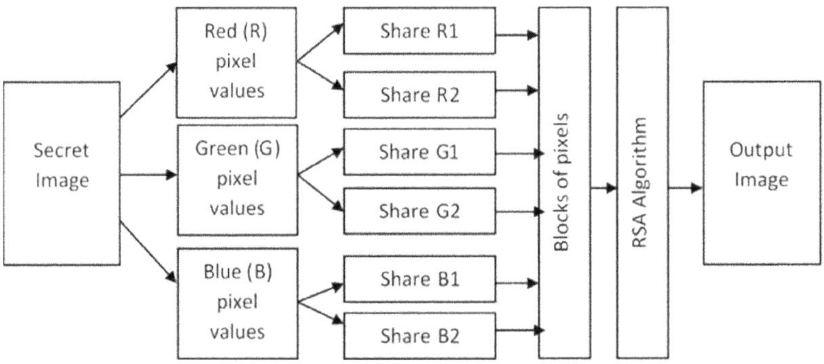

Figure 3.3 RSA-based VSS model [21].

security requirements while encrypting and decoding secret images using fundamental arithmetic operations. The (*n*, *m*, *l*)-MMSIS (Multilevel Multi-Secret Image Sharing) technique allocates the "*m*" shares generated from "*n*" individual secret images to "*m*" participants distributed across "*l*" different levels. The (*v*, *z*)-LAMSIS method uses polynomials and advanced visual cryptography to securely share multiple secret images, preventing cheating and allowing for perfect reconstruction of those images. A dependable (*k*, *n*)-threshold polynomial-based secret image sharing method (RPSIS) [26] is introduced, demonstrating resilience against noise in shadow images. The share is generated using random numbers, with its value according to the checksum of the shares of other pixels. The universal share, an arithmetic-based multi-secret image-sharing system, transforms n secret images into n shares. It employs a unique value-selection function to designate a separate value for each sharing location. A new Multiple Gray Scale Secret Image Sharing (MSIS) method is proposed in [28] to safely transmit multiple grayscale secret images to the target, which utilizes color cover images to increase security. Also, it lowers the number of shares and the coverage needed. Three functions of the proposed MSIS are share generation, share the revealing stage, and share signification, as shown in Figure 3.4. Comparative analysis reveals that the suggested MSIS efficiently improves security features, communicates quality, and optimizes the revealing process stage, but falls behind in sharing secret color images due to the complexity of pixel expansion.

All previous schemes need to consider the problem of encrypting and recovering secret images over a cloud network. The security of multimedia content delivered via the cloud has grown in importance in this multimedia era. Information can be transferred across the cloud via several different public communication methods from one location to another. As a result, the security of multimedia data transmitted over the cloud presents significant difficulties. Multimedia content in the cloud needs more protection than traditional methods to reveal the content quickly, especially in the case of the MSS scheme. A significant challenge in the cloud environment is developing a complex transmission model to maintain service dependability and security due to cloud computing services' real-time and ubiquitous

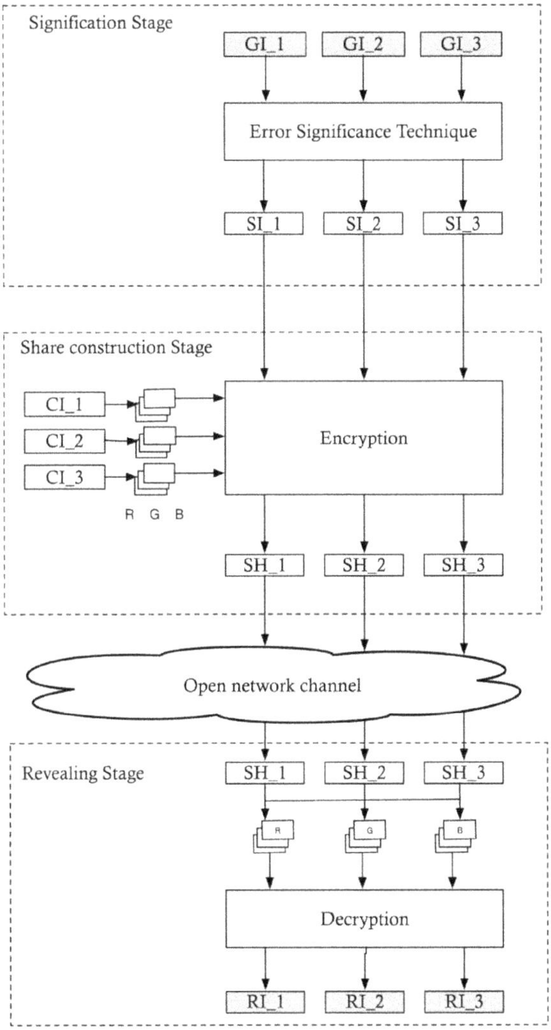

Figure 3.4 MSIS model [28].

requirements. It appears insecure because a third party typically stores the data transmitted over the cloud. Numerous approaches have been put forth so far to provide images with enhanced security. However, these methods are too insecure and only applicable to single secret images for use with cloud-based user data. Users have threatened to upload their secret images to the cloud to communicate. Therefore, specific approaches are instantly needed to protect sensitive data in the form of multi-secrets in the cloud environment from attackers or against unauthorized duplication and alteration [29].

Mainly, the secret sharing schemes proposed for the cloud environment deal with storing and securing the key (private and public), but not the secret content. To solve confidentiality, availability, and performance in cloud storage, [30] proposed CloudStash, which protects secret data for low-cost cloud storage and multithreading. Still, it applies the secret sharing to a single content (as a file) and only uses the cloud to share the participant shares. Hence, it has not executed the secret sharing scheme within the cloud-based Biometric security model, which employs an Elliptic encryption technique to safeguard user privacy [31].

A unique DNA (Deoxyribonucleic Acid)-based encryption system was presented for the protection of multimedia information in a cloud setting. A unique one-dimensional chaotic map is employed for the encryption of multimedia.

3.2 Challenges of Secret Sharing Scheme

Many significant achievements have been made to provide multimedia security through secret sharing schemes. There are several challenges and requirements associated with developing an effective secret sharing scheme. Hence, SSS presents the following challenges and requirements.

Security: There is a trade-off between the various techniques used for the secret image-sharing technique. The benefit of Multi SSS schemes over Single SSS schemes is that several shares can be used to share a lot of information. But it becomes a challenge to manage the multi-secret image data in terms of complexity, computation, and multilevel security.

Dynamic Participation and SSS: The scheme must be designed to handle dynamic participation (such as joining or leaving the scheme) while maintaining security. While secret sharing in hierarchical groups has been extensively examined, current approaches must address a specific situation in which three workers are required to authorize a bank transfer, with the condition that at least one must be a unit manager. Therefore, it is necessary to resolve the above problem with regard to participation.

Trust Issue: In most SSS, the dealer and the participants are assumed to be trustworthy. However, this is challenging, as a corrupt dealer might give a particular participant a fake shadow, or a spiteful participant might provide others with a fake share. Dealer and participant privileges-based SSS are applied in these circumstances. So, it is required to have a trusted channel between the dealer and participants.

Quality Issue: Some secret image sharing (SIS) methods result in shares with less secretive dimensions while lowering the total security factor. Maintaining the size and quality is difficult simultaneously.

Storage and Computation: Most researchers cannot construct secret image sharing that can exchange shares of various sizes. Also, many current schemes cannot provide completely randomized shares. Some methods combine the XOR procedure with different techniques like additive modulo operation, secure hash function, etc., to solve this issue, which may consume a lot of computational and storage resources.

Loss of Data Shares: Sizes are more significant than secrets; specific schemes still experience issues with pixel expansion. Simultaneously sharing multi-secret content poses a significant challenge, even with high security measures in effect. It is also challenging for the SSS to withstand a noise attack on secret image content. As noise can easily affect secret content, the information contained in the secrets will be lost.

3.3 Mathematics Background of Secret Schemes

SSS are security techniques designed to partition a secret into multiple components, also referred to as shares, and allocate them to various participants. The original secret can only be recovered by combining a specified number (threshold) of these shares. This ensures that unauthorized participants, who possess fewer than the minimal threshold of shares, have no knowledge about the secret. The underlying mathematics of SSS is rooted in polynomial interpolation, finite fields, and combinatorial principles.

3.3.1 Mathematical Foundations of Secret Sharing Schemes

The fundamental prerequisites for secret sharing schemes are as follows:

3.3.1.1 Finite Fields and Modular Arithmetic

Finite fields, denoted as Fp where p is a prime number, are used to implement secret sharing schemes. These fields allow addition, subtraction, multiplication, and division to be performed modulo p.

Definition: Finite Field F_p A finite field F_p consists of elements $\left\{0,1,2,\ldots,p-1\right\}$, where addition and multiplication are performed modulo p, ensuring a closed algebraic structure.

For example, in F_7, we have:

$$3+5\equiv 1 \ mod \ 7, \ \ 4\times 6\equiv 3 \ mod \ 7$$

Finite fields form the foundation of Shamir's secret sharing scheme.

3.3.1.2 Polynomial Interpolation

The most well-known and mathematically elegant scheme is Shamir's Secret Sharing, proposed by Adi Shamir in 1979. It is based on a fundamental principle from algebra known as Lagrange interpolation.

Secret Representation Using **Polynomials**: Shamir's (t, n)-threshold scheme encodes a secret S as the constant term of a polynomial of degree (t–1), where t is the threshold required for reconstruction:

$$f\left(x\right)=S+a_1x+a_2x^2+\bullet\bullet\bullet+a_{t-1}x^{t-1} \quad mod \ p \tag{3.1}$$

where $a_1,a_2,\ldots,a_{t-1}$ are randomly chosen coefficients from F_p.

- **Share Generation**: The dealer generates n shares by evaluating $f\left(x\right)$ at distinct nonzero points:

$$\left(x_i,y_i\right)=\left(x_i,f\left(x_i\right) mod \ p\right) \tag{3.2}$$

where $x_i\neq 0$ and x_i is uniquely assigned to each participant.

Example: A dealer wants to share a secret $S=123$ among five participants such that at least three participants (i.e., $t=3$) are required to reconstruct the secret. The secret sharing is performed in a finite field F_{251} (i.e., modulo 251).

Constructing the Polynomial

Since we need a (3, 5)-threshold scheme, we construct a random polynomial of degree $t-1=2$:

$$f(x)=S+a_1x+a_2x^2 \mod 251 \tag{3.3}$$

whcrc:

- $S=123$ (the secret)
- $a_1=45, a_2=67$ (randomly chosen coefficients). Thus, the polynomial becomes:

$$f(x)=123+45x+67x^2 \mod 251 \tag{3.4}$$

Generating Shares

Evaluating $f(x)$ at five distinct nonzero points x_i:

Each participant receives a share (x_i, y_i): Table 3.2 respresents the values of the function.

(1, 235), (2, 112), (3, 34), (4, 140), (5, 218)

Reconstructing the Secret using Lagrange Interpolation

Suppose three participants $(x_1, y_1)=(1,235),(x\_2, y\_2)=(2,112),(x\_3, y\_3)=(3,34)$ come together to reconstruct S.

Using Lagrange interpolation, the secret is recovered as:

$$S=f(0)=\sum_{j=1}^{t}\Sigma\, yj.\ell j(0) \mod 251 \tag{3.5}$$

where the **Lagrange basis polynomial** is:

$$l_j(x)=\prod_{k=1,k\neq j}^{t}\frac{x-x_k}{x_j-x_k} \mod 251 \tag{3.6}$$

Table 3.2 Generated Shares for Participants

x_i	$y_i=f(x_i) \mod 251$
1	235
2	112
3	34
4	140
5	218

Computing basis polynomials:

$$\ell_1(0) = \frac{(0-2)(0-3)}{(1-2)(1-3)} = \frac{6}{2} = 3 \, mod \, 251$$

$$\ell_2(0) = \frac{(0-1)(0-3)}{(2-1)(2-3)} = \frac{6}{2} = 3 \, mod \, 251$$

$$\ell_1(0) = \frac{(0-2)(0-3)}{(1-2)(1-3)} = \frac{6}{2} = 3 \, mod \, 251$$

Now, reconstructing the secret:

$$S = (235 \times 3) + (112 \times 248) + (34 \times 1) \, mod \, 251$$

$$S = 705 + 27776 + 34 \, mod \, 251$$

$$S = 28515 \, mod \, 251$$

$$S = 123$$

$S = 123$ is successfully reconstructed.

Secret Reconstruction via Lagrange Interpolation: Using Lagrange Interpolation, the polynomial $f(x)$ can be reconstructed as follows: Given any t shares (x_j, y_j), the polynomial $f(x)$ can be reconstructed uniquely using Lagrange Interpolation:

$$f(x) = \sum_{j=1}^{t} y_j . \ell_j(x) \tag{3.7}$$

Here, t shares are (x_j, y_j),. By evaluating at $x = 0$, we recover the secret:

$$S = f(0) = \sum_{j=1}^{t} y_j . \ell_j(0) \tag{3.8}$$

Example Calculation:

Let the threshold of (3, 5) with the secret $S = 123$ be used as the dealer selects:

$$f(x) = 123 + 45x + 67x^2 \bmod 251 \tag{3.9}$$

The shares are:

$$(1,235),(2,112),(3,34),(4,140),(5,218)$$

Using any three shares, the secret can be reconstructed using Lagrange interpolation.

3.3.1.3 Chinese Remainder Theorem (CRT) in Secret Sharing

The Chinese Remainder Theorem (CRT) is another mathematical approach for secret sharing based on modular arithmetic.

- **CRT-Based Secret Sharing**: Let the secret S be represented as a system of congruences:

$$S \equiv a_1 \bmod m_1$$

$$S \equiv a_2 \bmod m_2$$

$$S \equiv a_n \bmod m_n$$

where $m_1, m_2, \ldots, m_n$ are pairwise coprime integers. The secret S can be reconstructed using the CRT formula:

$$s = \sum_{i=1}^{n} a_i M_i y_i \bmod M \tag{3.10}$$

where:

$$M = m_1 m_2 \ldots m_n \tag{3.11}$$

$$M_i = \frac{M}{m_i} \tag{3.12}$$

$$y_i = M^{-1} \bmod m_i \quad (\text{modular inverse}) \tag{3.13}$$

CRT-based schemes are used in verifiable secret sharing and multi-secret sharing.

3.3.1.4 Combinatorics in Access Structures

While Shamir's scheme is a threshold scheme (any t out of n can reconstruct), not all applications follow such a rigid rule. Some scenarios require more flexible access structures, where only specific groups of participants are allowed to reconstruct the secret.

Example:

Groups A and B together can access the secret.
Groups A, C, and D can also access it.
But Groups A and C cannot.

Defining and managing these groups falls under combinatorics, the branch of mathematics concerned with counting and arrangements. Designing secret sharing schemes for such arbitrary access structures involves monotone Boolean functions and sometimes matroids and access graphs.

3.4 Types of Secret Scheme

SSS can be classified according to different criteria, such as the number of shares, the assigned weights, the privileges of participants, the mathematical techniques employed, and the size of the shares.

These classifications help in designing secure and efficient secret sharing mechanisms suited for various applications, including cloud security, distributed systems, and secure multiparty computations. Understanding these types and their characteristics is essential to choosing an appropriate scheme for a given security requirement. Figure 3.5 illustrates the classification of SSS based on various criteria, highlighting different approaches and their characteristics in secure data distribution.

- **Number of Shares Based SSS**: The number of shares may be single or many secret shares, a multi-secret sharing scheme [13, 14].
- **Share's Weight-Based SSS**: Some weight value is given to the shares. Like same weighted shares have the same weight, and multi-weighted shares have multiple weighted shares to participants. For instance, the voting system is where the

Secret Sharing Schemes Classification		
	Number of shares based SSS	Single SSS
		Multisecret SSS
	Shares' weight based SSS	SSS with same weighted shares
		SSS with multi-weighted shares
	Shares' changeability based SSS	Proactive SSS
		Dynamic SSS
		Veto based SSS
	Dealer's and participant's priveleges based SSS	Computational SSS
		Verifiable SSS
		Robust SSS
	Techniques based SSS	Polynomial based SSS
		Chinese Remainder Theort (CRT) based SSS
		XOR based SSS
		Visual Cryptograpgy based SSS
		Counting based SSS
	Shares size based SSS	Same size shares based SSS
		Different size shares based SSS

Figure 3.5 SSS classification.

chairman is granted the authority (or weight) of two or three votes among the other participants [16].

- **Dealer's and Participant's Privileges-Based SSS**: The classification of secret sharing based on the permissions granted to the dealer and participants. Based on the rights granted to the dealer and participants, this SSS categorization enables the reconstruction of shares using integrity and confidence [17].
- **Techniques-Based SSS**: The SS can be categorized based on the arithmetic methods employed like polynomial interpolation, CRT, X-OR based, etc. [18, 19].
- **Share** Size Based **SSS**: It is based on the size of the share to check whether the share is equal or different [19].

More specifically, the literature presents that the SSS for an image can be divided into the following categories based on the number of shared secrets: Single SSS, in which only one secret image is present and shared. Multi SSS, when more than one secret image may be exchanged, the secret sharing technique supports sharing multiple secret images. Figure 3.6 shows the secret sharing schemes for an image that can be used for single secret sharing and multi-secret

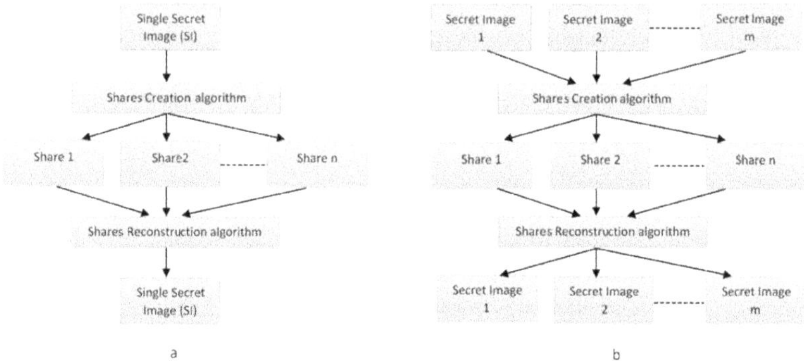

Figure 3.6 (a) Single secret sharing and (b) multi-secret sharing.

sharing (MSS) [13]. Both the schemes for secret sharing are broken into two different phases.

3.4.1 Multilayered Secret Sharing Scheme

The Multilayered Secret Sharing Scheme (MLSS) provides the security of extracted secret text data via a multi-step approach. In the first step, preprocessing of the text is done for the keyword extraction method. Subsequently, encryption methods are employed to secure the extracted textual data, providing confidentiality and integrity. Every phrase or token is encrypted with a cryptographic technique. The encrypted text data is partitioned into several shares via an SSS, with the shares allocated to various parties to improve security. To address this problem, SSS permits the division of your secret into several segments, which can be allocated to designated individuals [21].

SSSs are cryptographic methods used in secure protocols like multiple-party computation, threshold cryptography, Byzantine agreement, key control, and attribute-based enciphering [20]. They recover the original secret text by combining shares. Blakley and Shamir [11] extended this idea to a (k, n) system, where n represents the total number of shares and k represents the minimum number needed to retrieve the secret. SSSs allow confidential details to be shared in a group without a single user having access. When required or additional members of the grouping cooperate, the secret will be recovered. Any media, including video, text, images, audio, and numbers, can contain the secret.

Numerous SSS methodologies [23, 24] exist to handle various forms of multimedia data. This work uses the XOR-based SSS methodology to secure text data. The MLSS scheme divides a secret input text into $n+1$ shares, where n represents the length of the text. The proposed MLSS approach minimizes the size of the textual data after preprocessing, extracting the most informative or disclosing keywords as depicted in Figure 3.7. Ensuring data security is crucial for information security. The primary level of data security is guaranteed using the secret sharing method, while the generated secret share is communicated as a binary file at the secondary level.

3.4.2 Threshold Cryptography

Threshold cryptography refers to the use of SSSs where a threshold number is required for the participants who must cooperate to reconstruct the secret. This property is particularly useful in multiparty computations and key management. Threshold schemes ensure that no single participant has control over the secret, enhancing security by distributing trust among multiple participants.

In Shamir's SSS, the threshold is determined by the degree of the polynomial. For a scheme to be secure, the threshold t must be carefully chosen to balance security with the number of participants. If fewer than t number of shares are combined, the secret cannot be obtained. This property is a direct result of the algebraic structure of the polynomial and the fact that any set of t shares can reconstruct the polynomial, but fewer shares provide no meaningful information [15].

3.4.3 Other Secret Sharing Schemes

Blakley's secret sharing scheme [12] is a method in which a trusted dealer distributes a secret among n participants in such a way that the secret can only be reconstructed when at least t participants cooperate. Each participant receives a piece of information called a share. If

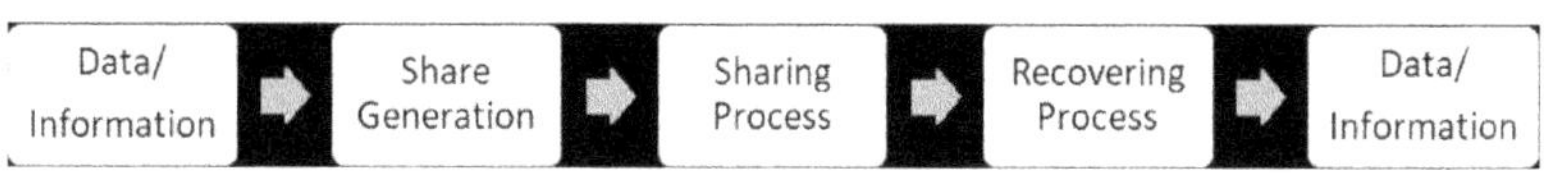

Figure 3.7 General secret sharing scheme steps.

fewer than t shares are combined, no information about the secret can be obtained.

This scheme is based on a geometric approach. Blakley assumed that the secret can be represented as a single point in a t-dimensional space. Each share corresponds to a hyperplane in this space. When t or more hyperplanes intersect, they meet at exactly one point, which represents the original secret. Therefore, reconstructing the secret is equivalent to finding the point of intersection of these hyperplanes. The coefficients defining the n different hyperplanes form the n shares distributed to the participants. Since the secret can be recovered only when a sufficient number of shares are combined, Blakley's scheme is classified as a linear threshold scheme, similar to Shamir's secret sharing scheme. Mathematically, Blakley's method can be represented using a system of linear equations of the form $Cx = y$, where the matrix C and vector **y** correspond to the equations of the hyperplanes. When computations are performed modulo a prime number p, the system is expressed as $Cx \bmod p = y$. By solving this system with enough shares, the secret point in the t-dimensional space can be successfully reconstructed.

Visual cryptography, introduced by Naor and Shamir [15], is another important scheme in which the message is split into shares that are images or visual objects. The secret can be visually recovered by stacking the shares, which is particularly useful for applications in image-based secrets, such as secure document sharing.

3.5 Characteristics of Secret Sharing Schemes

Secret sharing schemes possess several fundamental characteristics that make them suitable for secure applications:

- **Threshold Property**: Secret sharing is based on a threshold mechanism, meaning that at least participants must collaborate to reconstruct the secret. If fewer than participants attempt reconstruction, they gain no information about the secret [11]. For example, in a scheme, any three participants can recover the secret, but two alone cannot.
- **Information-Theoretic Security**: Many secret sharing schemes offer unconditional security, meaning that an adversary with fewer than t shares cannot deduce any information about the secret, even with unlimited computational power

[12]. For instance, in Shamir's SSS, the secret is hidden within a polynomial, making it impossible to determine the secret without at least t points.

- **Redundancy and Fault Tolerance**: The secret is divided among multiple participants, ensuring that even if some shares are lost or corrupted, the secret can still be reconstructed by a valid subset of participants [27]. For example, in cloud storage, secret sharing can be used to store data fragments across multiple servers so that data loss from a few servers does not result in complete data loss.
- **Perfect Secrecy**: A well-designed secret sharing scheme guarantees that any unauthorized subset of participants (fewer than t) gains zero information about the secret, ensuring maximum confidentiality [11].
- **Verifiability**: Some SSS, such as verifiable secret sharing (VSS), verify the correctness of shares and prevent the reconstruction of false secrets [25, 26]. There are no chances for a malicious participant to access the sensitive information.
- **Computational Efficiency**: Some of SSS balance security and computational efficiency, which makes them suitable for real-time applications [27]. For example, XOR-based secret sharing can work efficiently when computational resources are limited.
- **Proactive and Dynamic Security**: Some advanced secret sharing schemes are dynamic in nature; for example, proactive secret sharing periodically updates shares to prevent long-term exposure to adversaries and therefore enhance overall security [22, 24].
- **Minimal Share Size**: The size of each share should be kept as small as possible in order to reduce storage and communication overhead without compromising security [11]. In mobile communication systems, the minimum size of each share helps to ensure efficient use of bandwidth with maximum security [14].

References

1. Furht, B., & Socek, D. (2003). *A Survey of Multimedia Security*. Comprehensive report on multimedia security.

2. Bamasag, O. O., & Youcef-Toumi, K. (2015). Towards continuous authentication in internet of things based on secret sharing scheme. In *Proceedings of the WESS'15: Workshop on Embedded Systems Security* (pp. 1–8). IEEE.
3. Hu, C., Zhang, F., Cheng, X., Liao, X., & Chen, D. (2013). Securing communications between external users and wireless body area networks. In *Proceedings of the 2nd ACM Workshop on Hot Topics on Wireless Network Security and Privacy* (pp. 31–36). IEEE.
4. Jain, A., & Soni, B. K. (2017). Secure modern healthcare system based on internet of things and secret sharing of IoT healthcare data. *International Journal of Advanced Networking and Applications, 8*(6), 3283.
5. Luo, E., Bhuiyan, M. Z. A., Wang, G., Rahman, M. A., Wu, J., & Atiquzzaman, M. (2018). PrivacyProtector: Privacy-protected patient data collection in IoT-based healthcare systems. *IEEE Communications Magazine, 56*(2), 163–168.
6. Chang, C.-C., & Li, C.-T. (2019). Algebraic secret sharing using privacy homomorphisms for IoT-based healthcare systems. *Mathematical Biosciences and Engineering, 16*, 3367–3381.
7. Panja, S., Chattopadhyay, A. K., Nag, A., & Singh, J. P. (2022). Fuzzy-logic-based IoMT framework for COVID-19 patient monitoring. *Computers & Industrial Engineering*, 108941.
8. Iftene, S. (2007). General secret sharing based on the Chinese remainder theorem with applications in e-voting. *Electronic Notes in Theoretical Computer Science, 186*, 67–84.
9. Benaloh, J. C. (1986). Secret sharing homomorphisms: Keeping shares of a secret secret. In *Conference on the Theory and Application of Cryptographic Techniques* (pp. 251–260). Springer.
10. Schoenmakers, B. (1999). A simple publicly verifiable secret sharing scheme and its application to electronic voting. In *Annual International Cryptology Conference* (pp. 148–164). Springer.
11. Shamir, A. (1979). How to share a secret. *Communications of the ACM, 22*, 612–613.
12. Blakley, G. (1979). Safeguarding cryptographic keys. In *Proceedings of the AFIPS 1979 National Computer Conference* (pp. 313–317). New York.
13. Bisht, K., & Deshmukh, M. (2021). A novel approach for multilevel multi-secret image sharing scheme. *The Journal of Supercomputing, 77*(10), 12157–12191.
14. Deshmukh, M., et al. (2019). Secret sharing scheme based on binary trees and Boolean operation. *Knowledge and Information Systems, 60*(3), 1377–1396.
15. Naor, M., & Shamir, A. (1994). Visual cryptography. In *Workshop on the Theory and Application of Cryptographic Techniques*. Springer.
16. Tassa, T. (2007). Hierarchical threshold secret sharing. *Journal of Cryptology, 20*, 237–264.
17. Ogata, W., Kurosawa, K., & Stinson, D. R. (2006). Optimum secret sharing scheme secure against cheating. *SIAM Journal on Discrete Mathematics, 20*(1), 79–95.

18. Guttikonda, P., & Mundukur, N. (2020). Polynomial-based secret sharing scheme for text, image, and audio. *Journal of the Institution of Engineers (India): Series B, 101*(5), 609–621.
19. Sridhar, S., & Sudha, G. F. (2021). Two in one image secret sharing scheme (TiOISSS) for extended progressive visual cryptography using simple modular arithmetic operations. *Journal of Visual Communication and Image Representation, 74*, 102996.
20. Khan, A. A., Shaikh, A. A., Cheikhrouhou, O., Laghari, A. A., Rashid, M., Shafiq, M., & Hamam, H. (2022). IMG-forensics: Multimedia-enabled information hiding investigation using convolutional neural network. *IET Image Processing, 16*(11), 2854–2862.
21. Saini, P., Kumar, K., Kashid, S., & Negi, A. (2023). MEVSS: Modulo encryption based visual secret sharing scheme for securing visual content. In L. Troiano, A. Vaccaro, N. Kesswani, I. Díaz Rodriguez, I. Brigui, & D. Pastor-Escuredo (Eds.), *Key Digital Trends in Artificial Intelligence and Robotics* (Lecture Notes in Networks and Systems, Vol. 670). Springer.
22. Herzberg, A., Jarecki, S., Krawczyk, H., & Yung, M. (1995). Proactive secret sharing or: How to cope with perpetual leakage. In *Advances in Cryptology—CRYPTO '95: 15th Annual International Cryptology Conference* (pp. 339–352). Springer Berlin Heidelberg.
23. Kashid, S., Kumar, K., Saini, P., Negi, A., & Saini, A. (2022). Approach of a multilevel secret sharing scheme for extracted text data. In *2022 IEEE Students Conference on Engineering and Systems (SCES)* (pp. 1–5). IEEE.
24. Kashid, S., Awasthi, L. K., Kumar, K., & Saini, P. (2023). NS4: A novel security approach for extracted video keyframes using secret sharing scheme. In *2023 International Conference on Computer, Electronics & Electrical Engineering & Their Applications (IC2E3)* (pp. 1–6). IEEE.
25. Pedersen, T. P. (1991). Non-interactive and information-theoretic secure verifiable secret sharing. In *Annual International Cryptology Conference* (pp. 129–140). Springer Berlin Heidelberg.
26. Feldman, P. (1987). A practical scheme for non-interactive verifiable secret sharing. In *28th Annual Symposium on Foundations of Computer Science (SFCS 1987)*. IEEE.
27. Stinson, D. R. (1992). An explication of secret sharing schemes. *Designs, Codes and Cryptography, 2*(4), 357–390.
28. Asmuth, C., & Bloom, J. (1983). A modular approach to key safeguarding. *IEEE Transactions on Information Theory, 29*(2), 208–210.
29. Ateniese, G., Francati, D., Nunez, D., & Venturi, D. (2021). Match me if you can: Matchmaking encryption and its applications. *Journal of Cryptology, 34*(3), 16.
30. Gutub, A., Al-Juaid, N., & Khan, E. (2019). Counting-based secret sharing technique for multimedia applications. *Multimedia Tools and Applications, 78*(5), 5591–5619.

31. McEliece, R. J., & Sarwate, D. V. (1981). On sharing secrets and Reed-Solomon codes. *Communications of the ACM, 24*(9), 583–584.
32. Beutelspacher, A. (1990). *How to Say 'No'*. In *Advances in Cryptology — EUROCRYPT 89*, vol. 434 of "Lecture Notes in Computer Science" (pp. 491–496). Springer-Verlag.

4
Text Encryption

4.1 Introduction to Text Encryption

The rapid acceleration of digital technologies has increased the need to secure digital content shared over unreliable networks. Protecting this data through encryption helps to shield it from unauthorized access [1,2]. Encryption involves converting the original data into coded form, which can be accessed only by authorized parties who possess the appropriate encryption key. An example of encryption can be seen in Figure 4.1. In this example, we can see that when a sender wants to transmit a confidential message, known as plaintext, over a network, it is first converted into an unreadable format; this process is referred to as encryption [3,4]. The key used by the sender to encode the data is called the encryption key. The encoded, unrecognizable form of the data is known as ciphertext. At the receiving end, the receiver can access the original content by decrypting the ciphertext using a decryption key.

Encryption algorithms are divided into two categories: (1) Symmetric Encryption Algorithms (Private key Encryption) and (2) Asymmetric Encryption (Public Key Encryption) [5,6]. If the same key is used for both the encryption and decryption processes, the algorithm is called a symmetric encryption algorithm, as shown in Figure 4.2. In contrast, if different keys are used for encryption and decryption, the algorithm is known as an asymmetric encryption algorithm [7,8] as shown in Figure 4.3. The two keys involved in encryption and decryption are the public key and private key. The public key is openly distributed, and anyone can use it for the encryption process.

On the other hand, the private key is kept secret, and only the receiver uses it to decrypt the message at the receiver's end. In

DOI: 10.1201/9781003500841-4

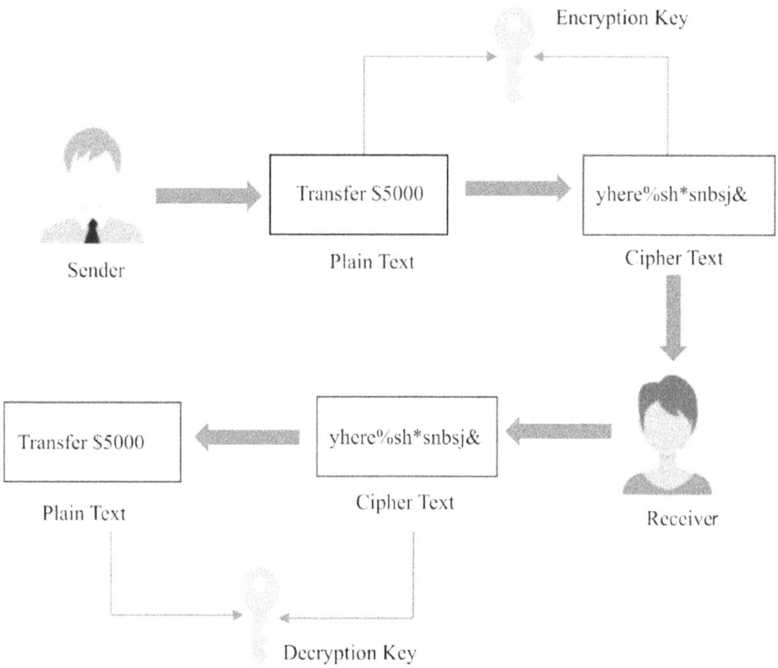

Figure 4.1 Encryption and decryption process example.

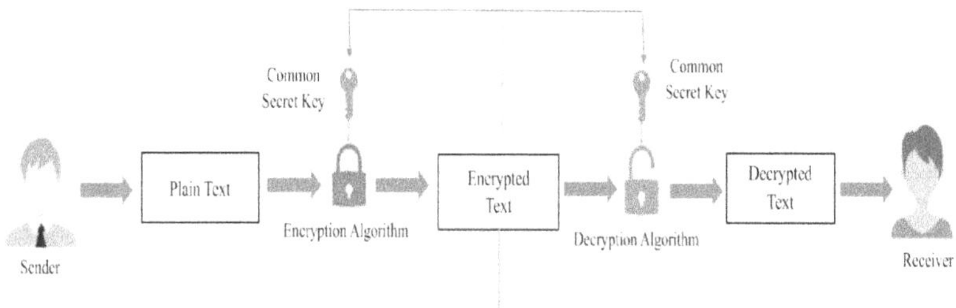

Figure 4.2 Symmetric encryption algorithm.

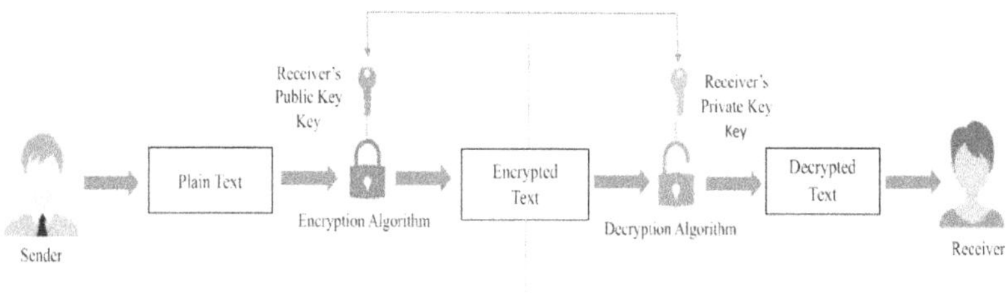

Figure 4.3 Asymmetric encryption algorithm.

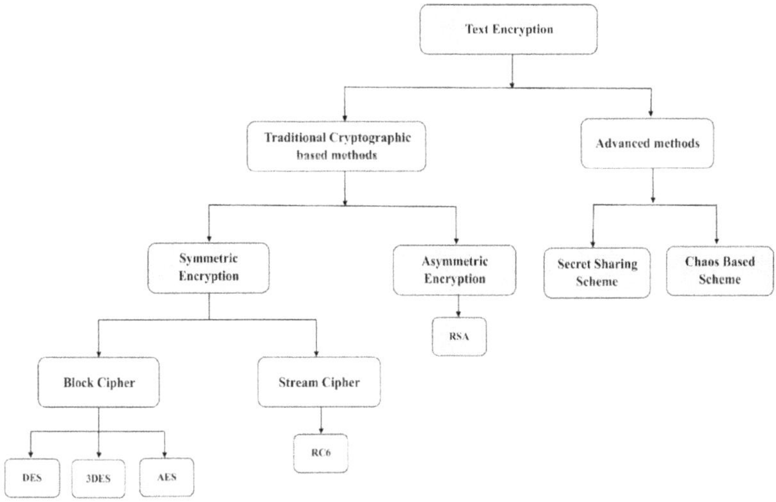

Figure 4.4 Text encryption algorithms.

asymmetric encryption algorithms, mathematical functions are used in encryption and decryption for the conversion of the original text into ciphertext.

Broadly, text encryption algorithms can be divided into traditional cryptographic-based encryption algorithms and advanced algorithms. Traditional encryption algorithms are further divided into symmetric and asymmetric encryption algorithms [8,9]. Secret sharing schemes and chaos-based encryptions are advanced encryption algorithms. During encryption, if the data is processed in fixed-size blocks, then the algorithms are called block ciphers [10,11]. The block may be of any size. DES (Data Encryption Standard) and AES (Advanced Encryption Standard) are examples of block ciphers [12,13]. Stream ciphers convert plain text into cipher text in bits or bytes. RC6 is an example of a stream cipher. The complete classification of various text encryption algorithms is presented in Figure 4.4.

4.2 Traditional Cryptographic-Based Text Encryption Methods

The two main categories of traditional encryption methods are symmetric and asymmetric key encryption [11]. The same secret key is utilized by symmetric encryption methods at both the sender and the recipient ends to encrypt and decrypt data. There are two types of symmetric encryption algorithms: block ciphers and stream ciphers.

One bit or one byte of the input data is encrypted at a time by a stream cipher. These are some examples of stream cipher algorithms: RC6. One block of plain text can be converted into another block of ciphertext using a block cipher [12]. A block has a size of either 64 or 128 bits. Some examples of block ciphers are DES and AES. In asymmetric encryption, the data is encrypted and decrypted using two distinct keys, referred to as the public key and private key. To encrypt data, the sender uses the recipient's public key; to decode data, the recipient uses its private key. Asymmetric key encryption algorithms include the RSA (Rivest-Shamir-Adleman) algorithm.

4.2.1 DES

By using the same key for both encryption and decryption, Data Encryption Standard (DES) encryption is symmetric. It is a block cipher, and the encryption block, or data size, is 64 bits. A 64-bit encryption key is employed. Because it encrypts data using 16 Feistel rounds, DES is also known as the Feistel cipher. Figure 4.5 depicts the architecture of DES. The steps for DES encryption are as follows:

1. The first permutation of 64-bit data.
2. Permuted 64-bit data is split into left and right data halves.
3. A 16 Feistel encryption round is applied to both the left and right data.
4. To obtain 64 bits of encrypted data, the left and right portions of the data are reconnected at the conclusion.

4.2.2 Triple Data Encryption Standard (3DES)

3DES works with 64-bit plaintext blocks at a time. In comparison to DES, 3DES offers improved security since it permits varied key sizes, ranging from 128 to 192 bits. We can say we repeat DES three times. Steps involved in 3DES encryption are as follows:

1. This algorithm generates three distinct keys.
2. The 64-bit plaintext goes through a first permutation.
3. Three levels of encryption are created by encrypting the plaintext three times, each time with a different key.
4. A final permutation is applied to produce the ciphertext.

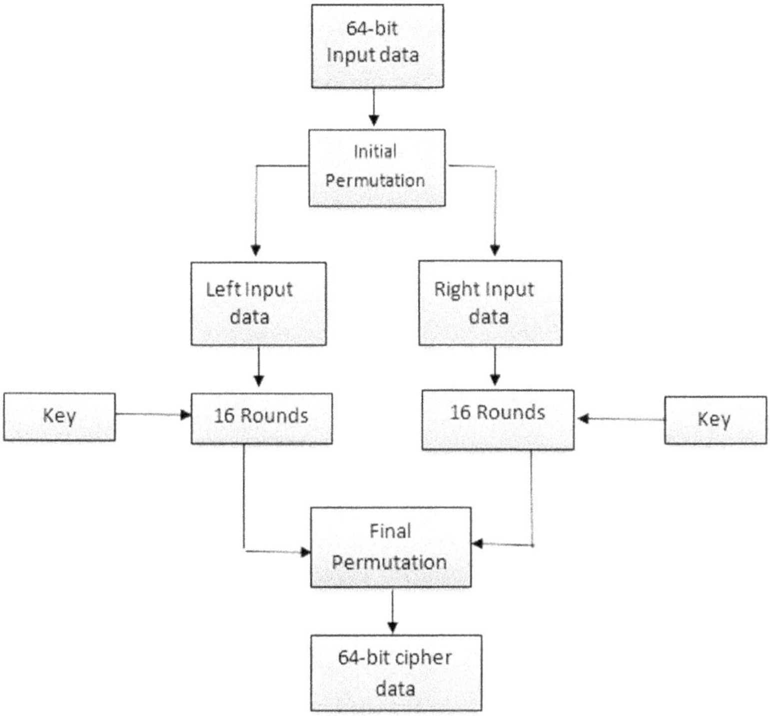

Figure 4.5 Architecture of DES.

4.2.3 Advanced Encryption Standard (AES)

A well-liked encryption technique for encrypting text, photos, and videos is called Advanced Encryption Standard (AES). AES has been the preferred method of video encryption in recent years due to its complexity and difficulty for attackers to decrypt. AES is a symmetric block cipher algorithm. Figure 4.6 represents the abstract view of the AES algorithm. Block ciphers offered by AES come in three varieties.

- **AES-128**

AES-128 uses a 128-bit key stream and 128 bits of input data to encrypt. Ten rounds are used to encrypt a single block of data. Each round involves transposition, substitution, and jumbling of the input data.

- **AES-192**

AES-192 uses a key length and an input data block of 192 bits. Twelve rounds are used to obtain the encrypted data.

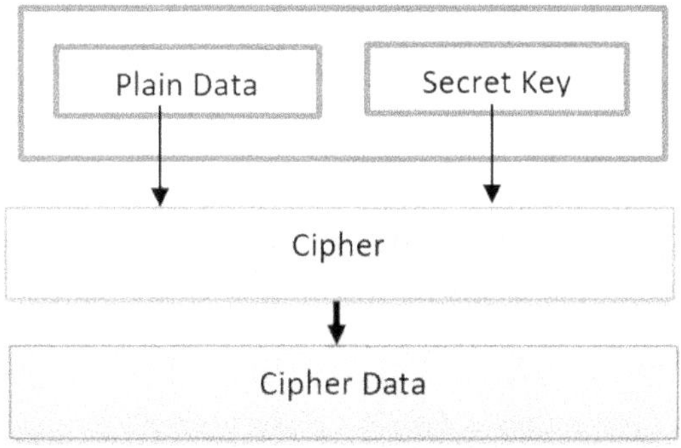

Figure 4.6 AES algorithm abstract view.

- **AES-256**

A-256 uses a key length and an input data block of 256 bits. It takes 14 rounds to encrypt the data.

Substitution, row shift, column mix, and add round key are the main operations of the AES algorithm. Figure 4.7 represents the architecture of the AES encryption algorithm.

4.2.4 RC6 Rivest Cipher 6 (RC6)

RC6 Rivest Cipher 6 (RC6) is a symmetric key cipher algorithm. This block cipher was developed from earlier iterations, such as RC5 and RC4. It supports varied key sizes.

1. The user-supplied symmetric key is used by the RC6 encryption technique to create a collection of round keys. The size of the key determines how many rounds are produced.

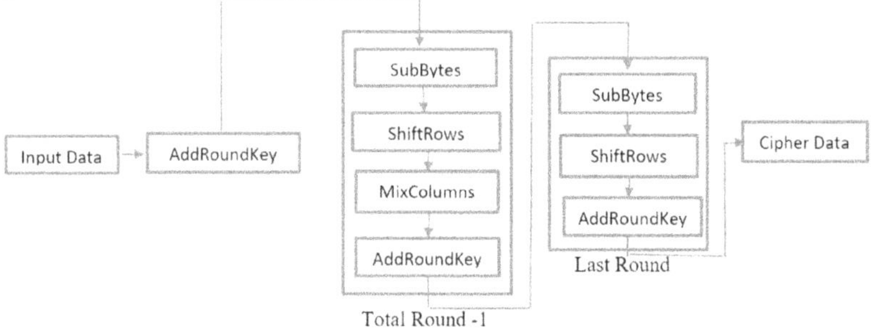

Figure 4.7 AES architecture for encryption.

2. After producing the round keys, plaintext is split up into 16-byte chunks.
3. In a sequence of rounds, the blocks are encrypted with the round keys. Substitution, permutation, mixing, and key addition are the four sub-steps that comprise each round. The output of one round is fed as input to the previous one.

4.2.5 Rivest, Shamir, and Adleman (RSA)

Since Rivest, Shamir, and Adleman (RSA) use separate keys for encryption and decryption, they are asymmetric key encryption methods. When sending and receiving data across a network, RSA is used to encrypt the data, and each party has a public and private key for encryption and decryption. The recipient's private key is used to decrypt the data after it has been encrypted using their public key. Thus, it is not required to exchange any keys in this particular situation. The RSA algorithm's operation is shown in Figure 4.8.

4.3 Secret Sharing Scheme-Based Text Encryption Algorithms

Secret sharing scheme-based text encryption algorithms enhance security by preventing unauthorized access and providing resistance against various attacks. The method of cryptographic encryption using secret sharing schemes (SSS) has emerged as an effective approach for enhancing the security, reliability, and integrity of sensitive textual information. Each part is saved in separate nodes or held by different individuals; therefore, reconstructing the original secret demands a predefined group and surpasses a fixed minimum threshold. For secure key distribution and data confidentiality challenges, this was proposed in 1979 by Adi Shamir and George Blakley. They

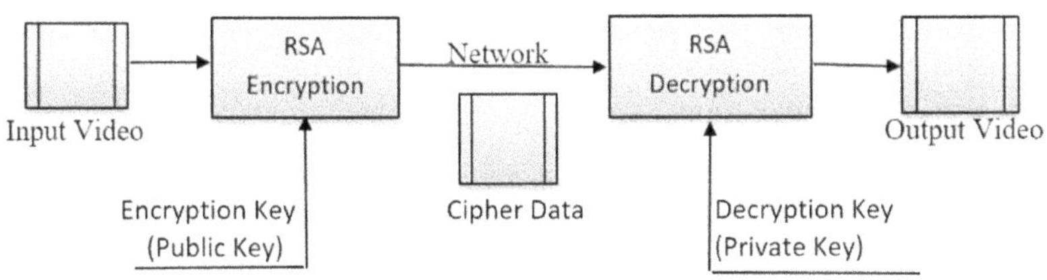

Figure 4.8 RSA algorithm.

focused on providing solutions for these issues. In these types of systems, recovering the original secret requires the minimum number of shares. Take, for instance, the (k, n) threshold system—the secret is reconstructed when k shares are collected out of n total available shares. Any attempt at combining fewer than k shares provides no useful information about the secret. It also ensures confidentiality and fault tolerance.

The primary concern is from the standpoint of security; secret sharing is to decrease risk exposure involved when the encryption keys or sensitive text content are stored in one location. There is a significantly lowered risk of unauthorized access, data corruption, or loss of keys when the shares are kept in numerous secure locations. Secret sharing arrangements also remove single points of failure, meaning operations are maintained even if some shares are lost or compromised [14].

4.3.1 Shamir's Secret Sharing Scheme (SSSS)

Shamir's Secret Sharing Scheme (SSSS) received considerable acclaim in modern cryptography for dividing a secret value among multiple holders. In SSSS, a secret is encoded into multiple shares, which are referred to as tokens. These tokens are allocated to the participants in a manner that a collaborative effort from a predefined number of token holders is required to reconstruct the secret [15].

This scheme is based on a (t, m) threshold structure where a secret is divided into m parts and out of these m parts, any t parts, with $t \leq m$, are sufficient to retrieve the original secret. If less than t tokens are received, the secret remains mathematically locked. The scheme is implemented using polynomial interpolation in finite fields, particularly Lagrange interpolation. A polynomial of degree $(t-1)$ is uniquely determined by t pairs of inputs and outputs, so a random polynomial of degree $m-1$ can be constructed freely in the form:

$$P(z) = s_0 + s_1 z + s_2 z^2 + \cdots + s_{t-1} z^{t-1} \tag{4.1}$$

where:

- s_0 represents the original secret,
- $s_1, s_2, \ldots, s_{t-1}$ are random coefficients selected from a finite field $\mathbb{F}_q$,

- and z denotes the input values at which the polynomial is evaluated.

The tokens are generated through the evaluation of a polynomial at m distinct, nonzero values of z.

Advantages:

- Secrecy: The secret is not accessible with partial data.
- Flexibility: Allows varying threshold limits.
- Mathematical Soundness: The interpolation process is proven to be accurate.
- Fault Tolerance: Share fragmentation preserves secrets even when portions are lost.

Limitations:

- Computational Overhead: When shares increase, computational cost increases.
- Share Management: Proper management of dividing the secret into shares and combining the shares back to form the secret is required.
- Collusion Threats: If k colluding bad actors take advantage of the secret, it can be rebuilt without permission.

Applications:

- Cryptographic Key Management: Keys can be split and distributed securely.
- Secure Voting Systems: Prevents manipulation by ensuring no single authority holds complete power.
- Secure Backups: Distributes critical data securely across different storage locations.
- Access Control Systems: Implements multiparty access controls.

4.3.2 Blakley's Secret Sharing Scheme

Blakley's secret sharing scheme uses a geometric view, in which the secret is seen as a single point in n-dimensional Euclidean space, and each person gets a hyperplane that goes through that point [16–19]. To recover the secret, a specified minimum number of k hyperplanes must be assembled; their mutual intersection produces a unique solution that reveals the point. If fewer than k hyperplanes are brought together, the resulting intersection leaves many possible candidates, so the original secret remains effectively masked. In more formal terms, the secret can be thought of as the coordinate vector:

$$\left(x_1, x_2, \ldots, x_n\right)$$

in an n-dimensional space, and each share corresponds to a hyperplane defined by the linear equation:

$$a_1 x_1 + a_2 x_2 + \cdots + a_n x_n = b \tag{4.2}$$

where:

- $a_1, a_2, \ldots, a_n$ are randomly selected coefficients,
- b is calculated using the secret's coordinates to ensure the hyperplane passes through the secret point.

When at least k such hyperplanes intersect, the original secret can be uniquely determined as the common solution to the system of equations. If fewer than k hyperplanes are available, the set of potential solutions becomes infinite, and no definitive information about the secret can be extracted.

Advantages:

- Geometric Representation: The scheme uses a geometric view that is easy to understand.
- Perfect Secrecy: If there are fewer than k hyperplanes, the secret stays safe.
- Flexibility: The scheme supports different threshold configurations depending on security requirements.

Limitations:

- Computational Complexity: It can be very expensive to solve big systems of linear equations.
- Storage Overhead: Representing hyperplanes may take up a lot of space, especially in higher dimensions.
- Collusion Risk: If k malicious participants collaborate, they can reconstruct the secret without authorization.

Applications:

- Secure Distributed Databases: Sensitive information is divided into parts and securely stored across distributed storage systems.
- Secure Backups: Compromised secrets cannot be uncovered easily, as the secrets are distributed among several storage nodes.
- Access Control: Supports multiparty systems in which no participant can independently view the secret.

Blakley's secret sharing scheme gives you a smart way to share secrets safely using geometry. Hyperplanes make sure that everything is completely private in a multilayered space while still being flexible. Even though it is hard to compute, the scheme is widely used in data backups, access control systems, and secure distributed systems. This plan is better than Shamir's plan, especially for geometric reasoning, because it is simple and strong. Different ways of computing might make Blakley's strategy better in the future.

4.3.3 Threshold Secret Sharing

All schemes derived from the methods of Shamir and Blakley[14,15,20] are encompassed under the broader model of cryptography known as threshold secret sharing. The goals of such methods are to divide a secret s into n parts, called shares $s1,\ldots,sn$, which are distributed among n designated participants. The secret *s* can only be reconstructed when a predetermined threshold *t* is achieved. This method provides additional safeguards, ensuring that the secret is protected even when some shares are lost or some are exposed. As long as the threshold number of valid shares is provided, reconstruction remains mathematically impossible. The model is denoted as (k,n), where:

- *k* is the minimum share threshold to recreate the original secret.
- *n* is the total number of shares given to participants.

The following is a mathematical simplification of threshold-based sharing under this model:

$$k \leq n \tag{4.3}$$

such that any subset of *k* valid shares can reconstruct the secret.

If there are fewer than *k* shares available, the reconstruction process becomes impossible from a mathematical and computational point of view, which keeps the system safe and private.

Advantages:

- Adaptable and Scalable: Changes thresholds and adjusts for more participants.
- Distributed Access Control: This stops a single point of failure or compromise.
- Fault Tolerance: The ability to deal with corruption or share loss without making secret recovery much harder.

Limitations:

- Collusion Risk: Malicious participants that meet the threshold can recover the secret without proper authorization.
- Share Management: Requires secure control of the share's storage and handling.
- Computational Overhead: Incur a notable amount of computation for reconstruction efforts.

Applications:

- Distributed Systems: Guarantees secure communication and proper access in distributed configurations.
- Fault-Tolerant Storage: Prevents data loss by partitioning critical data into multiple nodes of a distributed system.
- Cryptographic Key Management: Divides an encryption key among multiple administrators in a manner that each can manage part of the key securely.
- Secure Cloud Storage: Safeguards sensitive information within cloud environments that span multiple jurisdictions.

Threshold secret sharing is one of the most flexible and near-foolproof ways to keep sensitive data safe. Its theoretical basis guarantees complete privacy and protection from some types of intrusion attacks. This model is becoming more popular in modern architectures like key management, fault-tolerant storage, and secure distributed systems because it is decentralized and can handle faults. Even though they can be hard to work with, threshold schemes are still seen as important for cryptography and information security because they can be used in many different ways and can be made larger.

4.3.4 Verifiable Secret Sharing (VSS)

The current model for sharing secrets is based on trust agreements, which assume that everyone will act honestly during the reconstruction and distribution processes. Some dishonest people might, however, make false shares on purpose to stop reconstruction or reach a specific goal. VSS has this solution, which lets participants verify the shares on their own without giving away any private information. This feature is very useful for using VSS in places where it is not safe, like secure multiparty computation protocols and blockchain technology. VSS has the following goals:

- Participants' shares are real; bad behavior can be found and stopped.
- The reconstruction process will work if the threshold condition is met.
- The reconstruction process will work if the threshold condition is met.
- If the threshold condition is satisfied, the reconstruction process will be successful.

Cryptographic methods like zero-knowledge proofs and commitments are used in verifiable secret sharing to ensure the accuracy and integrity of the shares. By using these methods, participants can confirm:

- That the dealer has consistently distributed shares.
- That the same secret polynomial or geometric structure is represented by each participant's share.

A common commitment scheme used in VSS is the Pedersen Commitment, which mathematically binds a value without revealing it. A typical commitment can be represented as:

$$C = g^s h^r \left(\mathrm{mod}\, p\right) \tag{4.4}$$

where:

- g and h are public generators of a cyclic group.
- s is the secret (or share value).
- r is a random value (to add unpredictability).

These commitments are shared publicly, enabling participants to verify the consistency of their shares.

Advantages:

- Detection of Malicious Behavior: Prevents dishonest participants from disrupting the scheme.
- Ensures Share Consistency: Each participant can verify their share independently.
- Improved Security: Adds an additional layer of trust through verification mechanisms.
- Fault Tolerance: Faulty or malicious shares can be detected and ignored during reconstruction.

Limitations:

- Computational Overhead: Verification mechanisms add computational complexity.
- Increased Communication Costs: Verifiable commitments require additional data exchange.
- Trust in the Dealer (If Non-distributed): A dishonest dealer can still disrupt the process.

4.3.5 Proactive Secret Sharing

In traditional secret sharing, the participants have to protect shares of secrets for a longer time. Due to the longer time, they are vulnerable to attacks. Proactive Secret Sharing (PSS) refreshes the shares frequently without changing the underlying secret. This technique ensures that even if a portion of shares is captured by an attacker, even then the secret is not accessible.

- Eliminating the possibility of a persistent attack slowly discloses bits of the secret over time.
- Through periodic share renewal, the attack lifetimes can be bounded, and hence, the system can be kept secure over time.

These types of systems are exemplified by cloud storage systems and key escrow services, where data must be protected for extended periods of time.

This can be represented as:

$$S_{i'} = S_i + R_i \left(\mathrm{mod} p\right) \tag{4.5}$$

where:

- $S_{i'}$ is the updated share.
- S_i is the current share.
- R_i represents fresh random noise applied to the share.
- p is a prime number defining the finite field.

Advantages:

- Protection against Long-Term Attacks: Regular updates make it difficult for adversaries to accumulate enough valid shares.
- Increased Resilience: The scheme adapts to changing security conditions through periodic refreshes.
- Fault Tolerance: Share corruption or exposure in one period does not compromise subsequent periods.

Limitations:

- Computational Overhead: Frequent share updates introduce significant computational costs.
- Communication Overhead: Redistributing updated shares may require substantial communication bandwidth.
- Synchronization Challenges: All participants must be synchronized during share updates.

4.3.6 All-or-Nothing Secret Sharing

In this method, all the participants are required to reform the secret; subsets are not allowed to form the secret. The secret becomes completely unrecoverable without full participation. This approach focuses on achieving maximum security since no subset of participants—regardless of size—can separate any portion of the secret without all shares being merged.

In an all-or-nothing scheme:

- The secret is divided into exactly n shares.
- No subset of fewer than n shares provides any information about the secret.
- Reconstruction of the secret is possible **only when all n shares are present**.

Mathematically, the scheme can be represented as:

$$S = F\left(S_1, S_2, \ldots, S_n\right) \tag{4.6}$$

where:

- S is the secret.
- $S_1, S_2, \ldots, S_n$ are the shares.
- F represents a reconstruction function that requires all shares.

If any single share (S_i) is missing, the reconstruction process fails entirely, and no partial information about the secret can be inferred.

Advantages:

- Maximum Security: Prevents unauthorized reconstruction by any subset of participants.
- Ensures Full Participation: Guarantees the presence of all stakeholders during secret recovery.
- Simplicity: The scheme is conceptually straightforward and mathematically clear.

Limitations:

- Lack of Flexibility: Requires all participants to be present, with no room for partial reconstruction.
- High Dependency on All Participants: A single missing share renders the secret irrecoverable.
- Scalability Issues: Managing large numbers of participants may become impractical.

Applications:

- Military Secrets: Information classified at this level is extremely sensitive and requires absolute protection.

- Government Documents: Restricted documents ensuring access control with shared highly classified materials.
- Diplomatic Communications: Restricted documents protecting confidential diplomatic correspondence.
- Nuclear Launch Codes: Information protecting critical systems from unauthorized access.

All-or-Nothing Secret Sharing is a special kind of cryptography that allows a secret to be divided into several parts, and each part is assigned to one of the participants. The twist is that every single one of the participants is needed to reconstruct the secret.

4.3.7 Performance Analysis of Various SSS-Based Encryption Techniques

The protection of sensitive and textual information in digital systems is critical in areas like secure communications, cloud computing, and financial activities. The three areas of confidentiality, integrity, and authenticity may be defended by using text encryption techniques. Any encryption scheme, like traditional, threshold, all-or-nothing, secret sharing, verifiable, or proactive, comes with its own pros and cons.

- Computational Efficiency: Measures the time and resources required for encryption and decryption processes.
- Scalability: Assesses the ability of the technique to handle increasing numbers of participants or larger datasets.
- Security Strength: Evaluates resistance to cryptographic attacks, including brute-force, replay, and insider attacks.
- Fault Tolerance: Examines the technique's resilience against share corruption, loss, or participant failure.
- Communication Overhead: Evaluates the additional bandwidth and data exchange required during encryption and decryption processes.
- Key Management: Considers the complexity of managing encryption keys or shares securely.

In Table 4.1, the selected encryption technique must be consistent with the system's security needs, computational capacity, required fault tolerance, and communication limits. For systems susceptible

Table 4.1 Performance Analysis of Text Encryption Techniques

TECHNIQUE	COMPUTATIONAL EFFICIENCY	SCALABILITY	SECURITY STRENGTH	FLEXIBILITY	FAULT TOLERANCE	COMMUNICATION OVERHEAD	KEY MANAGEMENT
Shamir's secret sharing	Moderate	High	High	Flexible (*k*-out-of-*n*)	Moderate	Low	Moderate
Blakley's secret sharing	Moderate	Moderate	High	Moderate	Moderate	Moderate	Moderate
Threshold secret sharing	Moderate	High	High	Flexible (*k*-out-of-*n*)	High	Moderate	Moderate
Verifiable secret sharing	High	Moderate	Very high	Moderate	High	High	Complex
Proactive secret sharing	High	Moderate	Very high	High	Very high	High	Complex
All-or-nothing secret sharing	High	Low	Maximum	None	Low	Low	Simple

to prolonged threats or hostile actors, proactive and Verifiable secret sharing stands out as a viable option.

4.4 Chaotic Maps-Based Text Encryption Algorithms

Chaotic maps are used to generate pseudorandom sequences that are utilized to encrypt textual data. Chaotic maps are sensitive to initial conditions, indicating the random numbers needed to create secure encryption keys, which makes chaos theory a suitable basis for the design of solid cryptographic algorithms [16,17]. Chaotic maps are mathematical functions that describe the evolution of chaotic systems, and they are essential for studying chaotic dynamics and its applications. It began with Henri Poincaré's contributions [18] to the three-body problem of celestial mechanics. Due to their sensitivity to initial conditions, the paths taken by three mutually interacting bodies under gravitational attraction can never fully be predicted, and even slight perturbations in initial conditions lead to course outcomes that can gravely differ from one another. Commonly, all chaotic map-based encryption schemes have a common architecture that consists of permutation and diffusion phases. The pseudorandom sequence or key will be used to change the position of data in the permutation stage [19]. In the next stage referred to as the diffusion phase, the value of data is modified by applying various operations using the same chaotic sequence.

References

1. Schneier, B. (2015). *Applied Cryptography: Protocols, Algorithms, and Source Code in C.* Wiley Publishing.
2. Mohamed, K. S., & Mohamed, K. S. (2020). Cryptography concepts: Confidentiality. In *New Frontiers in Cryptography: Quantum, Blockchain, Lightweight, Chaotic and DNA* (pp. 13–39). Springer.
3. Sanchez, J., Correa, R., Buenaño, H., Arias, S., & Gomez, H. (2016, March). Encryption techniques: A theoretical overview and future proposals. In *2016 Third International Conference on eDemocracy & eGovernment (ICEDEG)* (pp. 60–64). IEEE.
4. Naser, S. M. (2021). Cryptography: From the ancient history to now, it's applications and a new complete numerical model. *International Journal of Mathematics and Statistics Studies*, *9*(3), 11–30.

5. Coles, M., & Landrum, R. (2009). Introduction to encryption. In *Expert SQL Server 2008 Encryption* (pp. 1–20). Berkeley, CA: Apress.
6. Hellegren, Z. I. (2017). A history of crypto-discourse: Encryption as a site of struggles to define internet freedom. *Internet Histories*, *1*(4), 285–311.
7. Syed, N. F., Shah, S. W., Shaghaghi, A., Anwar, A., Baig, Z., & Doss, R. (2022). Zero trust architecture (zta): A comprehensive survey. *IEEE Access*, *10*, 57143–57179.
8. Alatawi, M., & Saxena, N. (2023, May). Sok: An analysis of end-to-end encryption and authentication ceremonies in secure messaging systems. In *Proceedings of the 16th ACM Conference on Security and Privacy in Wireless and Mobile Networks* (pp. 187–201). ACM.
9. Orman, H. (2015). *Encrypted Email: The History and Technology of Message Privacy*. Springer International Publishing.
10. Reyad, O., Mansour, H. M., Heshmat, M., & Zanaty, E. A. (2021, March). Key-based enhancement of data encryption standard for text security. In *2021 National Computing Colleges Conference (NCCC)* (pp. 1–6). IEEE.
11. Khadam, U., Iqbal, M. M., Alruily, M., Al Ghamdi, M. A., Ramzan, M., & Almotiri, S. H. (2020). Text data security and privacy in the internet of things: Threats, challenges, and future directions. *Wireless Communications and Mobile Computing*, *2020*(1), 7105625.
12. Merkle, R. C. (1978). Secure communications over insecure channels. *Communications of the ACM*, *21*(4), 294–299.
13. Borisov, N., & Mitra, S. (2008). Restricted queries over an encrypted index with applications to regulatory compliance. In *Applied Cryptography and Network Security: 6th International Conference, ACNS 2008, New York, NY, USA, June 3–6, 2008. Proceedings 6* (pp. 373–391). Berlin Heidelberg: Springer.
14. Al Ebri, N., Baek, J., & Yeun, C. Y. (2011, December). Study on Secret Sharing Schemes (SSS) and their applications. In *2011 International Conference for Internet Technology and Secured Transactions* (pp. 40–45). IEEE.
15. Dawson, E., & Donovan, D. (1994). The breadth of Shamir's secret-sharing scheme. *Computers & Security, 13*(1), 69–78.
16. Patel, N. (2019). Your personal health information may have been compromised: Using encryption to prevent data breaches on end-user devices. *Hofstra Law Review*, *48*, 563.
17. Arachchi, H. K., Perramon, X., Dogan, S., & Kondoz, A. M. (2009). Adaptation–aware encryption of scalable H. 264/AVC video for content security. *Signal Processing: Image Communication*, *24*(6), 468–483.
18. Bhatt, C., Tiwari, C., Thalal, B. S., Vishnoi, A., Joshi, K., & Singh, T. (2024, March). Secured multi-platform communication application using advanced encryption standard algorithm. In *2024 10th International Conference on Advanced Computing and Communication Systems (ICACCS)* (Vol. 1, pp. 483–487). IEEE.

19. Karthick, R. (2024). Advanced threat detection in backup systems: AI, encryption, and role-based access control. In *International Conference on Emerging Computational Technologies*. Eternal Scientific Publication.
20. Judijanto, L. (2024). Data security in computers: An introduction to the concept of encryption. *International Journal Of Humanities, Social Sciences And Business (INJOSS)*, *3*(3), 416–425.

5
Image Encryption

5.1 Introduction

The advancement in the field of science and computer technology has extensively increased the transmission of digital images. In various fields such as military, medical, remote sensing, legal, and intellectual property, there is a high level of confidential and sensitive information in the form of digital images [1]. Image encryption can be utilized to protect the data from potential threats. Image encryption converts the original image into an unrecognizable format using a secret key. The unrecognizable format is in the form of noise and is called a cipher image. The decryption process uses the same process in reverse order to decrypt the image [2]. Based on the number of keys used in the encryption process, we can classify image encryption into two types: (1) private key or symmetric key image encryption, as shown in Figure 5.1, and (2) public Key or asymmetric image encryption. In private key image encryption, the same key is used to encrypt and decrypt the digital image, as shown in Figure 5.2. This key must be kept secret and shared only between the communicating parties. Private key image encryption methods such as AES (Advanced Encryption Standard) are generally faster and computationally less intensive [3]. In the case of public key image encryption, two different keys are utilized for encryption and decryption. The public key can be shared openly, allowing anyone to encrypt an image, while the private key is kept secure and used by the authorized party to decrypt the image. RSA is one of the most widely used asymmetric encryptions. The two types of encryption schemes are presented in Figures 5.1 and 5.2 [4].

DOI: 10.1201/9781003500841-5

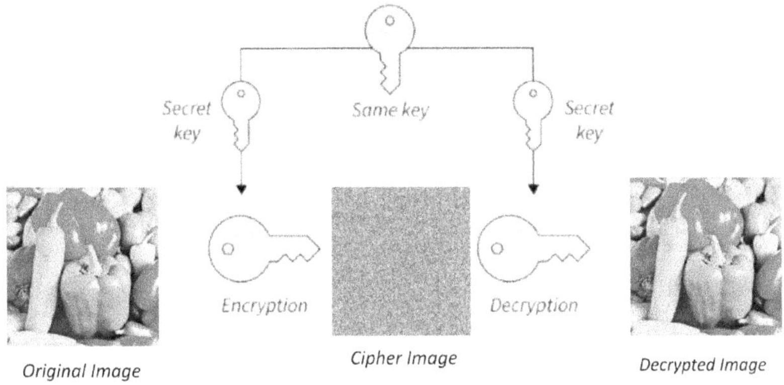

Figure 5.1 Private or symmetric key image encryption.

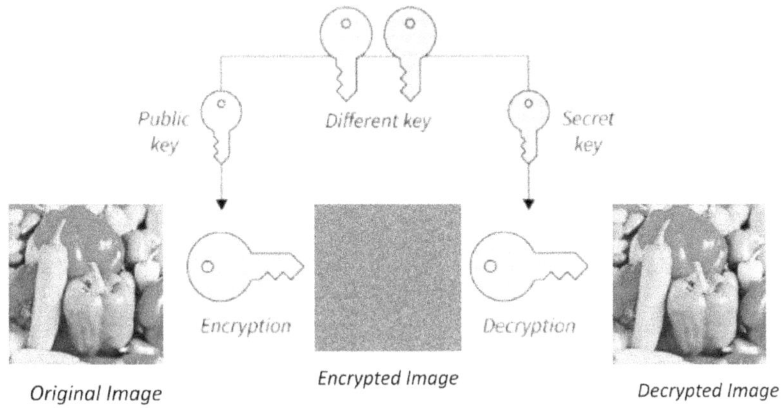

Figure 5.2 Public or asymmetric key image encryption.

5.1.1 Image Encryption Approaches

Figure 5.3 shows a number of image encryption algorithms, classified into four major areas: Optical Domain, Transform Domain, Spatial Domain, and Compressive Sensing. All the domains make use of unique methods to encrypt image data. Amplitude phase retrieval, position multiplexing, and phase truncation are used in the Optical Domain. the Transform Domain encodes images using mathematical transformations such as wavelet, gyrator, and the Fresnel transform. The Spatial Domain employs direct pixel-level methods such as chaotic maps, elliptic curves, DNA encoding, and so on. Metaheuristics and Compressive Sensing combine compression and encryption at the same time, providing a lightweight and effective defense that can be

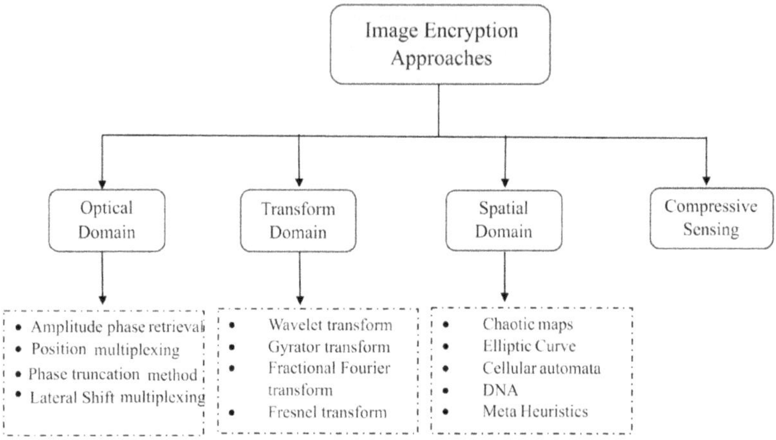

Figure 5.3 Image encryption approaches.

used in real-time applications and resource-restricted contexts. All these varied approaches are appropriate to address the changing needs of security of images in this digital era [5].

5.2 Need for Image Encryption

Nowadays, in the digital era, images have been ranked as one of the most popular kinds of data, which is highly utilized at the personal, professional, and organizational levels of communication. Whether it is social media platforms and cloud storage, medical records and surveillance systems, or any other sphere, the sharing of images is inevitable. Nonetheless, such extensive dissemination is also attributable to a high number of privacy and security threats. The need, therefore, exists to come up with strong image encryption mechanisms. Block ciphers include mainly the Data Encryption Standard (DES) and the Advanced Encryption Standard (AES). They suit mainly textual information and cannot be useful to encrypt image information [6]. These are some of the major reasons why image encryption is essential:

5.2.1 Data Complexity and Data Volume

5.2.1.1 New Cyber Threats

Increasing the efficiency in Resource-Stressed Environments: As the Internet of Things (IoT) experiences a wider scope, there is an increased concern to protect images that are retrieved using Internet of Things (IoT) gadgets, such as smart cameras, sensors, and drones. The device in question is likely to run in an environment of limited power, storage, and processing capacity. Thus, strategies that are energy-efficient and lightweight encryption approaches are necessary to be established [6].

5.2.1.2 Compliance and Privacy

In today's digital world, images have become one of the most widely shared types of data, used extensively in personal, professional, and organizational communication. From social media platforms and cloud storage to medical records and surveillance systems, the sharing of images is essential in many domains. However, this widespread sharing also associates significant privacy and security risks. Therefore, there is a requirement to develop robust image encryption techniques. Data Encryption Standard (DES) and Advanced Encryption Standard (AES) are widely used block ciphers. They are primarily designed for textual data and are not suitable for encrypting image data [6]. Here are some key reasons why image encryption is crucial:

Increased Data Complexity and Volume: Images are now high-resolution data of large volume: files which demand high computing. High-resolution and/or dimensional image data is not efficiently handled as compared to the conventional methods of encryption. Real-time applications such as video streaming on the Internet or surveillance video monitoring can be carried out with the help of new methods of encryption, capable of supervising an extensive amount of data in a timely manner, without delays [6].

Emerging Cyber Threats: Cyberattacks are becoming more advanced today and are targeting and taking advantage of the weaknesses in the traditional encryption methods. Existing encryption algorithms are vulnerable to attack methods such as brute force, statistical analysis, and differential cryptanalysis, which can easily crack [6].

Improving Efficiency in Resource-Constrained Environments: As the Internet of Things (IoT) experiences a wider scope, there is an increased concern to protect images that are retrieved using Internet of Things (IoT) gadgets, such as smart cameras, sensors, and drones. The device in question is likely to run in an environment of limited power, storage, and processing capacity. Thus, strategies that are energy-efficient and lightweight encryption approaches are necessary to be established [6].

Enhanced Security Requirements for Privacy and Compliance: Legal and compliance requirements of privacy have increased in security. The modern privacy regulations and legal structures have advanced in terms of security requirements. Modern privacy laws and regulations, such as the General Data Protection Regulation (GDPR) and Health Insurance Portability and Accountability Act (HIPAA) impose high levels of security. In order to conform to these standards, the encryptions should ensure that the security is robust to safeguard personal information [6].

Need for Real-Time Encryption in Streaming and Surveillance: Surveillance and streaming services are now heavily reliant on real-time encryption to secure video and image data on the fly. Traditional encryption methods are often too slow to handle the high-speed processing demands of live video encryption, especially when dealing with large data streams [6].

Security for Emerging Technologies: Data shared or stored in fields such as augmented reality (AR) and virtual reality (VR) also need to be secure to prevent its unauthorized access [6].

5.3 Image Encryption Using Chaos Theory

Chaos theory studies the behavior of dynamic systems that are highly sensitive to initial conditions. The phenomenon is commonly known as the "butterfly effect." In a chaotic system, a small change in the starting conditions can lead to vastly different outcomes, resulting in high unpredictability and randomness. These properties make chaos theory a valuable asset in cryptography, especially for applications requiring secure and unpredictable patterns, like image encryption [7].

The fundamental properties of chaotic systems that make them suitable for cryptography include the following:

- **Deterministic Behavior with Unpredictability**: Chaotic systems are deterministic but appear random, making them ideal for cryptographic purposes.
- **Sensitivity to Initial Conditions**: Small variations in the starting parameters of a chaotic system led to significantly different outcomes, enhancing security.
- **Ergodicity**: The system eventually explores a wide range of states, ensuring that encrypted images have a high degree of randomness.

5.3.1 Architecture of Chaos-Based Image Encryption Schemes

In Figure 5.4, the chaos-based encryption methods use a chaotic map to generate a highly random chaotic sequence that is used in the encryption process. Mainly, the chaos-based encryption comprises two phases: Permutation and Diffusion. Permutation is used to scramble the positions of pixels, whereas Diffusion is used to change the value of pixels. The chaotic sequence is used in the permutation and diffusion steps during encryption [7].

Key Generation and Parameter Initialization: Cryptographic keys are generated for initializing the chaotic maps. These keys typically consist of initial conditions and control parameters for the chaotic functions. A unique feature of chaos-based encryption is its reliance on initial parameters for chaotic systems. These variables define the chaotic behavior and randomness in the encryption process. A slight change in any of such initial conditions (encryption keys) results in an entirely new encrypted result. This increases the security of the

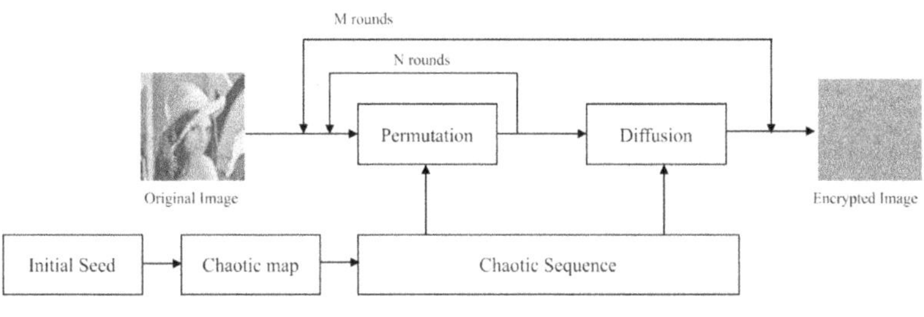

Figure 5.4 Chaos-based image encryption.

scheme. The keys and the initial conditions hold much importance in the security of any encryption scheme based on chaos. Thus, to construct a secure chaos-based cryptosystem, the selection of the initial parameters is a compulsory task. An attacker might manage to obtain the initial conditions; they might also endanger the security of the whole system as they often have chaotic maps [7].

Permutation: The permutation stage is required in order to defeat the spatial correlation between pixels. The resulting image in this stage is a disruption of the original image, in terms of the existing structure and patterns, due to the chaotic system altering the location of the pixels. This technique hides any visual clues that potential assailants could usually use to examine the content. A chaotic map such as the Baker Map, Logistic Map, or Arnold Cat Map produces a rule or set of rules on how to rearrange the pixel positions. It is with this sequence that the positions of pixels are rearranged. Each color channel can also be permuted independently to add complexity. The pixel position scrambling is unique to each encryption, and it ensures that the original image cannot be exposed [7].

Diffusion Stage: After permutation, the diffusion stage modifies the pixel values based on chaotic sequences, effectively spreading the influence of each pixel across the entire image. This stage ensures that minor changes in the input image or encryption key result in significant alterations throughout the entire encrypted image, known as the avalanche effect. Chaotic maps, such as Henon or Logistic maps, generate random values that are used to alter the intensity or color values of each pixel. The chaotic sequences generated during this step are combined with pixel values, either by addition, XOR operations, or other mathematical transformations, to ensure that the image data is thoroughly diffused. In the case of color images, diffusion is applied independently to each color channel to further enhance the encryption complexity [7].

5.3.2 Classification of Chaos-Based Image Encryption Schemes

The classification of chaos-based image encryption methods is categorized according to their integration with other techniques. The first category, Only Chaos-based Confusion-Diffusion, relies solely on the intrinsic unpredictability of chaotic systems to scramble and diffuse image data. The second, chaos combined with AES, enhances traditional encryption by embedding chaos to increase complexity and resistance to attacks. The chaos + DNA computing approach uses principles of molecular biology alongside chaos theory to encode data at the nucleotide level, improving security. Lastly, chaos integrated with cellular automata leverages the dynamic behavior of cellular automata combined with chaotic maps for lightweight, efficient, and secure image encryption, particularly suited for real-time and embedded systems [8].

The random nature of chaotic maps builds secure cryptosystems. There are several ways to apply chaotic maps in image encryption. Some encryption methods solely use chaotic maps in their confusion-diffusion procedures, while others combine chaotic maps with other methods. Based on the technology with which chaotic maps are combined, we can categorize chaos-based image encryption methods as shown in Figure 5.5.

Only Chaos-Based Confusion-Diffusion: Many encryption schemes directly use the chaotic maps in the confusion and diffusion procedure. The chaotic map equations are iterated using some initial seed to generate random chaotic values. The generated chaotic values can be used in several ways, such as a pseudorandom secret key, a hash function, an S-Box, a random sequence for pixel scrambling and modification [8].

Chaos Combined **with AES**: Advanced Encryption Standard (AES) is a secure image encryption algorithm. To improve its efficiency, researchers have integrated AES with chaotic systems such as Neupane et al. [1] proposed a hybrid encryption algorithm that integrates chaotic maps with the AES encryption standard. The approach

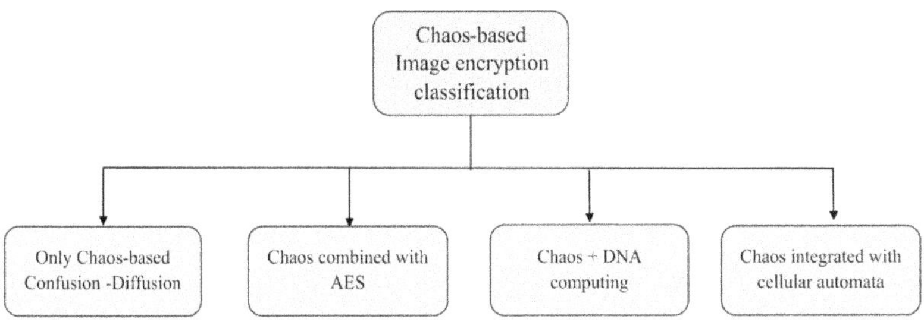

Figure 5.5 Chaos-based image encryption classification.

utilizes a three-dimensional chaotic map to generate a series of bit sequences across three planes: X, Y, and Z.

The Chaos Combined with DNA-Based Image Encryption Algorithm: The interconnection of chaos and DNA-based encoding is the future law of image encryption technique. When considering the chaos that is sensitive to initial conditions and its unpredictability, chaos is applied in the generation of random sequences or keys needed in encryption. A DNA encoding DNA image replacement system is a biological implementation based on DNA encoding, which converts the value of pixels to a sequence of the DNA nucleotide bases (A, T, C, G). This two-tier technique improves protection with chaotic sequences used to scramble and substitute the pixels, and DNA functions like XOR, addition, or complement would give a layer of encryption based on the natural concepts of DNA. The combination of the techniques results in a very strong encryption scheme since brute-force attacks are very unlikely to succeed, provides spacious key spaces, and guarantees intricate encryption strategies applicable to sensitive image data [8].

Chaos Integrated with Cellular Automata: Cellular automata (CA) are grid-based computational systems on which every cell modifies its state according to particular rules and according to the state of neighboring cells. These systems are parallel and quite dynamic in nature, and thus, they are appropriate for undertaking operations such as the scrambling of data and the production of keys during encryption. When used together, chaotic maps and cellular automata provide a powerful security arena for image encryption. Chaotic messages are normally applied to generate pseudorandom keys or scramble the pixels in the image, and cellular automata operations are carried out, making the data even more hidden under rules. This two-fold strategy increases the cryptanalytic resistance and provides high security during the transmission of sensitive images [9].

5.4 Secret Sharing Schemes-Based Encryption of an Image

Image encryption is a process of transforming data images to a format that cannot be read or deciphered by unauthorized persons. Large image files and other special requirements related to visual data transmission, however, may challenge traditional encryption algorithms as they have a high rate of redundancy and spatial correlation of pixels. An interesting solution is encryption-based secret sharing. In secret sharing, one shares some data into different parts or shares in such a way that only a given combination of shares can restore the initial data. This will be very secure against unauthorized access, since in the event that the shares are intercepted, they do not expose unauthorized users to information unless they have reached the established requirements. Secret Image Sharing Image Encryption Schemes (SSS) fall into a number of categories [10].

5.4.1 *Threshold Secret Sharing Scheme (TSS)*

Threshold secret sharing scheme is a cryptographic process in which a secret value is shared into a plurality of shares (or portions), such that any subset of shares is able to recover the initial secret. This subgroup is known as the threshold that determines how many shares one needs to obtain the secret. The system is also very sturdy, since it guarantees that only in case a maximum number of shares (equal to or greater than the threshold) would be available would the original data be attained, whereas any less would give no clues about the secret. Areas of application include secure data storage, image encryption, mutually distributed systems, and image encryption [11].

5.4.2 *Verifiable Secret Sharing Scheme (VSS)*

Secret sharing is a cryptographic scheme in which the shares that are created ensure that the data is secure, but a Verifiable Secret Image Sharing Scheme (VSISS) goes further to ensure that each separate share is easily verified to be genuine. In contrast to classical secret sharing schemes in which the validity of shares is based on trust that the shares were created properly and not altered, a VSISS offers a way to authenticate shares before allowing them to be used to reconstruct the image. Secret sharing is a technique that divides data into multiple parts, or "shares," so that only a specific combination of these shares can reconstruct the original information. This approach is highly resilient against unauthorized access because even if some shares are intercepted, they reveal no information unless the required threshold is met. The Secret Image Sharing Image Encryption Schemes (SSS) can be classified into several categories [10,12, 13].

5.5 Performance Analysis

There are different types of encryption evaluation metrics to test the effectiveness of image encryption algorithms against different types of attacks. These encryption metrics include Histogram Deviation, Irregular Deviation, Entropy, number of pixels change rate (NPCR), unified average changing intensity (UACI), Histogram Uniformity, and so on. This section discusses these metrics. Figure 5.6 shows the diagrammatic classification of these parameters [14].

Histogram Deviation: The given histogram deviation maximizes the difference between the plain image and the cipher one. It determines the quality of the process of encryption. The deviation value of the histogram is supposed to be larger in order to give a good quality of the encryption. In order to obtain the histogram deviation, we, firstly, obtain the histogram of the plain image and of the cipher image. A difference is then determined between the two created histograms by the following equation:

$$H_D = \frac{(d_0 + d_{255})/2 + \sum_{i=1}^{254} d_i}{M \times N} \tag{5.1}$$

where d_i is defined as the amplitude of the absolute difference at gray level i.

Deviation from Ideality: It determines how well the encryption scheme is. It is specified as the capacity of an encryption to reduce the amount of disparity of the cipher image with the ideal value. Ideally, the encrypted image (C_1) should have a completely uniform distribution of the histogram [1]. The deviation from ideality (I_D) is defined as:

$$I_D = \frac{\sum_{C_I=0}^{255} \left| H(C_1) - H(C) \right|}{M \times N} \tag{5.2}$$

where $H(C)$ is described as the histogram of the cipher image. $H(C_1)$ is ideal value of the cipher image histogram. Mathematically, $H(C_1)$ is defined as:

$$H(C_1) = \begin{cases} \frac{M \times N}{256}, & 0 \le c_1 \le 255 \\ 0, & \text{otherwise} \end{cases} \tag{5.3}$$

Chi-Square Analysis: The distribution of the encrypted image in the histogram is checked with the help of chi-square analysis. The test described by chi-square is defined as:

$$X = \sum_{i=1}^{k} \frac{(N_i - NP)^2}{np} \tag{5.4}$$

where N_i is defined as the number of pixels in the ith interval, N is defined as the total number of pixels, and $P = 1$. The chi-square creates a number P, and the value of the P lies between $[0,1]$.

Histogram Uniformity: The number of occurrences of gray level pixels of an image is plotted as a bar graph that is called a histogram. The horizontal and vertical axes are used in plotting the histogram. The horizontal axis has the gray level of the image. A horizontal axis value starts with zero, which increases to include the amount of gray pixels. The y is the vertical axis, which is the frequency of repeats of the pixel of the image [1]. As a rule, the histogram of a cipher image must offer the following two available characteristics: (1) the distribution of the cipher image ought to be even. (2) The histogram of higher and lower cipher images and the original image must differ.

Kolmogorov–Smirnov Test: Kolmogorov–Smirnov test, also known as the KS test, is a method of comparing the probability distribution of the function $f(x)$ and the theoretical value of the distribution

$$D = \max\left|f(x) - g(x)\right| \tag{5.5}$$

The system is chaotic; then the value of the Kolmogorov–Smirnov test is positive. A larger value of the Kolmogorov–Smirnov test shows complex chaotic behavior.

Statistical Attack: During a statistical attack, the attacker violates the strategy of encryption by using the correlation coefficient (CC) and entropy of the image

- **Information Entropy**: Information entropy is the measure of the randomness and unpredictability of an image, and it is defined as:

$$E(i)=\sum_{j=0}^{2^N-1} p(I_j)\log_2 \frac{1}{p(I_j)} \tag{5.6}$$

where $p(I_j)$ is the probability of random variable I_i. The value of information entropy should be 8.

- **Correlation Coefficient**: The relationship between the neighboring pixels of the image is characterized by the correlation coefficient (CC). The best outcome of CC is almost zero in delivering a good quality of image encryption method. Mathematical: It can be shown as:

$$c_{i,j}=\frac{\operatorname{cov}(i,j)}{\sqrt{A(i)}\sqrt{A(j)}} \tag{5.7}$$

$$\operatorname{cov}(i,j)=\frac{1}{M}\sum_{k=1}^{M}\left(x_k-B(x)\right)\left(y_k-B(y)\right) \tag{5.8}$$

$$A(x)=\frac{1}{M}\sum_{k=1}^{M}(x_k-B(x))^2 \tag{5.9}$$

$$B(x)=\frac{1}{M}\sum_{k=1}^{M}x_k \tag{5.10}$$

In this case, $c_{i,j}$ represents the CC, M represents pixel pairs chosen at random, and i,j represents the two neighboring pixels. $A(x)$ is the variance of x and $B(x)$ is the expectation of x.

Key Sensitivity: Key sensitivity means all the inaccurate decryption output, even when one makes the slightest change in a shared key during the encryption or decryption procedure. In order to analyze the significant sensitivity of the proposed scheme, initially, the encrypted image is obtained using a shared key and applying the suggested encryption procedure to the image. Afterwards, a single fragment of such a common identical key is changed in a random location, and the already predicted cipher picture is interpreted. The decrypted image generated during the decryption process using an altered key is highly noisy and unintelligible. The significant degradation in the recovered image confirms the strong key sensitivity of the proposed encryption algorithm.

Differential Attack: The two cipher images obtained by an attacker enable him to execute a differential attack. The former photo is a cipher photo which is produced by the original photo. Small changes in the pixels of the image in the initial image also generate another cipher image. The attacker tries to exploit the circumstance that, in case we provide input data which has a certain predefined alteration, then a certain alteration in the output pattern must occur. The cryptanalysis of the encryption algorithm is made on the basis of the modification between two input images that are already predetermined by the attacker. The two parameters that are used to test the efficiency of the proposed image encryption scheme against differential attack are known as the number of pixels change rate (NPCR) and Unified average changing intensity (UACI), which is explained below.

Unified average changing intensity (UACI) [3] indicates the difference between the average intensity of the two images. The higher value of the UACI is good because it shows that encryption is good. It is defined mathematically as follows:

Avalanche Effect: Avalanche effect is the one used to determine the efficiency of the diffusion mechanism. A modified image (I_M) is generated by making changes to one bit in the original image (I) to find out the avalanche effect. Afterwards, the original image and edited image are then coded. Cipher images C_1 and C_2 are produced out of the original image and the altered image, respectively. The difference between C_1 and C_2 is almost half of the total length of the image. Next, the encryption algorithm is good at diffusion.

Chosen/Known Plaintext Attack: A Chosen Plaintext Attack (CPA) considers that the attacker chooses some plain images and produces their cipher image with the help of the encryption process. The primary aim of the selected plaintext attack is to get blind information, such as the secret key. Nevertheless, there is the Known Plaintext attack (KPA) as a model of attack where the attacker has both the plain image and its cipher image produced upon the encryption. The enemy derives the secret data, such as the secret key. The conventional diffusion and confusion methods include a secret key alone. The identical keystream is used with this secret key with a large number of images, i.e., the secret key in many images does not change.

- **Number of Pixel Change Rate**: Number of pixel change rate(NPCR) [2] fixes how the minimal alteration of the pixel value of the original picture causes alteration of the cipher image. It must be superior with an increase in value in the encryption of an image. The original image is used to form the cipher image (C_1). The cipher image C_2 will be formed with a minor adjustment in the value of a pixel of the already used original image. Mathematically, the expression to attain the NPCR value can be:

$$\text{NPCR} = \frac{1}{X \times Y} \sum_{i=1}^{X} \sum_{j=1}^{Y} N(i\ j) \times 100\% \tag{5.11}$$

where:

$$N(i,j) = \begin{cases} 0, & C_1(i,j) \neq C_2(i,j) \\ 1, & \text{otherwise} \end{cases} \tag{5.12}$$

- **Unified Average Changing Intensity**: Unified average changing intensity (UACI) [3] indicates the difference between the average intensity of the two images. The higher value of the UACI is good because it shows that encryption is good. It is defined mathematically as follows:

$$\text{UACI} = \frac{1}{X \times Y} \sum_{i=1}^{X} \sum_{j=1}^{Y} \frac{|E_1(i,j) - E_2(i,j)|}{255} \times 100\% \tag{5.13}$$

Here, $E_1(i,j)$ and $E_2(i,j)$ are two encrypted images.

Avalanche Effect: Avalanche effect is the one used to determine the efficiency of the diffusion mechanism. A modified image I is generated by making changes to one bit in the original image (I) to find out the avalanche effect. Afterwards, the original image and edited image are then coded. Cipher image C_1 and C_2 are produced out of the original image and the altered image ($AltI$), respectively.

The C_1 and C_2 difference is almost half of the total length of the image. Next, the encryption algorithm is good at diffusion.

NIST Randomness Test: The National Institute of Standards and Technology (NIST) created the test suite (NIST SP 800-22 Rev. 1a) for the randomness test. The randomness test is a parameter to evaluate the performance of the statistical properties of the cipher image. The test suite contains 15 different tests that are used to identify the non-randomness that exists in the cipher. This test calculates the *P*-value, and the resultant *P*-value should be greater than 0.01 for the success of this test.

Brute-Force Attack: The attacker attempts to calculate all the possible combinations to decrypt the cipher image. The focus of the adversary is to guess the correct secret key. The minimum size of key space to defend against the brute-force attack should be 128-bit.

Decryption Parameters

A good encryption scheme should output the image very close to the original or the same as the original after decryption; i.e., minimum loss should be there while performing decryption. Figure 5.7 describes these metrics.

- **Bit Correct Ratio (BCR)**: The number of bit errors present in the plain image and cipher image is known as BCR. Mathematically, BCR is represented as:

$$\mathrm{BCR} = 1 - \frac{\sum_{m,n}^{m\times n}, P(x\ y) \oplus D(x,y)}{m \times n} \tag{5.14}$$

The pixel at location (x, y) is represented by $P(x, y)$ and $D(x, y)$ in the plain and decrypted video frame. The value of BCR should be between 0 and 1.

- **Mean Square Error (MSE)**: MSE finds the square of the average difference between the original and cipher frame. The formula used to define MSE is given by:

$$\mathrm{MSE} = \frac{1}{a \times b} \sum_{x=1}^{a}, \sum_{y=1}^{b} L(x,y) - M(x,y)]^2 \tag{5.15}$$

Here a and b represent row and column, respectively. The pixel at location (x, y) is represented by $L(x, y)$ in the original image and $M(x, y)$ the cipher video.

- **Mean Absolute Error (MAE):** MAE calculates the average absolute differences between original video frame pixels and cipher video frame pixels. MAE between two pixels should have a large value. The formula to find Mean Absolute Error (MAE) is as follows:

$$\text{MAE} = \frac{1}{a \times b} \sum_{x=1}^{a}, \sum_{y=1}^{b} \left| L(x\ y) - M(x, y) \right| \tag{5.16}$$

Here $L(x, y)$ and $M(x, y)$ is the intensity of the pixel at the position (x, y) of the plain frame and the encrypted frame.

- **Structure Similarity Index Measure (SSIM):** It assesses the visual quality and structural information of an image or video frame. It calculates how similar an image or video frame is to a reference image. The pixel metrics of the original and encrypted video frames are denoted by $P_x(i, j, k)$ and $C_x(i, j, k)$, respectively. The following formula is utilized to calculate the Structural Similarity Index Measure (SSIM):

$$\text{SSIM} = \frac{\left(2\mu_{P_x}\mu_{C_x} + C_1\right)\left(2\sigma_{P_xC_x} + C_2\right)}{\left(\mu_{P_x}^2 + \mu_{C_x}^2 + C_1\right)\left(\sigma_{P_x}^2 + \sigma_{C_x}^2 + C_2\right)} \tag{5.17}$$

Here, the mean of P_x and C_x is given by μ_{P_x} and μ_{C_x}. The variance of P_x and C_x is $\sigma_{P_x}^2$ and $\sigma_{C_x}^2$ respectively. The covariance of $\sigma_{P_xC_x}$ is given by x and y. $C_1 = (k_1L)^2$ and $C_2 = (k_2L)^2$. We set $k_1 = 0.01$ and $k_2 = 0.03$ and L is equal to the range of pixels.

- **Root Mean Square Error (RMSE):** It finds the average of the error value between corresponding pixels of a plain video frame and a cipher video frame. The formula to calculate RMSE is as follows:

$$\text{RMSE} = \sqrt{\text{MSE}} = \sqrt{\frac{1}{a \times b} \sum_{x=1}^{a} \sum_{y=1}^{b} [L(x,y) - M(x,y)]^2} \quad (5.18)$$

Here a and b represent row and column, respectively. The pixel at location (x, y) is represented by $L(x, y)$ in the original image and $M(x, y)$ cipher video.

- **Peak-Signal-to-Noise Ratio**: To evaluate the quality of the encrypted image in comparison to the original image, Peak-Signal-to-Noise Ratio (PSNR) is utilized. The formula used to calculate it is as follows:

$$\text{PSNR} = 10 \times \log_{10} \frac{255 \times 255}{\sqrt{\text{MSE}}} \quad (5.19)$$

A higher quality of reconstructed image/video frame should have a high PSNR value.

- **Signal-to-Distortion Ratio (SDR)**: The "noise" or "distortion" is unintended changes or degradation introduced during the encryption process. The Signal-to-Noise Ratio (SNR) measures how well the original image's information is preserved compared to the introduced distortions or changes during encryption. The mathematical formula to calculate SDR is as follows:

$$\text{SDR} = 10 \times \log_{10} \left(\frac{\sum_{i,j} L(i,j)^2}{\sum_{i,j} \left[L(i,j)^2 - M(i,j)^2 \right]} \right) \quad (5.20)$$

Here $L(i, j)$ and $M(i, j)$ is the plain and decrypted video frame pixel at position (i, j).

References

1. Kaur, M., & Kumar, V. (2020). A comprehensive review on image encryption techniques. *Archives of Computational Methods in Engineering, 27*(1), 15–43.

2. Kumari, M., Gupta, S., & Sardana, P. (2017). A survey of image encryption algorithms. *3D Research*, *8*, 1–35.
3. Islam, M., Shah, M., Khan, Z., Mahmood, T., & Khan, M. J. (2015, December). A new symmetric key encryption algorithm using images as secret keys. In *2015 13th International Conference on Frontiers of Information Technology (FIT)* (pp. 1–5). IEEE.
4. Mohamad, M. S. A., Din, R., & Ahmad, J. I. (2021). Research trends review on RSA scheme of asymmetric cryptography techniques. *Bulletin of Electrical Engineering and Informatics*, *10*(1), 487–492.
5. Liu, Z. (2018). *Comparative Evaluations of Image Encryption Algorithms*. Auckland University of Technology.
6. Mohammad, O. F., Rahim, M. S. M., Zeebaree, S. R. M., & Ahmed, F. Y. (2017). A survey and analysis of the image encryption methods. *International Journal of Applied Engineering Research*, *12*(23), 13265–13280.
7. Zhang, B., & Liu, L. (2023). Chaos-based image encryption: Review, application, and challenges. *Mathematics*, *11*(11), 2585.
8. Tuli, R., Soneji, H., Vahora, S., Churi, P., & Bangalore, N. M. (2022). PixJS: A novel chaos-based approach for image encryption. *Concurrency and Computation: Practice and Experience*, *34*(17), e6990.
9. Turgut, O. E., & Turgut, M. S. (2024). Chaotic gradient based optimizer for solving multidimensional unconstrained and constrained optimization problems. *Evolutionary Intelligence*, *17*(3), 1967–2028.
10. Saha, S., Chattopadhyay, A. K., Barman, A. K., Nag, A., & Nandi, S. (2023). Secret image sharing schemes: A comprehensive survey. *IEEE Access*, *11*, 98333–98361.
11. Lou, T., & Tartary, C. (2008). Analysis and design of multiple threshold changeable secret sharing schemes. In *Cryptology and Network Security: 7th International Conference, CANS 2008, Hong-Kong, China, December 2–4, 2008. Proceedings* 7 (pp. 196–213). Springer Berlin Heidelberg.
12. Stadler, M. (1996, May). Publicly verifiable secret sharing. In *International Conference on the Theory and Applications of Cryptographic Techniques* (pp. 190–199). Berlin, Heidelberg: Springer Berlin Heidelberg.
13. Chandramouli, A., Choudhury, A., & Patra, A. (2022). A survey on perfectly secure verifiable secret-sharing. *ACM Computing Surveys (CSUR)*, *54*(11s), 1–36.
14. Ahmad, J., & Ahmed, F. (2010). Efficiency analysis and security evaluation of image encryption schemes. *Computing*, *23*(4), 25.

6
Audio Encryption Strategy

6.1 Introduction to the Audio and Its Encryption

Audio: sound that is recorded and saved by a machine (such as a recorder or a digital sound player) that uses a magnetic device or a laser to record on a specially coated surface. The sound waves are analog in nature and have amplitude and frequency [1]. The analog waves are now converted into a digital signal (binary data) by two main processes, sampling and quantization. Sampling refers to capturing brief instants from the wave at constant time intervals, and quantization refers to assigning a numerical value to each captured instant to depict its magnitude [2]. Audio has become ubiquitous in daily human life, providing a wide range of applications in education, entertainment, healthcare, etc. [3]. In education, it improves learning with audiobooks, language training, and e-learning formats. In entertainment, sound enhances experiences with music, podcasts, and immersive sound in gaming and movies. Healthcare also depends on audio for telemedicine, mental health apps, and making information available for the visually impaired. Audio sound is influenced by several important factors.

- **Sample Rate**: It refers to how many audio snapshots, or samples, are taken every second when sound is recorded or played back. It is measured in Hertz (Hz) or kilohertz (kHz), where 1 kHz equals 1,000 samples per second. A higher sample rate means more samples are captured, leading to a more accurate reproduction of the original sound. For example, the standard sample rate of 44.1 kHz (used in CDs) captures 44,100

DOI: 10.1201/9781003500841-6

samples per second, which is sufficient to reproduce high-quality sound that the human ear perceives as natural. Higher sample rates, such as 48 kHz or 96 kHz, are used for even greater precision, especially in professional audio and video production.

- **Bit Depth**: Bit depth refers to how much information is stored for each individual audio sample. It directly affects the dynamic range of the audio, which is the difference between the quietest and loudest sounds that can be captured or played back without distortion. A higher bit depth captures more detail, allowing both very soft and very loud sounds to be recorded more accurately. For instance, 16-bit audio, which is standard for CDs, provides 65,536 possible levels of sound, offering a good balance between quality and file size. However, 24-bit audio, commonly used in professional recording studios, provides over 16 million levels, allowing for even greater accuracy and a wider dynamic range, especially important in environments requiring high-quality audio, like film scoring or mastering tracks.
- **Channels**: Channels refer to the number of separate audio streams used to create sound. Audio can be mono (single channel) or stereo (two channels). The textbook in both cases is mono audio, where the same sound comes out of all speakers, perfect for voice recordings, telephone calls, etc. Stereo sound—two channels, left and right—comes through both a set of earbuds and headphones, bringing a feeling of direction, including hearing a sound from overhead or behind you, a standard in music and entertainment. Higher tier formats like surround sound, e.g., 5.1 (5 speakers and 1 subwoofer) or 7.1 (7 speakers and 1 subwoofer), construct a more realistic, 3D soundscape using the multiple speakers. These mediums are also commonly used in home theaters, cinemas, and gaming to achieve a more immersive acoustic experience.
- **Compression**: Compression shrinks large raw audio files for easier storage. Compression is all about the compromise of file size and quality to everyone's needs and tastes. Just as with video, raw audio files are quite large and, therefore, are compressed to a common audio format such as MP3, AAC,

or FLAC. Compression codecs such as MP3 and AAC shrink file size by eliminating minor audio details that are harder to perceive, but still provide high-quality sound that's perfect for most listening and streaming purposes. Lossless compression formats, such as FLAC or ALAC, don't remove any of the audio information from the original recording, resulting in better sound quality for those seeking uninhibited listening. However, compressed formats still have a general equivalence to make uncompressed formats smaller and more convenient to use, but leave less high sound quality because of the file's increasing size. Compression algorithms are designed to reduce file size by simplifying audio data, making it more efficient to store and transmit. While compressed audio is convenient and widely used, especially for casual listening, there is often a trade-off between file size and audio fidelity.

6.1.1 Audio Encryption

In Figure 6.1, the audio technology is vital in fields like communication, entertainment, education, and security. To protect audio data, ensure privacy, and prevent unauthorized access during transmission or storage, audio encryption is essential [4]. Encryption is crucial for applications like voice calls, recordings, streaming media, and confidential data embedded in audio files (e.g., steganography). Audio encryption refers to the process of securing audio data by converting

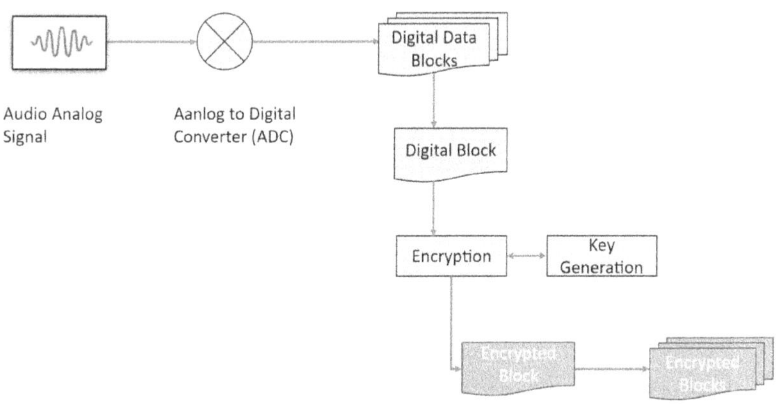

Figure 6.1 Architecture of audio encryption.

it into an unreadable format using cryptographic algorithms. Audio encryption involves the following steps.

- **Audio Conversion**: To convert analog audio data to digital data, a general process referred to as the Analog-to-Digital Conversion (ADC) is used.
- **Encryption Process**: The audio data is encrypted by the audio encryption during transmission and storage, so that the audio data in a readable form is transformed into an unreadable form based on the encryption algorithm. In symmetric encryption, a single key takes part in both processes: encryption and decryption of the audio data; therefore, achieving high speed and less complexity of operation [e.g., AES (Advanced Encryption Standard)]. But preserving the key securely among the communicating parties is a difficult task. On the other hand, asymmetric encryption (method) consists of two totally separate keys, one of which is a private key and the other is a public key: the public key can be distributed freely and widely, whereas the private key is kept secret to its respective owner (e.g., RSA algorithm). This technique provides secure communication even if the public key is disclosed.
- **Ciphertext Generation**: It is the process of designing an encrypted (ciphertext) version of a digital audio signal based on a cryptographic algorithm. This process starts by using the selected encryption (symmetric or asymmetric) and the encryption key used. The algorithm takes plaintext, the original audio data, and jumbles it in such a way that it becomes secure and unreadable. A ciphertext obtained in this way tends to have the property that the audio data can only be obtained from other than the original form by decrypting the ciphertext with an appropriate private key. Converting to an encrypted form is an important step in securing audio for privacy while in transit or at rest.
- **Decryption**: In the decryption phase, the cryptographic algorithm undoes the effect of encryption, recovering the original audio from its encrypted form. It is the transformation of an encrypted audio file (ciphertext) into its original, unencrypted state (plaintext) by using a decryption key. This

process secures the original audio data through protection between individuals with the right keys only.

6.2 Need for Audio Encryption

Audio encryption is very important because of the exploding audio data that is transmitted, stored, and downloaded over diverse platforms in the present digital world [5, 6]. It grants users full privacy and security on sensitive audio content, such as phone calls, recordings, or streaming media, preventing unauthorized access, interception, or alteration. Encryption also preserves data integrity and confidentiality, which is essential for securing communication and storage [7]. Some requirements for audio encryption are as follows:

- **Privacy for Confidential Content**: The audio material sometimes contains confidential and/or private information such as conversations, conferences, or personal messages. The content is encrypted so that it can be accessed only by those who have been given permission to access it. Audio encryption prevents intruders from being able to receive audio files or streams and intercept existing ones and listen to them—which keeps eavesdropping and manipulation of this data to a minimum.
- **Legal and Regulatory Compliance**: Many industries (for example, healthcare, finance) are bound by rigorous privacy regulations like HIPAA or GDPR that demand that audio communication is encrypted. Encrypting audio is a way for organizations to obey these rules so that private information in audio itself remains secure and meets legal compliance standards.
- **Safe Transfer Over Networks**: When audios are transmitted over the internet or other networks, it can be intercepted by hackers. Encryption acts like a protective shield, protecting audio by jumbling it into garbled code as it is transmitted. That is, if you intercept that sound, you should not be able to understand it because it should be encrypted. Only someone with the corresponding decryption key. can restore it to its original form, leaving the audio you create secure and private.

- **Intellectual Property Protection**: Artists such as musicians, podcasters, and businesses need to keep content encrypted to avoid theft and distribution of their content without proper permissions. If the audio file is obtained by unauthorized persons, they may make illegal copies or redistributions, resulting in economic losses. Encryption enables content creators to control who can access their work so that no one hears it who should not.
- **Prevent Data Alteration**: The voice data files are also kept in the original state using encryption. If a person tries to modify an encrypted audio file, they can no longer read it. This is particularly crucial when the audio content's integrity is of the essence, such as in a courtroom or secured messages.
- **Sensitive Communication Confidentiality**: In specific audio communication cases, which are highly secure, like corporate meetings or private conversations, the encryption of these communications adds an element of confidentiality. These conversations, if they are encrypted, cannot be eavesdropped on or recorded by unauthorized persons.

6.2.1 Types of Audio Encryption

Figure 6.2 Audio encryption. This covers a variety of approaches designed to protect audio data. Audio encryption is a process of

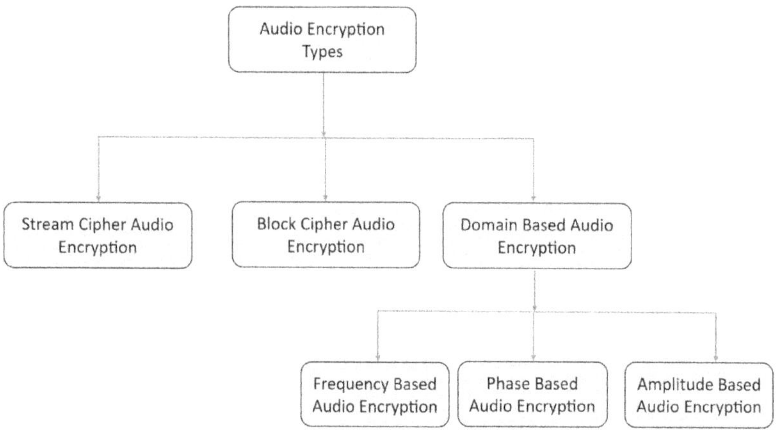

Figure 6.2 Different approaches for audio encryption.

securing audio files and streams during transmission with an encryption algorithm. Stream ciphers, block ciphers, and domain-specific techniques like amplitude-based, phase-based, and frequency-based are among the main techniques used for audio encryption. All such methods find specific applications depending on the characteristics of the audio data under consideration and the assumed security needs.

Stream Cipher Encryption: Stream cipher processes an audio stream without breaking it into fixed-size blocks [8]. This method operates on an audio bit-to-bit or byte-to-byte basis, which makes it particularly appropriate for real-time encryption, such as with live audio streaming or voice communication. Salsa20 [9] or ChaCha20 are stream cipher encryption algorithms that are better and more recent.

Benefits

- Low Latency: It can quickly encrypt and decrypt, making fit for live audio streaming and real-time communication.
- Performance: Needs less processing power, suitable for resource-limited devices.
- Ease of Integration: More straightforward to integrate into applications that may need to encrypt data at loop; however, no one can really tell.

Drawbacks

- Key Management Issues: Most of these stream ciphers use different keys in order to keep the session secure.
- Errors Sensitivity: A single error in the keystream can completely disrupt the decryption.
- Security: Older stream ciphers, such as RC4, are susceptible to attack if they are not well implemented.

Applications

- VoIP (Voice Over Internet Protocol) Services: Secure communication between people talking, utilizing applications such as Skype and Zoom.
- Live Audio Streaming: Secures and delivers high-quality real-time live streams.
- IoT Devices: Preserves persistent audio streams in connected devices such as digital assistants.

Block Cipher Encryption: Block ciphers are 128 or 256-bit blocks of input audio processed separately or in combination with previous (blocks of) data [10]. This approach is useful when you need to encrypt stored audio files or when you are working with structured streaming data. Block ciphers offer versatility with multiple modes of operation, such as CBC (Cipher Block Chaining), which ensures security by chaining blocks together, and GCM (Galois/Counter Mode) that integrates encryption and data integrity. The most famous example here is AES; it is still the gold standard in block ciphers due to its being fast as well as secure. Block Ciphers—since they need a fixed-size block of data to encrypt or decrypt— are not ideal for real-time audio encryption. This block-based processing can contribute to (some) transmission delay, so block ciphers are less suitable for real-time streaming or applications that need low latency, including VoIP. Therefore, they are more suitable to be used in stored audio files or chunk-based streaming services where the speed is less important.

Benefits

- Security: High service level security via robust algorithms and modes of operation. Perfect for Static Data Protect your stored audio archives such as music libraries, podcast collections, or digital recordings.
- Adaptable: Can be used with various encryption algorithms for improved security or performance, depending on the use case.
- Versatility: Can work with various encryption modes, enhancing security or performance depending on the use case.
- Data Integrity: Several block cipher modes, such as GCM, guarantee the integrity of the data as well as encryption.

Drawbacks

- Latency: A delay can be induced even in the processing of fixed-sized blocks (e.g., in real-time operation).
- Computationally Intensive: It is computationally expensive, thus more inappropriate for resource-constrained devices.
- Complex implementation: There is some complexity associated with some modes (e.g., CBC, GCM), and if implemented incorrectly, it can result in attacks.

Applications

- Stored Audio Files Security: Relevant audio files (e.g., voice recordings, copyrighted music, etc.) are protected during storage.
- Stream-Styling Platforms: Encrypts audio in pieces for secure playback with services such as Netflix and Spotify.
- Digital Rights Management (DRM): Ensures copyrighted audio is accessible only to authorized users.

Frequency-Based Encryption: Frequency-based encryption works by converting the audio signal from the time domain to the frequency domain using methods like FFT (Fast Fourier Transform). In this process, the audio signal is broken down into its frequency components, and encryption is applied to these components. Since audio is understood by humans in terms of its frequency, encrypting these parts makes the audio unintelligible without the correct decryption key.

Benefits

- Preserves Audio Characteristics: Frequency-based encryption allows the encrypted audio to maintain its overall audio characteristics, making it suitable for high-quality audio signals like music and complex soundscapes.
- Selective encryption is available (e.g., encipher only major frequencies).
- Good for applications such as streaming, in which there is a premium on computational efficiency.
- Frequency domain encryption suits compressed audio as most audio codecs (e.g., MP3, AAC) are also frequency-based; therefore, it is easy to plug in integration.

Drawbacks

- High Computational Cost: Moving from the time to the frequency domain of audio, e.g., using the FFT (Fast Fourier Transform), incurs high computational cost, which is not favorable for real-time applications or systems with limited computation/energy resources.

- Noise Sensitivity: May be sensitive to noise or distortion in the transmit or storage process, which can reduce the information content of the encrypted Single Nucleotide Polymorphisms (SNP) and render the depth decryption process more complex.
- Additional Latency: There may be additional delay introduced due to the processing tasks of converting and encrypting the frequency components, which can be a problem for real-time audio scenarios (especially applications such as VoIP or live streaming).

Applications

- Digital Rights Management: For copyright protection of music and audio recordings distributed through digital channels.
- Military Secure Transmission: Protects voice-moving communications over secure military communication links, including commands and surveillance recordings, to mask and protect sensitive information from interception and decoding by adjacent adversaries.
- Telemedicine: Preserves private data, for example, encrypted medical records (e.g., heart sounds or speech therapy sessions) to keep the confidentiality in telemedicine systems.
- Audio Watermarking: Audio watermarking for copyright protection by embedding encrypted frequency domain watermarks to trace and prove ownership of music tracks.

Phase-Based Encryption: Phase-based encryption method operates by introducing distortion only in the phase of the signal while preserving its magnitude (or amplitude). Which is to say the loudness and tone of the sound are not altered, and the adjustments are not audibly obvious. Since these phase changes are relatively unobtrusive and do not alter the audio's perceived quality, the straight quality is maintained, yet the signal is protected from being pirated. The method is especially effective in the sharing of private audio as it allows for strong encryption without sacrificing user experience.

Benefits

- Inaudible to the Human Ear: Phase changes are typically inaudible to human hearing so that the encrypted audio still sounds like the original and is perfectly suited for applications where fidelity is a must.

- Magnitude Preserving: Since only the phase is changed and the amplitude is left intact, it is compatible with standard playback systems, and decoding requires no specialized hardware or software.
- High Security: The encryption ensures that the flowing ciphertexts do not make sense to unauthorized listeners, as the information is warped in a phase that is hard to recover without possessing the encryption key.
- Low Complexity: In phase-one based encryption, the computational complexity is lower than that associated with phase and amplitude-based methods, which translates into good real-time performance.

Drawbacks

- Types of Compatibility Problems Regarding Advanced Processing: Since phase-based encryption is based on the modification of audio phases, any kind of transformation of the audio can degrade the encrypted data. Moreover, the computational cost could become much higher, especially when the input signal is large, or it needs to work in real time, which would result in possible time lagging of the processing.
- Hard to Implement for the Complex Signals: To correctly encrypt and decrypt phase information without any mistakes with respect to complex audio signals, it may be difficult to technically encrypt and decrypt the phase information with more precise algorithms.
- Lack of Perceptual Enrichment: The method does transmit audio but does not improve it, i.e., remove noise and improve quality, so it cannot be used in use cases requiring audio perception improvement.
- No Compression Gains: It does not compress the audio, so other compression is necessary for storage or transmission, adding processing complexity.

Applications

- Voice Commands Protection in IoT: Protects confidential audio commands from appliances such as intercoms and security systems, which secures audio in streaming services.

- Gaming and Entertainment: Protects team communications in multiplayer games from being intercepted by rival gamers, and guards access to premium audio content within games and virtual events.
- Academic and Research Data Security: Secure transmission of audio data for research studies and sensitive audio data collected in experiments and surveys.

Amplitude-Based Encryption: This method modifies the amplitude (loudness/quietness) of an audio signal in a fashion that is abnormal for the human auditory system [11]. This is done in a controlled way, such that the original sound is still unintelligible to someone who does not know how to decrypt it. The essential idea of amplitude-based encryption is to adapt the sound intensity but to preserve the frequency and phase components of an audio signal such that anyone who wants to regenerate or recognize the original signal should have the decryption key. This process is easier than phase-based or frequency domain-based encryption; however, as it operates on the OR of the two aspects of the audio signal (either the amplitude) rather than the complicated frequency/phase component. But even for all its crudeness, it can still serve to offer reasonable security in some applications, especially in cases where sophisticated encryption algorithms are not required.

Benefits

- Simplicity: It is easy to realize and computationally less expensive than more complex encryption methods such as phase-based or frequency domain-based encryption.
- Computationally Low Complex: Minimal requirement on computational resources, i.e., it adds only amplitude modifications to the original audio signal and is suitable for low-complexity or real-time encryption scenarios.
- Nearly Zero Effect on Playback Equipment: The encrypted audio does not have any effect on frequency and phase, so the playback hardware can be common ordinary hardware by adjusting the volume level alone, and it achieves high compatibility with most systems.

Drawbacks

- Insecurity of the Coded Amplitude Information: The good security performance of amplitude scrambling is generally believed to be inferior to that of higher-order fusion, or phase/frequency-domain encryption. Amplitude scrambling alone may be too weak against attacks when statistical properties can be easily predicted. Large random gain factors may lead to excessive distortion and may have a negative impact on audio quality.
- Lack of Robustness: The encrypted data based on this might not be robust against noise or distortion. Because it raises and lowers the volume, environmental noise can disrupt the encrypted signal, making it hard for someone to decrypt it properly.
- Not for Complex or Sensitive Applications: It may not be appropriate for delicate data and privacy settings, and applications that require heavy-duty encryption. Higher-level security needs may call for more complex techniques, e.g., phase or frequency-based encryption.

Applications

- Voice Assistants: Voice commands and discussions with smart devices (e.g., Alexa, Google Assistant) can be protected by an amplitude-based encryption protecting them from unauthorized access.
- Secure Communication: This layer is for applications designed to secure personal communication, such as encrypted voice calls on mobile phones or secure messaging systems. Communication systems in which real-time is of the essence.

The following Table 6.1 compares encryption techniques based on their complexity, perceptual quality, security, applications, and real-time feasibility.

6.3 Role of Audio Encryption in the Digital Era

Audio encryption is an essential factor for providing privacy and security in the digital world in different fields. High-quality audio

Table 6.1 Comparison of Audio Encryption Techniques

Aspect	**Stream Cipher**	**Block Cipher**	**Frequency Based**	**Phase Based**	**Amplitude Based**
Complexity	Low to moderate	Moderate to high	Moderate	Moderate	Low
Perceptual quality	High	High	High (if selective encryption)	High	Medium (if excessive scrambling)
Security	High (depends on key)	Very high (with strong keys)	High (depends on key/ algorithm)	High	Medium
Application	Real-time audio streams	Securing stored audio files	Streaming, VoIP, DRM	Streaming, DRM	Low-power devices
Real-time feasibility	Very high	Moderate	Moderate to high	Moderate	High

encryption is a technical prerequisite but also a key part of the digital trust mechanics of audio-driven technologies that guide our modern digital society. It keeps private communications, like voice calls and teleconferences, secure and private. In the entertainment sector, encryption is used to protect music, podcasts, and audiobooks from piracy by letting only authorized users access them. It secures users' private data, such as voice assistants and wearables, defends users against cyber threats and data privacy laws, and makes it easier for relevant agencies to cooperate during offensive cyber operations. Encryption allows secure access to live streaming and broadcasting, ensuring only eligible users have access to events with the help of Digital Rights Management (DRM) that prevents piracy and redistribution of content. Besides, audio encryption can improve cybersecurity by protecting money transfers that are established on voice from cyberattacks such as man-in-the-middle (MITM) interception, so its application is critical for trust and security in this digital era.

Key aspects of Audio Encryption:

- Privacy: Secure sensitive communications, including voice calls, meetings, and conference calls from unauthorized access and eavesdropping.
- Keep Original Metadata: Presets of music, podcast, and audiobook are available to choose from to classify audio files automatically, so that you do not need to do this manually.
- Privacy: Protects voice data from smart devices such as Alexa, Google Home, and wearables and ensures privacy regulation and cybersecurity protection.
- Identification and Trust: Empowers safe voice authentication for financial transactions and biometric verification, and with that also guarantees no data breach and the prevention of fraud.
- Broadcast and Streaming Security: Secures limited access to live events, webcasts, webinars, and streaming while using Digital Rights Management (DRM) to stop theft, piracy, or unauthorized use.
- Cybersecurity Maturation: Protect audio communications and put more guardrails in place across the broader digital

security structure to help prevent man-in-the-middle attacks. These considerations underscore the critical need for audio encryption to establish a foundation of privacy, security, and confidence in the digital world of today.

6.4 Audio Encryption Using Chaos Theory

Standard symmetric encryption algorithms such as DES [12], AES [13], and RSA [14] are not suitable for real-time audio encryption, though they provide strong security. This is because there are several problems. For one, audio data is of great volume; traditional encryption algorithms' overhead is great, which can make it very difficult for real-time applications to operate. Secondly, symmetric algorithms have limited key sizes, they are exposed to brute-force attacks, and the redundancy of encrypted signals is also considered, which affects the quality of the signal. Third, the computational power and time complexity of these algorithms are very high because complex operations are carried out therein. Fourth, it is always necessary to preserve the perceptual quality of audio in audio usage, but the traditional cipher always deteriorates the content of audio. Another major factor is that asymmetric encryption is too slow for encryption to be applied directly to audio. In recent years, chaotic systems have been discussed as promising for audio encryption, as they have good behaviors in tackling these problems [15].

In Figure 6.3, the intuitive rationale of employing chaotic maps in encryption is linked with the fact that chaotic systems, though deterministic, are very sensitive to initial conditions and control parameters. This renders these parameters and those conditions perfect as keys in a cipher scheme. Furthermore, the low cost of manufacturing

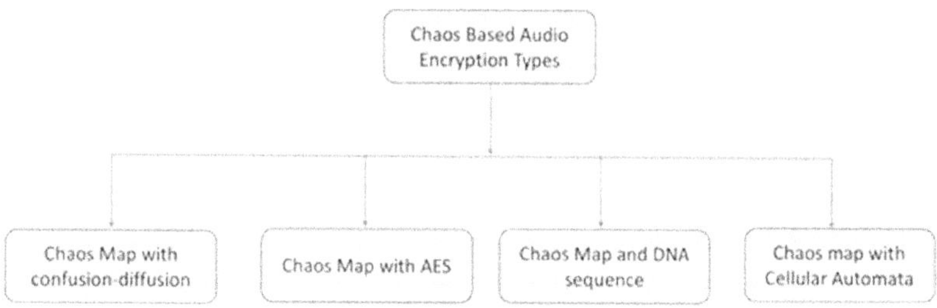

Figure 6.3 Chaos-based audio encryption types.

chaotic signals encourages us to apply them in the domain of audio encryption algorithms [16]. AN also slouch for the fact that generation of a chaotic signal typically requires little by way of computation (certainly when compared to conventional cryptographic channels that utilize cryptographic algorithms, e.g., AES, DES, all of which can require substantial resources). The low cost of chaotic signals is the principal reason that chaos is suitable for real-time applications like audio encryption, where processing power and speed are necessary [17]. The chaos-based audio encryption can be divided into several categories depending on the type of chaotic map used, the method to encrypt (e.g., scrambling or diffusion) [18], the synchronization scheme implemented, and the mathematical operations applied to mix the audio data with chaotic signal [19].

Audio Encryption with Chaos Techniques Using Confusion and Diffusion: The low-rate waveform coding covers a large body of what is known as chaos-based encryption schemes. Chaos mappings, such as the logistic map and the Lorenz system, can produce, to some extent pseudorandom sequences making use of the extreme sensitivity to the initial conditions. In this approach, confusion shuffles the positions of audio samples using chaotic index mapping, obscuring the original structure, while diffusion modifies the sample values by XOR or arithmetic operations with the chaotic sequence, spreading small changes across the entire signal [20]. In 2017, Sathiyamurthi et al. [21] proposed a speech encryption approach based on chaotic shift keying. This scheme utilized LM, Tent, Quadratic, and Bernoulli maps. The authors argued that the encryption scheme offered a strong diffusion and confusion mechanism for speech communication. Due to the random and sensitive features of chaotic maps, the method has the advantages of high security and anti-attack. It is lightweight and suitable for use in various applications, including secure audio transmission and digital rights management.

AES-Based Audio Encryption with Chaos Maps: The audio encryption with the mixture of chaos maps and AES is a hybrid system that brings the chaos system's unpredictability and the information security characteristics of modern cryptography. At the first stage of this method, the chaotic system shuffles the audio samples' positions in such a way that their structure becomes unrecognizable. Then, the AES, a commonly used symmetric encryption algorithm, enciphers the randomized audio data for protection purposes. Reddy et al. [22] for WAV audio format applied the AES technique. Here, a pseudorandom number generator (PRNG) sequence and chaotic CA rule are XORed with the AES-encrypted audio. This also frustrates pattern recognition that may be attempted on the cipher, greatly increasing the security of the entire encryption [23]. The hybrid one takes advantage of the lightweight high-speed characteristics of the chaos image for preprocessing and the strong resistance of AES against brute-force and statistical attack [24]. The dual-layer encryption mechanism guarantees that secure audio transmission and storage are achieved while maintaining a high level of security, efficiency, and stability for real-time applications.

Chaotic Systems and DNA Sequence Transformation Audio Encryption: Audio encryption by chaos map and DNA approach is an innovative key by chaos theory and DNA rules to increase encryption strength. In this model, the audio signal is sampled and then the binary form of it is encoded into DNA strands with DNA rules A, T, C, and G. Chaos maps manage the confusion process, which consists of disordering the DNA encoded data, and the diffusion step, which alters the sequence by the DNA addition, subtraction, or XOR data values by chaotic keys [25]. The mixture of chaos and DNA encoding adds more complexity to the encrypted result, and therefore an attempt to break the encryption by brute force or cryptanalysis is highly resisted. In 2019, Wang et al. [26] proposed an audio encryption system using the DNA approach. In the presented approach, the initial value of the chaotic map is set by the hash value of the audio. The DNA encoding and the authors employed the mixed system for scrambling and diffusion. It is lightweight in computation, high in security, and sensitive to slight perturbations of the key, which suits applications in secure audio communication and storage for modern communication systems.

Cellular Automata with Chaos Maps: The fusion of chaos maps and CA-based audio encryption is a strong hybrid mechanism for confidential communication. Cellular automata, which are characterized by their simple rule structure evolution, and chaos maps, which are known for their sensitivity and randomness, are integrated to increase the robustness of the proposed encryption scheme. An analog audio source is first converted into digital, and a chaotic sequence is obtained using maps such as the logistic and Henon map for the audio samples shuffle (confusion). They are then followed by cellular automata over the permuted data with a fixed set of evolution rules, which further transform values and allow for complete diffusion. CA's recursive structure may cause a slight change to propagate widely, and chaos maps generate higher randomness in the encryption process [27]. It adds to the system multilayered complexity, and it is this complexity that is, in the first place, the most secure against attacks. George et al. [28] compressive 28 with LFSR and 2DCA linear feedback shift register (LFSR) and two-dimensional classical cellular automata in a 28 for efficient realization of a compressive sensing-based audio encryption. The authors utilized a secure measurement matrix with linear feedback shift registers (LFSR).

An LFSR random bit stream generator is adopted for generating the initial state matrix of cellular automata. Lightweight and high performance, the combination encryption scheme is more suitable for protecting audio in real-time scenarios.

6.5 Audio Encryption Performance Metrics

Audio encryption performance investigation. Audio encryption performance evaluation has centered around the efficient and effective encryption of audio data for secure transmission or storage, as shown in Figure 6.4. This includes evaluation of computational measures such as encryption/decryption speed, resource utilization, and energy consumption, for real-time and large applications. The quality of the audio is also considered, as we want to preserve the original signal after decrypting it. One important feature is the security strength against brute force or ciphertext modification. Furthermore, aspects such as scalability, support for different types of compression, as well as possibilities of hardware acceleration are considered to strike a balance between security and performance.

Performance evaluation of audio encryption is mainly classified according to the efficiency of both encryption and decryption operations, with the worst being the basic operations that guarantee the confidential and safe treatment of the audio data. For encryption speed, you will be more concerned with the speed at which the audio data can be converted into an unreadable secure format without losing

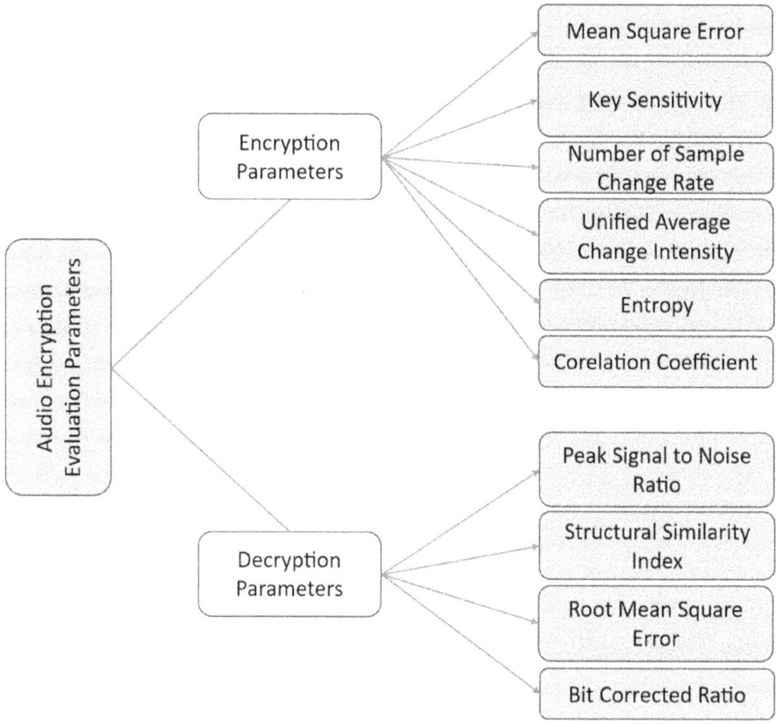

Figure 6.4 Audio encryption and decryption performance evaluation parameters.

much of the sound quality and without a long latency for input and output. Decryption quality, however, measures how the encrypted audio signal can be correctly and quickly reversed to its original content. This must be achieved while maintaining the integrity and quality of the audio signal and synchronizing the signals in real time.

Mean Squared Error (MSE): MSE is a critical metric for evaluating the quality of encrypted audio. By comparing the original and encrypted audio signals, MSE quantifies the amount of distortion introduced during the encryption process. A high MSE in dB (typically above 30 dB) indicates that the encryption algorithm has good immunity to attacks, maintaining a close resemblance to the original audio and ensuring that minor changes in the input lead to significant, unpredictable differences in the encrypted output (the avalanche effect). It can be calculated by:

$$\mathrm{MSE} = \frac{1}{N}\sum_{i=1}^{N}(x_i - y_i)^2 \tag{1}$$

where x_i and y_i are the values of the original audio sample and encrypted audio sample, respectively, at ith position. N is the total number of samples in the audio signal.

Key Sensitivity: Key sensitivity is a critical property of encryption algorithms that evaluates how dependent the encrypted output is on the encryption key. A good encryption algorithm should produce entirely different encrypted outputs when the key is changed, even slightly. Let's say you have a key length of n bits. There are 2^n possible keys. When we alter just one bit in the key, the difference in ciphertext should be substantial, with approximately 50% of the bits altered, reflecting a dramatic change in the output. This ensures that the encryption system is secure against brute-force attacks, where an attacker might try small variations of the key to decipher the encrypted data.

In cryptography, the key length is one of the most important factors influencing the security of a system. While longer keys offer more security, for example, if you use a 64-bit key, there are 2^{64} possible combinations of keys, but with a 128-bit key, there are 2^{128} combinations. The larger the key length, the more time and computational power are required for an attacker to successfully perform a brute-force attack.

Key sensitivity is tested by altering the encryption key and comparing the resulting ciphertexts using metrics like number of sample change rate (NSCR) and UACI. High values in these metrics indicate that the encryption algorithm is highly sensitive to key changes, causing significant differences in the output.

Number of Sample Change Rate (NSCR): The Number of Sample Change Rate (NSCR) is an important parameter to assess the quality of an audio encryption scheme by determining the percentage of change in audio samples after processing has been performed on the audio sample. The higher the NSCR value, the lower the quality of the processed audio sample. It estimates the percentage of samples in the encrypted audio in which they do not coincide with the original ones. From a mathematical point of view, NSCR is calculated in such a way that it compares each sample of the original and encrypted audio files, determining how many of them are varied. The NSCR can be written mathematically as follows:

$$\text{NSCR} = \frac{\sum_{x,y}, D(x, y)}{M} \times 100\% \tag{2}$$

where:

$$D(x, y) = \begin{cases} 1, & \text{if} C_1(x, y) \neq C_2(x, y) \\ 0, & \text{if} C_1(x, y) = C_2(x, y) \end{cases} \tag{3}$$

M = Total number of samples, and C_1, C_2 are original and encrypted audio signal values. If the NSCR value is greater and essentially close to 100%, then the encryption technique has strongly tampered with the primary audio so as to make it unrecognizable, thus ensuring its security. Such a property is crucial to secure the audio file against differential attacks; otherwise, small variations in the input might be exploited to infer addictive properties or defects of the encryption scheme itself. A low NSCR means that many samples appear unchanged, which in turn emphasizes vulnerabilities in the encryption algorithm. By guaranteeing a high NSCR, the encryption methods bring sufficient uncertainty and randomness, which makes it extremely difficult for eavesdroppers to acquire the original signal. It means that NSCR is a good indicator of encryption quality and resistance.

Unified Average Change Intensity (UACI): The Unified Average Change Intensity (UACI) is a measure of change between two distinct audio signals (usually, between the original sound and its encrypted) [1]. It is used to determine to what extent the process of encryption changes the audio data. A larger UACI value means that the applied encryption has made a more pronounced effect on the audio, which is typically desired in terms of cryptographic strength. The UACI is calculated using the following formula:

$$\text{UACI} = \frac{1}{N}\left(\frac{\sum_{i,j}, \left|C_1(i\,j) - C_2(i, j)\right|}{\alpha}\right) \times 100\% \tag{4}$$

where N = Total number of audio samples , $C_1(i, j)$ and $C_2(i, j)$ are the audio samples of the original audio and the encrypted audio signal at position (i, j) in two different ciphered audio signals. α is the maximum possible value that a sample can take. For 8-bit audio, for instance, $\alpha = 255$. For 16-bit audio, $\alpha = 65535$ etc. This is to compensate for the bias between the two samples. A higher UACI value indicates the audio signal has been heavily modified/re-encrypted. This is good because it means that the algorithm is successfully "mixing" the audio in such a way that it becomes harder for an attacker to extract meaningful specifics about the encrypted audio. So let's claim you estimate UACI on two sound signals, and together with the estimates of their respective UACI as 40%. This implies that the average intensity of the original and encrypted signals has been distorted by 40%. This means that the encryption is good; the audio is deformed enough.

Entropy: Entropy is an important statistic to approximate the randomness and unpredictability in an encrypted speech signal. In cryptography, the desire is to have the encrypted data look like random noise so attackers can't find patterns or meanings lingering in the encrypted data. The randomness is measured by entropy based on the probability distribution of the encrypted audio values. Mathematically, it can be defined by:

$$H(X) = \sum_{i=0}^{N} P(X_i) \log_2 \frac{1}{P(X_i)} \tag{5}$$

Here, $P(x_i)$ is the probability of occurrence of the audio sample value at x_i and N is the number of possible distinct sample values that can be taken on by the audio signal. When entropy is high at close to 8, it means there is a uniform distribution of probability, in such a way that any value is just as likely to show up as any other. This randomization is such that the encrypted audio is immune to statistical attacks in which attackers search for patterns in the encrypted data. The former indicates a low entropy, and thus part of the encrypted signal shows predictable patterns and is hence less secure.

Correlation Coefficient (CC): Correlation coefficient (CC) is a metric for measuring the dependency or relationship of two audio signals, in general, the original audio and its encrypted version [2]. This measure may be useful in evaluating the secrecy of an encryption algorithm, depending on how much the algorithm obscures patterns in the original signal. The mathematical equation to find the correlation coefficient (CC) is denoted as r_{pq}:

$$r_{pq} = \frac{\operatorname{cov}(p,q)}{\sqrt{D(p)\cdot D(q)}} \tag{6}$$

where:

$$\operatorname{cov}(p,q) = \frac{1}{m}\sum_{i=1}^{m}(p_i - E(p))(q_i - E(q)) \tag{7}$$

$$D(p) = \frac{1}{m}\sum_{i=1}^{m}(p_i - E(p))^2 \tag{8}$$

$$E(p) = \frac{1}{m}\sum_{i=1}^{m} p_i \tag{9}$$

where p_i and q_i are the values of the original signal p and encrypted signal q at the ith position, $E(p)$ and $E(q)$ are the means of p and q respectively. m is the total number of samples.

$CC = 1$: Perfect correlation (implies weak encryption as original speech patterns are clearly retained). $CC = 0$: No correlation (the case for strong encryption, as the encrypted sound is completely random).

6.6 Audio Decryption Performance Metrics

In judging the performance of audio decryption, some parameters are employed to compare the vessel audio signals with the decrypted ones. Performance measurement metrics are used to evaluate the quality of the reconstructed audio after passing through the encryption/decryption process. These are some of the common 4–5 key metrics used:

Peak Signal-to-Noise Ratio (PSNR): Peak Signal-to-Noise Ratio (PSNR) is a common metric for evaluating the quality of the recovered audio that measures the distortion or noise induced during the encryption and decryption. It is the quotient of the maximum signal power entering before and after processing and the noise (the power difference between original and decrypted audio). It is frequently employed as a measure of the quality of a signal. The PSNR is a decibel (dB) based value, such that higher values are better than lower values and represent less audio distortion. Mathematically, PSNR is calculated as:

$$\mathrm{PSNR} = 10\log_{10}\frac{\mathrm{MAX}^2}{\mathrm{MSE}} \tag{10}$$

where MAX is the highest possible value by a signal—255 for 8-bit audio, 32767 for 16-bit audio (it also works for other popular systems, like 32-bit float or 24-bit). MSE (Mean Squared Error) quantifies the square of the difference between the original signal and the decrypted audio signal. If PSNR is larger than zero, it means the noise between the original and decrypted audio is small. For such applications, where high quality is crucial, e.g., in music, broadcasting, or telecommunications, even minor distortions may affect the user's experience. For example, auditory encoding can be viewed as acceptable for high-quality audio when the PSNR is above 30 dB and closely near perfect reconstruction of the original audio signal when it is closer to 40 dB or beyond. The SNR is particularly important where the clarity and usability of the decrypted audio are more important, such as in the field of telecommunications, music, and broadcasting.

Structural Similarity Index Measure (SSIM): The SSIM is a measure to check the perceptual quality and structure of the decrypted audio. It is proposed to simulate the way people perceive differences as changes in sound, including the relational structure between the original signals and the recovery signals in terms of amplitude, frequency, and phase. In contrast to conventional approaches, such as PSNR, which only consider pixel-wise or sample-wise variation, SSIM compares the perceived similarity by calculating the structure of the audio signal. A higher SSIM value means there are more similar pixels in two images, and it is a value between 0 and 1. A value of 1 indicates that the decrypted audio matches the original; that is, the encryption/decryption process did not greatly alter the audio. Conversely, a value closer to 0 indicates that the decrypted audio has diverged substantially from the original.

$$\mathrm{SSIM}(x, y) = \frac{(2\rho_x\rho_y + C_1)(2\sigma_{xy} + C_2)}{(\rho_x^2 + \rho_y^2 + C_1)(\sigma_x^2 + \sigma_y^2 + C_2)} \tag{11}$$

where ρ_x, ρ_y are means of signal of x, y, σ_{xy} is covariance between x and y, σ_x^2, σ_y^2 are variance of the signal x and y, respectively. SSIM measures by evaluating three factors: luminance (amplitude), contrast (IOR various), and structure (frequency pattern). These latter elements are assembled into a single index, which gives the global perceptual similarity. The SSIM is, thus, especially useful in subjective testing in that it corresponds most closely with human hearing: any decline in audio fidelity would be evident to the listener.

Root Mean Square Error (RMSE): RMSE evaluates the average difference between the original and decrypted audio samples. The less the RMSE, the better the decrypted audio resembles the original, and vice versa. Good decryption is usually achieved with a small RMSE, meaning that the audio after decryption is audible and intelligible. Therefore, RMSE helps assess the effectiveness of an encryption scheme in maintaining the original audio's integrity.

$$\text{RMSE} = \sqrt{\text{MSE}} \tag{12}$$

where MSE (Mean Squared Error) is the average squared difference between the original and decrypted audio signals.

Bit Corrected Ratio (BCR): Bit Corrected Ratio (BCR) is a metric used to assess the accuracy and integrity of decrypted audio after encryption, transmission, and potential distortion from noise. It measures how closely the decrypted audio matches the original audio by evaluating bit-level differences. Specifically, BCR quantifies the proportion of bits in the decrypted audio that are correct when compared to the original signal.

$$\text{BCR} = 1 - \frac{\sum_{i=1}^{\text{length}} A(i) \oplus D(i)}{\text{size}} \tag{13}$$

where $A(i)$ and $D(i)$ is the bit values at position i in the original audio signal and decrypted audio signal, respectively.

When $\text{BCR} = 1$, it indicates that the decrypted audio is identical to the original, with no errors introduced during encryption and decryption. This suggests that the encryption and decryption processes have successfully preserved the audio's integrity. On the other hand, $\text{BCR} = 0$ indicates that all bits in the decrypted audio are incorrect, meaning the audio is completely distorted and unrecognizable.

Ideally, the BCR value should be close to 1, signifying that the decrypted audio closely resembles the original. A higher BCR value is indicative of a more successful encryption-decryption process with minimal distortion, while a lower BCR points to potential issues in the system, such as excessive noise or error propagation.

6.7 Applications of Audio Encryption

In the digital age, with soundproof data security in high demand in industries. From protecting private corporate meetings to supporting secure financial deals, secured audio contributes significantly to secure transactions in personal/professional lives [29]. In the following, we present the many real-life usages of audio encryption and how its importance is increasing in multiple sectors. This section presents the various applications of audio encryption and its growing importance across different sectors.

- Audio Copyright Protection: With the explosive popularity of online digital media streaming services, copyright protection of audio content has been increasingly important. Audio encryption is widely applied in DRM schemes to protect the unauthorized copying and distribution of digital music, audiobooks, and podcasts. This in turn ensures that the content is only accessed and played by licensed users.
- Online Banking and Safe Transactions: In various bank systems, voice recognition is included as an extra authentication method. To prevent voice spoofing and unauthorized users, authentication is achieved by the encrypted voice, which is secure. Encrypted speech is also used in secure financial transactions, where voice commands are used for transfer and payment.
- Private Corporate meetings: Companies and MNCs fall back on encrypted audio conferencing for such secretive discussions on mergers, acquisitions, strategic planning, etc. Encryption stops industrial espionage and makes sure no sensitive information leaks to opponents or black hats.
- Media and Broadcasting: Radio and television broadcasting organizations deploy encryption to limit access to

pay-per-view content. Pay-TV and satellite radio are examples of services that encrypt audio broadcasts to allow access to only those who are authorized with a decryption key.

- Emergency Response Teams: Police and disaster relief workers depend on secured voice communications for dispatch and coordination. Protected voice for emergency, so that intruders cannot grasp, use, or manipulate emergency commands.
- Aerospace and Defense Communications: The aerospace and defense sectors use encrypted audio to prevent eavesdropping between pilots and air traffic controllers and ground crews. Military-grade encryption ensures private conversations and mission-critical information are protected from possible adversaries.
- Smart Home and IoT Security: As smart home devices and IoT devices are more often using voice commands and smart assistants, audio encryption is necessary to avoid eavesdropping from cyber attackers. It has encrypted voice commands to make sure only the authorized person is able to communicate with smart home devices
- Police and Surveillance: Encrypted audio is adopted by police for operational acts. It is also deployed in monitoring systems to secure valuable records that could serve as legal evidence. Curran encryption means only authorized personnel can access vital audio information.
- Healthcare and Telemedicine: Patient privacy is very important in the healthcare industry. Secure audio communication allows for encrypted doctor-patient communication via telemedicine. It also prevents health care providers from talking about private patient information and then ending up with a data breach.
- Secure Voice Communication: One of the important uses of audio encryption will be in secure communication. Enterprises, governmental authorities, and military deployments use encrypted voice communications to secure sensitive information and resist eavesdropping to encrypt VoIP (Voice over Internet Protocol) calls, and encrypted messaging apps to make sure confidential conversations stay secret.

References

1. Sharma, G., Umapathy, K., & Krishnan, S. (2020). Trends in audio signal feature extraction methods. *Applied Acoustics*, *158*, 107020.
2. Pulkki, V., & Karjalainen, M. (2015). *Communication Acoustics: An Introduction to Speech, Audio and Psychoacoustics*. John Wiley & Sons.
3. Takahashi, N., Gygli, M., & Van Gool, L. (2017). Aenet: Learning deep audio features for video analysis. *IEEE Transactions on Multimedia*, *20*(3), 513–524.
4. Gandhi, R. A., & Gosai, A. M. (2015). A study on current scenario of audio encryption. *International Journal of Computer Applications*, *116*(7), 13–17.
5. Christenson, P. G., & Lindlof, T. R. (1983). The role of audio media in the lives of children. *Popular Music & Society*, *9*(3), 25–40.
6. Wyman, R. (1966). Audio media in music education. *Music Educators Journal*, *52*(4), 105–108.
7. Zhou, X., Chao, W., & Shao, X. (2023). A study of encryption for multimedia digital audio security. *International Journal of Advanced Computer Science and Applications*, *14*(2), 581–585.
8. Belmeguenai, A., Ahmida, Z., Ouchtati, S., & Djemii, R. (2017). A novel approach based on stream cipher for selective speech encryption. *International Journal of Speech Technology*, *20*, 685–698.
9. Afdhila, D., Nasution, S. M., & Azmi, F. (2016, September). Implementation of stream cipher Salsa20 algorithm to secure voice on push to talk application. In *2016 IEEE Asia Pacific Conference on Wireless and Mobile (APWiMob)* (pp. 137–141). IEEE
10. Albahrani, E. A. (2017, March). A new audio encryption algorithm based on chaotic block cipher. In *2017 Annual Conference on New Trends in Information & Communications Technology Applications (NTICT)* (pp. 22–27). IEEE.
11. Lie, W. N., & Chang, L. C. (2006). Robust and high-quality time-domain audio watermarking based on low-frequency amplitude modification. *IEEE Transactions on Multimedia*, *8*(1), 46–59.
12. National Bureau of Standards. (1999). *Data Encryption Standard* (FIPS PUB 46–3). Federal Information Processing Standards Publication. Gaithersburg, MD: National Institute of Standards and Technology, vol. 46, no. 3, pp. 1–22.
13. Daemen, J., & Rijmen, V. (2001, March). Rijndael: The advanced encryption standard. *Dr. Dobb's Journal, 26*(3), 137–139.
14. Rivest, R., Shamir, A., & Adleman, L. (1978). A method for obtaining digital signatures and public-key cryptosystems. *Communications of the ACM, 21*(2), 120–126.
15. Rahul, B., Kuppusamy, K., & Senthilrajan, A. (2023). Chaos-based audio encryption algorithm using biometric image and SHA-256 hash algorithm. *Multimedia Tools and Applications*, *82*(28), 43729–43758.
16. Dai, W., Xu, X., Song, X., & Li, G. (2021). Audio encryption algorithm based on chen memristor chaotic system. *Symmetry*, *14*(1), 17.

17. Roy, M., Chakraborty, S., & Mali, K. (2024). Audio encryption framework based on chaotic map and DNA encoding. *Applied Acoustics*, 224, 110152.
18. Shannon, C. E. (1949, October). Communication theory of secrecy systems. *Bell System Technical Journal, 28*(4), 656–715.
19. Sathiyamurthi, P., & Ramakrishnan, S. (2017, September). Speech encryption using chaotic shift keying for secured speech communication. *EURASIP Journal on Audio, Speech, and Music Processing, 2017*(1), 2–11.
20. Belazi, A., El-Latif, A. A. A., & Belghith, S. (2016, November). A novel image encryption scheme based on substitution-permutation network and chaos. *Signal Processing, 128*, 155–170.
21. Sathiyamurthi, P., & Ramakrishnan, S. (2017). Speech encryption using chaotic shift keying for secured speech communication. *EURASIP Journal on Audio, Speech, and Music Processing, 2017*, 1–11. https://doi.org/10.1186/s13636-017-0118-0.
22. Reddy, A. S., Achar, D. N., Mol, M. S., & Panda, N. (2024, June). Audio Encryption Using AES and Cellular Automata. In *2024 15th International Conference on Computing Communication and Networking Technologies (ICCCNT)* (pp. 1–6). IEEE.
23. Lin, C. H., Hu, G. H., Chan, C. Y., & Yan, J. J. (2021). Chaos-based synchronized dynamic keys and their application to image encryption with an improved AES algorithm. *Applied Sciences*, 11(3), 1329.
24. Reddy, A. S., Achar, D. N., Mol, M. S., & Panda, N. (2024, June). Audio encryption using AES and cellular automata. In *2024 15th International Conference on Computing Communication and Networking Technologies (ICCCNT)* (pp. 1–6). IEEE.
25. Naskar, P. K., Paul, S., Nandy, D., & Chaudhuri, A. (2019, September). DNA encoding and channel shuffling for secured encryption of audio data. *Multimedia Tools and Applications, 78*(17), 25019–25042. https://doi.org/10.1007/s11042-019-7696-z.
26. Wang, X., & Su, Y. (2020). An audio encryption algorithm based on DNA coding and chaotic system. *IEEE Access, 8*, 9260–9270. https://doi.org/10/1109/ACCESS.2019.2963329.
27. Souyah, A., & Faraoun, K. M. (2016, October). An image encryption scheme combining chaos-memory cellular automata and weighted histogram. *Nonlinear Dynamics, 86*(1), 639–653.
28. George, S. N., Augustine, N., & Pattathil, D. P. (2015). Audio security through compressive sampling and cellular automata. *Multimedia Tools and Applications, 74*, 10393–10417. https://doi.org/10.1007/s11042-014-2172-2.
29 Fotso, S. B. N., Atchoffo, W. N., Nzeukou, A. C., & Talla Mbé, J. H. (2025). Enhanced security in lossless audio encryption using zigzag scrambling, DNA coding, SHA-256, and Hopfield networks: A practical VLC system implementation. *Multimedia Tools and Applications, 84*(23), 27091–27125.

7

VIDEO ENCRYPTION STRATEGY

7.1 Introduction to Video and Video Summarization

Whether for sharing information, education, or entertainment, video is an amazing technology that has permeated every aspect of our daily lives. Fundamentally, video is just a series of pictures, or frames, that are displayed one after the other at such a rapid pace that our brains and eyes are led to believe that there is smooth motion. Imagine paging through a picture book with a moving object in a slightly different location on each page. It appears as though the object is moving if you flip quickly enough! That's exactly how video works. Videos usually come with sound, which makes the experience even richer and more engaging [1].

There are a few key factors that determine how a video looks and feels:

Frame Rate: This is how many frames (images) are shown per second. It is measured in frames per second. A higher frame rate means more frames are shown per second, and the video appears smoother [2].

Resolution: The amount of visual detail present in an image or video frame is called resolution. It gives the pixel arrangement horizontally and vertically. A higher resolution means more pixels are used to represent visual content.

Aspect Ratio: Aspect ratio tells the shape of visual content. It refers to the proportional relationship between the width and height. For example, a 4:3 aspect ratio produces a square-like frame, which was used in old televisions.[3] The **16:9**

DOI: 10.1201/9781003500841-7

aspect ratio is for high-definition televisions and streaming platforms.

Color Depth: Color depth refers to the number of bits used to represent color of a single pixel. A higher color depth means more color per pixel. Of course, video files can be huge, especially if they have a high resolution and frame rate. That's why we use special file formats like MP4 and AVI to compress the videos, shrinking their size without losing too much quality. This task is effectively performed by compression techniques such as H.264 and HEVC (H.265) [4], allowing us to store and stream videos online without requiring an infinite amount of data.

7.1.1 Video Encryption

Video encryption jumbled the content of the video file and locked it to prevent its unauthorized access. A video that has a noise-like structure with some random data that is unrecognizable is the output of a video encryption scheme. Only the authorized users possessing the correct secret key can access the video content. The architecture of the video encryption scheme is shown in Figure 7.1. We can consider a scenario where we are supposed to share video content secretly, as the content is being shared on a publicly open network that is not secure.

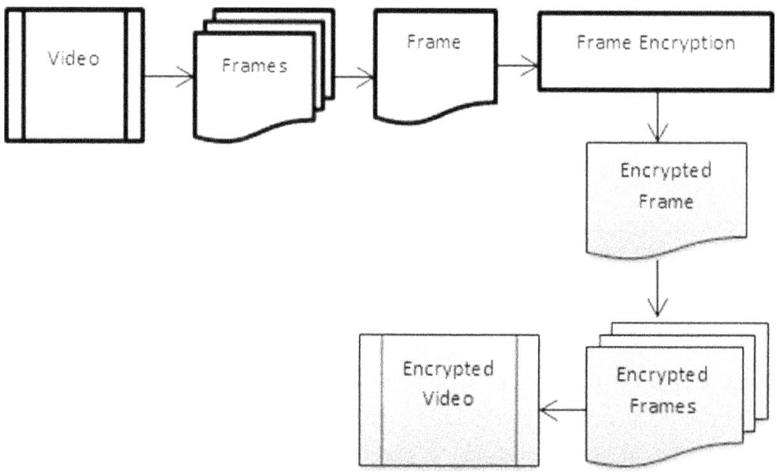

Figure 7.1 Architecture of video encryption.

Video encryption is the best method to protect it from attackers. To encrypt the video, we extract frames from the video and encrypt each of them using an encryption algorithm. Only users possessing the appropriate credentials or keys can unlock the video and view it [4–7]. AES is widely used due to its balance between security and efficiency. When applied in video encryption, AES achieves real-time performance with minimal quality loss.

7.1.1.1 Need for Video Encryption

- **Confidentiality and Access Control**: The video encryption limits the access of video information and ensures that the authorized users who are authenticated are the only ones able to access it. It is noteworthy to encrypt the video content since it has sensitive and personal information. When encrypted, such content is secure against unauthorized access, but without encryption, such content is at risk of unauthorized accessibility, which presents substantial threats in terms of privacy, espionage, or data leaks.
- **Regulatory Compliance and Data Protection Laws**: Stringent legislation and regulations: Government undertakings such as regulatory compliance and data protection legislation are, in some cases, stringent laws and regulations implemented in all sectors, such as healthcare and finance, to secure sensitive video data. Regulations like GDPR (General Data Protection Regulation) in Europe and HIPAA (Health Insurance Portability and Accountability Act) in the healthcare sector, take adequate security-related measures in guarding the videos. Encryption plays a role. It is a great principle to apply these laws and regulations.
- **Dashboard Video Transmission**: Real-time or transmission of much-stored video or live Streaming is required to be secured since it is continuously being sent forth over shared networks or public networks. Cyber criminals are ever busy intercepting or tamper with this valuable video information, which can be intercepted or tampered with. Encryption distorts the video streams into data streams that cannot be read in transit and makes any interception using keys that do not accomplish proper decryption.

- **Protection for Intellectual Property and Control over Piracy**: In the case of content creators, the digital video sources should be secured by distributors and media platforms; the protection of digital video sources is necessary to protect intellectual property rights and income. There is encryption against unauthorized replication that reveals and consequently stops piracy.

  It is significant in industries such as film production, online education, and subscription-based streaming.
- **Preventing Data Tampering**: Encryption also ensures that videos remain in their original format. An encrypted video becomes unreadable if someone attempts to change it. This is essential in circumstances where the authenticity of the video is crucial, such as secure communications or court cases.
- **Ensuring Confidentiality in Sensitive Communications**: Encryption guarantees that the topics being discussed remain private during sensitive video meetings, such as private conversations or corporate conferences.

7.1.2 Types of Video Encryption

The two main classes of video encryption methods are selective and full encryption. Each approach comes with its own pros, cons, and real use cases. In this chapter, we will explore selective and full video encryption, including how each works, where they are most useful, and why one is better.

Full Video Encryption: Imagine full video encryption as wrapping the entire video in a protective layer. Every single part of the video, from the images to the audio and even background data, is fully secured [8]. This is the best way to keep the video safe, ensuring that no part of it can be accessed without the proper key.

Benefits:

Total Protection: Every part of the video is secured, leaving nothing vulnerable.

Easy to Implement: Since the whole video is encrypted, there's no need to decide which parts need protection; it's all covered.

Drawbacks:
Slower Processing: Encrypting the entire video takes more time and computing power, especially for large, high-resolution videos.

Inflexibility: Not every video needs such a high level of protection, so full encryption might not always be necessary.

Selective Video Encryption: Selective Encryption is the method to encrypt only a subset of video streams. The main goal of selective encryption is to reduce the computational complexity and select a significant part of the video to encrypt. [9]. Some elements within a video frame that are typically encrypted in selective encryption include headers, motion vectors, transform coefficients, intra and inter prediction data, and bitstream syntax elements.

Benefits:
High Efficiency: Selective encryption is highly efficient because it is faster and we are required to encrypt only a subset of the video frame.

Flexibility: There are several syntax elements, motion vectors, and coefficients that can be encrypted in selective encryption.

Less Security: In the case of selective encryption, only a subset of video undergoes encryption; therefore, selective encryption is less secure.

Complexity: The complexity lies in finding the subset of video that has to be encrypted in selective encryption.

7.1.3 Video Summarization

Video summarization is a process of automatically generating the key points or summary of a video. The summary may be a set of key frames known as a static summary or a short video clip known as a dynamic summary. The summary is more informative, reduces time, and shows only important content. Video summarization helps to reduce storage requirements, bandwidth requirements, and processing time. It has applications in surveillance, medical imaging, and video lectures learning platforms. Video summarization helps to extract and present only the most relevant content from a video. Summarization helps in

7.1.4 Types of Video Summarization

Two main categories of video summarization techniques exist:

Summarization Using Keyframes: In this technique, summarization is done by selecting key frames based on color, motion, texture, or scene changes. Imagine looking through a photo album, where every image documents an important moment. It is straightforward, but it functions best in videos that contain distinct, clear moments, such as surveillance footage.

Segment-Based Summarization (Video Skimming): This technique extracts brief video clips rather than merely still photos. It's similar to viewing a brief trailer that compiles the most memorable moments. Video skimming is excellent for documentaries and sporting events, where the actions and movements are the main events.

7.1.5 Techniques in Video Summarization

To handle the large volume of video data, researchers have developed several intelligent methods to summarize the video content.

Clustering-Based Techniques: In this technique, the visual and semantic characteristics of video frames are analyzed to identify similarities among them and group them into clusters. From each cluster, a representative frame or segment is selected to effectively summarize and represent the content of the entire video.

Attention-Based Methods: These are the methods that give emphasis to the best video segments that are engaging and informative. These algorithms take into consideration high-motion areas, spectacular visual differences, or salient objects. These algorithms allow drawing highlights that intuitively catch the attention of the viewer's attention.

Graph-Based Approaches: In this approach, videos are in the form of graphs, and nodes refer to videos. They correspond with scenes or events, and edges represent temporal or contextual relations. By examining the composition of this graph, one can identify important moments that are the pillars of this story. It is more appropriate, especially when one wants to summarize long form or intricate information, e.g., films or television documentaries.

Deep Learning Methods: Sophisticated neural networks like Convolutional Neural Networks (CNNs) and Recurrent Neural Networks (RNNs) have demonstrated very successful results on video summarization tasks. These models are able to learn hierarchical features and time patterns, inferring on a large labeled video corpus, which makes them identify contextually significant information.

7.2 Video Encryption Using Chaos Theory

Think about the world in which even the tiniest change can mean a great difference, like in: how a butterfly flapping its wings in Brazil may cause a tornado in Texas. The chapter of mathematics called chaos theory, which analyzes complicated systems, is the consequence of this concept, where the system is extremely sensitive to initial conditions. Video encryption is one of the many real-world applications of chaos theory.

What does this signify for you, then? You have undoubtedly come across video encryption, whether you were aware of it or not, if you have ever watched a YouTube tutorial, taken part in a video call, or streamed a movie online. Data is jumbled during the encryption process to prevent unwanted access. However, conventional encryption techniques can occasionally be predictable or subject to intrusions [10–12]. The application of chaos theory improves the security of video encryption by introducing an element of unpredictability that is practically impossible to break. Video encryption is made considerably more difficult for unauthorized parties to crack by adding an element of unpredictability brought about by chaos theory. According to chaos theory, even a small alteration to the initial circumstances can have radically different results. When chaotic maps are used in encrypting video, even a minor modification to the key can fundamentally alter the way of encrypting video.

Chaotic Maps: In chaos theory, chaotic maps are referred to as mathematical functions that generate intricate and unpredictable patterns. Chaotic maps are of two types: one-dimensional and multidimensional. One-dimensional chaotic maps such as the logistic, tent, and sine maps are defined by a single variable and a single control parameter. Multidimensional, on the contrary, is a 2 1/2- dimensional space. The chaotic maps include a variety of variables and control parameters. They provide a more complex order and increased sensitivity to a starting point. All these properties of chaotic maps render them very useful and suitable for scrambling video data in a quite controlled, but seemingly random manner. Chaotic maps can edit the video content through simple calculation of math but are almost impossible to decode the same without the appropriate key. The strength of chaos-based encryption lies in two fundamental rules: confusion and diffusion. Confusion is the method of covering the relation between the original and video information that is encrypted [13]. Such is accomplished by chaotic systems by scrambling the video information, which blurs any rational correlation, and makes it extremely hard for the attacker to undo. Design the encryption without precisely specifying the parameters of the chaotic map. Diffusion, on the one hand, guarantees that no matter how minor the change in the video, like altering one of its elements, there will be adverse effects. Pixels move all through the stream of the encrypted data [14]. It implies that minor changes in the input data cause drastic changes in the encrypted data, hence increasing the encryption.

The chaotic systems are computationally simple and thus they are specifically appropriate in real-time in high-speed and security-oriented applications; speed and security are part and parcel. With the further development of the research, the popularity seems to be on the part of chaotic map-based techniques compared to the conventional cryptographic multimedia security. Video protection using secret sharing schemes.

7.2.1 Secret Sharing Schemes the Basics

In its essence, a secret sharing scheme is aimed at disseminating pieces of a secret, e.g. an in encrypted video, across (or distributed among) many entities or storage points. This will mean that despite the fact that a couple of them might be involved, the others are vindicated. When his or her shares are compromised or being shared, then the original video is not shared.

The threshold of shares can be attained. Such an approach not only increases data confidentiality but also brings in flexibility in access control and fault tolerance. They have developed several methods of secret sharing, each of which is characterized by certain differences. It would be appropriate in various applications.

1. Shamir Secret Sharing: This is a cryptographic scheme that relies on polynomial interpolation, enabling a secret to be shared so that any t out of n shares can reproduce the original. It provides powerful mathematical security and adaptable thresholds and it is ideal on portable video protection systems.
2. Blakley Secret Sharing: This is a secret sharing scheme that is founded on the intersection of hyperplanes coded and decoded secrets in a multidimensional space. Even more than, but nevertheless not so frequently used, as it is an interesting geometric way of securing data partitioning suggested by Shamir.

7.3 Use Secret Sharing Schemes to Protect Video

Secret sharing protocol increases the data security through scattering of sensitive information into various parts. They are called shares, and one particular share does not unveil anything significant on its own. The threshold refers to a predetermined number of shares; when a combination is made, it is only then that the shares become effective. In a crucial way, this strategy enhances the security of large and small box storage and video transmission.

7.3.1 The Basics of Secret Sharing Schemes

In its essence, a secret sharing scheme is aimed at disseminating pieces of a secret, e.g., an encrypted video, across (or distributed among) many entities or storage points. This will mean that despite the fact that a couple of them might be involved, the others are vindicated.

When his or her shares are compromised or being shared, then the original video is not shared. Researchers have developed several methods of secret sharing, each of which is characterized by certain differences. It would be appropriate in various applications.

1. **Shamir's Secret Sharing**: This is a cryptographic scheme that relies on polynomial interpolation. It enables a secret to be shared so that any t out of n shares can reproduce the original. It provides powerful mathematical security and adaptable thresholds, and it is ideal for portable video protection systems.

2. **Blakley's Secret Sharing**: This is a secret sharing scheme that is founded on the intersection of hyperplanes to encode and decode secrets in a multidimensional space. Even more than, but nevertheless not so frequently used as. It is an interesting geometric way of securing data partitioning suggested by Shamir.
3. **Visual Secret Sharing**: A scheme specifically adapted toward visual material is visual secret sharing. It partitions an image into fragments or video frames converted to transparencies (shares) that need to be superimposed to see the first one. VSS is especially practical on human-verifiable systems in which computational resources are limited.
4. **XOR-Based Secret Sharing**: These secret sharing mechanisms rely on XOR operations and are useful in lightweight sharing methods. It is simple and fast to share data secretly using XOR-based secret sharing schemes.

7.3.1.1 Shamir's Secret Sharing for Video Security

Polynomial interpolation is the main method that is applied to finite fields in Shamir's secret sharing scheme. This method is robust and divides the video content into several shares. At least n shares, called thresholds, are required to reconstruct the video file. The brief steps involved are the following:

- The video data is first converted into a binary format.
- A polynomial of degree $k-1$ is generated using the video data as coefficients.
- Each share is created by evaluating the polynomial at different points.
- These shares are then distributed to different locations or participants.

To reconstruct a video, at least k shares are needed. The approach proves its robustness because using fewer shares won't be able to reveal the original video content.

Applications:

- Corporate Security: Securing the video meetings is a part of corporate security. Video encryption protects the video meetings and prevents unauthorized access.

- Healthcare: Protecting patient video consultations during telepresence and medical records, diagnosis reports are the applications of video encryption in the health sector.

Advantages:

- High level of security due to the mathematical complexity.
- Flexible threshold settings allow for customized security levels.

Challenges:

- Computational intensity can be a drawback for large video files.
- Requires careful management of shares to prevent data loss.

7.3.1.2 Blakley's Secret Sharing for Secure Video

Blakley's secret sharing scheme offers a geometrically intuitive and mathematically rigorous alternative to polynomial-based secret sharing. Rooted in linear algebra, this method represents the secret as a point in a multidimensional space and constructs shares as hyperplanes that intersect precisely at that point. This approach is very safe and helpful when redundancy is crucial. This is how it operates:

- The video data is transformed into a point in high-dimensional space.
- Hyperplanes are constructed such that their intersection defines this point.
- Each share corresponds to a point on one of these hyperplanes.

To reconstruct the video, the required number of shares (each representing a different hyperplane) must be combined to find the intersection that reveals the original video data.

Applications:

- Government Communications: All the video content that is being shared among various government agencies is protected using video encryption schemes.
- Cloud Storage: Video encryption algorithms are also used to secure content that is available on cloud storage.

Advantages:

- Strong security due to the geometric complexity.
- Effective in environments where high redundancy is needed.

Challenges:

- Complexity in managing and understanding high-dimensional data.
- Requires careful configuration to ensure the system's reliability.

7.3.1.3 Threshold Visual Secret Sharing for Video

Threshold Visual Secret Sharing (VSS) is a specialized cryptographic technique designed for visual content, making it particularly effective in the domain of video security. Unlike traditional text-based secret sharing methods, VSS works by splitting visual frames of a video into multiple shares, which are often unintelligible on their own but visually reconstruct the original frame when the required threshold number is combined. It functions as follows:

- Video frames are converted into binary images.
- These images are split into visual patterns or shares using a VSS algorithm.
- The original video can only be reconstructed by overlaying the required number of shares.

Applications:

- **Surveillance Systems**: The video content captured by surveillance cameras can only be viewed by authorized personnel once the encryption algorithm is applied to it.
- **Media Archives**: Video content that is in the form of priceless archives is also protected using video secret sharing schemes.

Advantages:

- Direct visual feedback on security.
- Easy implementation for video frames or static images.

Challenges:

- Limited to visual data; not suitable for all types of video content.

- Reconstruction quality may vary depending on the number of shares.

7.3.1.4 XOR-Based Secret Sharing for Video

XOR-based secret sharing offers a simple yet effective method for securing video data, especially in scenarios where speed and low computational overhead are priorities. This approach relies on the exclusive OR (XOR) operation, a fundamental binary logic function, to generate and later reconstruct secret shares. This is how it operates:

- The video is converted into binary data.
- This data is split into several parts, and XOR operations are used to create shares.
- The original video can be reconstructed by performing XOR on the required number of shares.

This approach is best in situations where speed is compulsory.

Applications:

- Real-Time Communication: Live stream videos can be encrypted using XOR-based secret sharing schemes.
- Personal Security: Stored video content on our personal drive or storage media can be secured using XOR-based secret sharing schemes.

Advantages:

- Fast and efficient.
- Simple implementation makes it accessible for various applications.

Challenges:

- Provides lower security compared to more complex methods.
- Limited applicability to binary data operations.

7.3.2 Practical Use of Secret Sharing Scheme to Video Security

Since they use the capability of fragmenting sensitive video information into distinct safe fragments, secret sharing schemes have experienced the most usage in the various industries where high levels of confidentiality, integrity, and access control are required. These solutions are also being incorporated in other industries in order to protect important video files and data against unauthorized use, malicious insiders, etc.

Government and Military Use: Classified video clips like surveillance records, intelligence briefings or debriefings of missions can be secured by breaking them into shares and providing each share to various government institutions or military outfits. It will reduce the exposure to the full disclosure of internal breaches and improve the security of operations, as it will entail interagency cooperation to have the entire contents.

Healthcare: Patient confidentiality is especially an issue of concern in telemedicine, surgical recordings, and other visual types of medical data. Sensitive information in a video, like a virtual consultation or a diagnostic video, can be shared using secret sharing among medical professionals who have authority. This will mean that only approved people will have the ability to reconstruct and access the data. Maintaining health privacy rules, such as HIPAA compliance.

Cloud Storage Solutions: With cloud computing emerging as the preferred method of storage of huge quantities of video content, the risk of breaches at the center has increased. Using secret sharing schemes, video information can be divided and kept in many cloud providers or geographical locations. This distribution will make only one service be favored with full accessibility. In this way, decreasing the likelihood of leakage of masses of information in the event of a breach.

Media and Entertainment: Media corporations are having a chance to utilize secret sharing to secure rich media products, for example, unreleased movies, exclusive interviews, or video promotions, when they are being developed and advertised. The complete content cannot even be accessed in case one of the shares is compromised. This renders the procedure perfect in ensuring that there is no leakage of the content and there is exclusivity on the content.

7.3.3 Challenges and Considerations

Although secret sharing schemes support an extremely secure process of sharing sensitive video data, there are a number of practical issues that arise when it comes to the implementation process. Planning needs to be done with consideration to computation, share allocation, and the reliability of a system to be used effectively. The main points to take into consideration are the following:

Complexity of Computation: Certain secret sharing schemes may be computationally demanding; some cases, especially those of Shamir and Blakley, are computationally complex when addressing large video files. One can have a high processing load on, e.g., encoding and decoding of high resolution or long duration video. This might become a block in a real-time scenario or on a device having limited computational facilities.

Share Management: The confidentiality and trustworthiness of secret sharing plans are very much dependent on the quality of the management of the shares. In the case of the loss of shares, corruption of shares, or illegal possession of the shares, the integrity of the whole system faces a threat. Strategies to carry out safe sharing of stocks and sending and recalling of the stocks should be in place, especially in the event of distributed pets or storage sites.

Cost: Implementation of secret sharing schemes may require a larger number of storage systems or instances in different physical points, which may lead to an augmentation in the infrastructure and maintenance overheads. Companies have to consider the implementation cost as an added expenditure compared to the security gains, particularly when scaling the system to enterprise or cloud-level video storage.

Data Recovery: Unlike in the traditional encryption techniques, whereby a single decryption key can be used to restore data, the secret sharing method depends on the existence of at least a provided threshold number of shares. In case the loss or damage of shares exceeds the permissible limit, the original video loses its existence. This is a risk that supports the idea of redundancy, backup plans, and excellent administrative effort behind the lifecycle management of every share.

7.4 Evaluation of the Video Encryption Methods' Performance

Designing strong and secure encryption systems that can successfully protect video content requires an understanding of these parameters as well as potential weaknesses. The different encryption and decryption parameters used to evaluate a cryptosystem's performance are shown in Figure 7.2. These factors shed light on how effectively an encryption scheme protects video data without sacrificing usability or performance.

7.4.1 Encryption Parameters

Several important parameters are frequently used to assess the effectiveness of encryption schemes. These parameters aid in determining how well the cryptosystem safeguards the video data, how much processing power is needed, and how resilient the system is to various attack types. We describe some of the most widely used encryption parameters below.

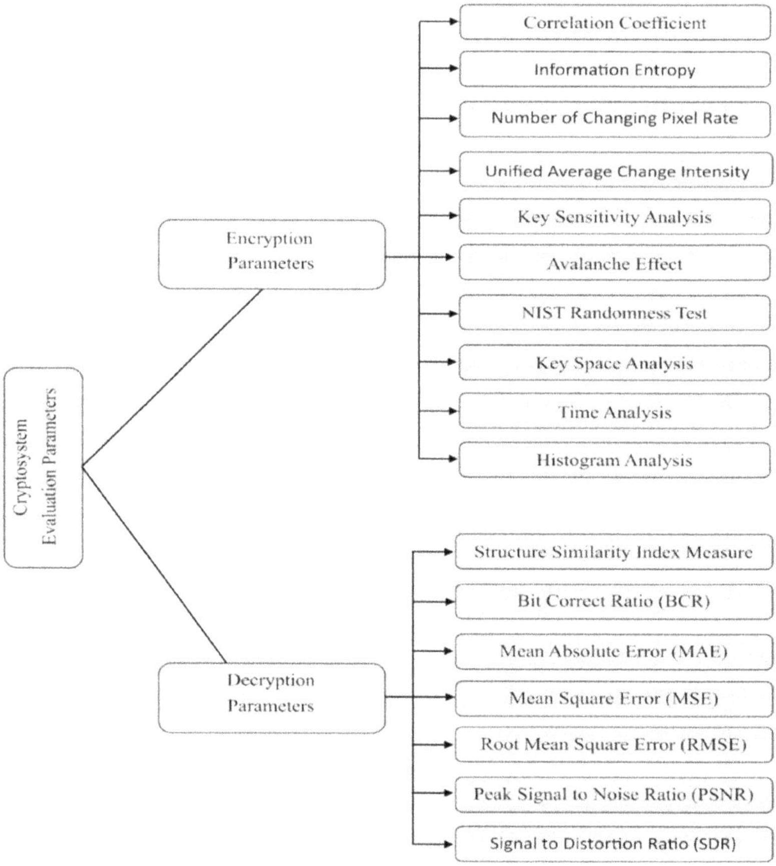

Figure 7.2 Encryption and decryption parameters.

Correlation Coefficient: This statistical measure characterizes the degree of relationship between two variables, in this case, between two pixels in an image or video frame [15–18]. It is a crucial parameter for assessing how encryption affects an image or video's visual qualities. A high correlation coefficient is the result of nearby pixels in an unencrypted video frequently having similar values. A well-thought-out encryption scheme, on the other hand, ought to drastically lower this correlation, suggesting that the original video content has been obscured by the encryption's successful pixel value randomization. Mathematically, the correlation coefficient can be determined as follows:

$$R_{xy} = \frac{\sum_{i=1}^{N}\left(x_i - \bar{x}\right)\left(y_i - \bar{y}\right)}{\sqrt{\sum_{i=1}^{N}\left(x_i - \bar{x}\right)^2 \sum_{i=1}^{N}\left(y_i - \bar{y}\right)^2}} \tag{7.1}$$

where x_i and y_i represent the pixel location of the initial video frame. A lower correlation coefficient signifies that pixels are not related, and attacks would not be able to extract any useful information from the encrypted video.

- **Information Entropy**

In video encryption, the presence of unpredictability in the video frame is measured by information entropy [19]. The higher entropy makes it harder for an attacker to crack or guess the cipher video frame. Mathematically, information entropy is computed as follows:

$$H(X) = -\sum_{i=1}^{n} P(x_i)\log_2 P(x_i) \tag{7.2}$$

Where $P(x_i)$ is the probability of the occurrence of a symbol. Entropy being high means it is unpredictable, which is advantageous for encryption. Conversely, low entropy indicates that the video is highly predictable. High entropy guarantees the security of the video content.

- **Number of Pixels Changing Rate (NPCR)**

The rate at which the number of pixels changes (NPCR) in video encryption, the "Number of Pixels Changing Rate" (NPCR) is a metric that quantifies how well an encryption algorithm jumbles the pixels in a video frame [20]. In essence, it indicates the number of pixels that have changed between the original and encrypted frames. According to the theory, a good encryption algorithm should alter a significant portion of the pixels, making it impossible for anyone to deduce the video's original content. The mathematical formula of NPCR is:

$$NPCR = \frac{1}{P \times Q} \sum_{l=1}^{P} \sum_{m=1}^{Q} X(l,m) \times 100\% \tag{7.3}$$

where: l and m are the number of pixel rows and columns. $X(l,m)$ is a function that compares the original pixel value with the encrypted pixel value. If the pixel values differ, $X(l,m) = 1$; if not, $X(l,m) = 0$. High NPCR indicates strong encryption [21].

- **Unified Average Change Intensity (UACI)**

Unified Average Change Intensity (UACI) measures the change in intensity of pixels before and after encryption [22]. The UACI is calculated as follows:

$$UACI = \frac{1}{P \times Q} \sum_{l=1}^{P} \sum_{m=1}^{Q} \frac{|E_1(l,m) - E_2(l,m)|}{255} \times 100\% \tag{7.4}$$

Where $E_1(l,m)$ and $E_2(l,m)$ represent the pixel values of the original and encrypted frames at position (l,m), respectively. High UACI indicates that the encryption has significantly altered the video content. Low UACI suggests that the encryption has not changed the intensity of pixels.

- **Key Sensitivity Analysis**

Key sensitivity analysis ensures that even a minor change in the key produces a different cipher video frame. To evaluate key sensitivity, we usually start by taking the original encryption key and then flipping a single bit of the key. The difference between the two ciphers generated by the original key and the changed key is analyzed. The encryption scheme is considered highly sensitive if the two ciphers are totally different [23].

- **Avalanche Effect**

The avalanche effect is a crucial concept in cryptography that describes how a small change in the input to an encryption algorithm (like changing just one bit in a plaintext or key) results in a significant and unpredictable change in the output (ciphertext). This ensures that even a tiny alteration in the input leads to a drastically different output, making it incredibly difficult for an attacker to infer the original input or key by analyzing the output.

To test the avalanche effect, in the video encryption, the plain frame of the video sequence is encrypted to obtain the cipher frame $(C1)$. The pixel value of the plain frame is changed by 1 bit to obtain the encrypted frame ($C2$). The difference between the two cipher frames before and after the change by 1 bit $(C1-C2)$ is obtained. If the obtained difference is large, we conclude that the scheme provides a high level of security [24].

- **NIST Randomness Test**

The NIST randomness test is a set of statistical tests developed by the National Institute of Standards and Technology (NIST) to evaluate the randomness of sequences, often used in cryptographic applications. When it comes to video encryption, ensuring that the encrypted video data appears random is crucial for security. The more random the encrypted video appears, the harder it is for attackers to decipher it. The NIST randomness test helps verify that the encryption process has effectively scrambled the video data to look completely random. The test consists of 15 different statistical tests given in Table 7.1. According to the probability P- value is calculated for each test. To pass the test, the P -value must be greater than 0.01. If the scheme passes all the tests, then it is considered random.

- **Keyspace analysis**

Keyspace analysis is all about examining the size of the keyspace to ensure it's large enough to protect your video from being decrypted by an unauthorized party.

To decrypt the cipher message, all possible combinations of secret keys are used by the attacker to perform a brute force attack [25]. Suppose a secret key of size p is used in the scheme. In this case,

Table 7.1 NIST 800-22 Test

S.NO	TEST NAME	NUMBER OF SEQUENCES WITH P-VALUE ≥ 0.01	NUMBER OF SEQUENCES WITH P-VALUE < 0.01	PROPORTION SUCCESSFUL	RESULT
1	Frequency test	992	8	0.992	Pass
2	Block frequency test	993	7	0.993	Pass
3	Cumulative sum test	997	3	0.997	Pass
4	Runs test	990	10	0.990	Pass
5	Random excursions variant test	986	14	0.986	Pass
6	Binary matrix rank test	983	17	0.983	Pass
7	Linear complexity test	989	11	0.989	Pass
8	Non-overlapping template matching test	987	13	0.987	Pass
9	Approximate entropy test	992	8	0.992	Pass
10	Random excursions test	987	13	0.987	Pass
11	Overlapping template matching test	988	12	0.988	Pass
12	Maurer's universal statistical test	987	13	0.987	Pass
13	Longest run of ones in a block	989	11	0.989	Pass
14	Discrete Fourier transform test	989	11	0.989	Pass
15	Serial test	988	12	0.988	Pass

the attacker would attempt all 2^p possible combinations to launch an attack on the system. Thus, having a large secret key size saves the system from being attacked by an adversary.

- **Time Analysis**

Time analysis in image and video encryption is all about understanding how quickly and efficiently the encryption and decryption processes can be performed. When you're working with large amounts of data, like high-resolution images or long videos, the time it takes to secure that data can be a critical factor.

The time required to encrypt and decrypt can be analyzed as follows:

The Algorithm Complexity: The time complexity of the algorithm measures the time taken by the algorithm in terms of input size. The complexity focuses on key operations of the algorithms.

Data Size: The file size is also a key attribute in the time required by the algorithm. Larger video files take more encryption and decryption time as compared to shorter video content.

Hardware Performance: A powerful hardware configuration takes less time compared to low-performance hardware.

Algorithm Optimization: Some optimized operations decrease the time required by the algorithm without compromising the security.

- **Histogram Analysis**

Histogram analysis is one of the methods of determining the effectiveness with which the process of encryption has scrambled the video data. This analysis uses histograms, or visual depictions of the distribution of pixel intensities across the frames of a video. These histograms provide a view of the frequency of each intensity value of pixels in the frame [26]. In the video, it is basically a graph with the x-axis representing the range of pixel intensity values (quite often 0 to 255 in 8-bit grayscale graphics) and the y-axis representing the frequency of that value. The value of the intensity of a frame. In an unencrypted video, the histogram may result in patterns, peaks, and valleys that relate to the contents of a video. If a video is realistically encrypted, the histogram of the video frames ought to show equal or random distribution of the pixel intensities, and it will have no particular pattern. The fact that the histogram is randomly distributed is an indicator that the process of encryption has indeed chaotically scrambled the original pixel values, and therefore, the original video material can hardly be found out by an outsider who has no access to the key.

7.4.2 Decryption Parameters

The quality of the decrypted video can be evaluated by such parameters as:

- **Structure Similarity Index Measure (SSIM)**: The Structure Similarity Index Measure (SSIM) is probably the most vital measure that is used to analyze the quality of the decrypted video with the original one. It is also essential in video encryption since it assists in determining the degree to which the structural data and quality of the video are maintained under encoding and decoding. SSIM considers changes in contrast, luminance, and structural information. The formula in Equation (7.5) is used to calculate SSIM. $Px(i,j,k)$ and $x(i,j,k)$ represent the pixel metrics of the original and encrypted video frames, respectively.

$$SSIM = \frac{\left(2\mu_{P_x}\mu_{C_x} + C_1\right)\left(2\sigma_{P_xC_x} + C_2\right)}{\left(\mu_{P_x}^2 + \mu_{C_x}^2 + C_1\right)\left(\sigma_{P_x}^2 + \sigma_{C_x}^2 + C_2\right)} \quad (7.5)$$

Hereμ_{P_x} and μ_{C_x} is the mean of P_x and C_x. The variance of P_x and C_x is $\sigma_{P_x}^2$ and $\sigma_{C_x}^2$, respectively. The covariance of $\sigma_{P_xC_x}$ is given by x and y. $C_1 = (k_1L)^2$ and $C_2 = (k_2L)^2$. Here $k_1 = 0.01$ and $k_2 = 0.03$ and L is equal to the range of pixels. A high SSIM value near 1 is desirable, and it suggests that the decrypted video is very similar to the original video. On the other hand, a low SSIM value indicates video content loss.

- **Bit Correct Ratio (BCR)**

BCR calculates the ratio of error bits to the total bits in an image or video frame. The BCR is computed by contrasting the bits from the original frame and the decrypted video frame. The BCR is expressed as a percentage to evaluate the change in original and decrypted pixel values. The BCR is calculated as follows:

$$BCR = \left(1 - \frac{Number\ of\ error\ bits}{Total\ number\ of\ bits\ in\ the\ frame}\right) \times 100\% \quad (7.6)$$

Here, **error bits give the difference between the original and encrypted pixel values**. A Higher BCR value means the decrypted frame closely resembles the original frame. On the other hand, a lower BCR indicates decryption errors.

- **Mean Absolute Error (MAE)**

MAE measures the average absolute differences between corresponding pixels in the original and encrypted frames. It is computed as follows:

$$MAE = \frac{1}{N}\sum_{i=1}^{N}\left|P_x(i,j,k) - C_x(i,j,k)\right| \tag{7.7}$$

Here: N is the total number of pixels in the frame, $P_x(i,j,k)$ is the original pixel value $C_x(i,j,k)$, and is the cipher pixel value. A high MAE value means high security.

- **Mean Square Error (MSE)**

The resemblance of the original video frame with the cipher video frame can be measured using Mean Square Error (MSE). It is defined as the average of the squared variations in the pixel intensities of the original and decrypted video frames. The goal to of calculating MSE is to quantify the amount of data that is lost or changed during the encryption and decryption processes. A lower MSE value suggests that the decrypted video is similar to the original. A higher MSE value indicates more distortion or information loss [27]. The formula for MSE is:

$$MSE = \frac{1}{a \times b}\sum_{x=1}^{a}\sum_{y=1}^{b}[(L(x,y) - M(x,y))]^2 \tag{7.8}$$

Here (x,y) is the location of the pixel represented by $L(x,y)$ in the original image and $M(x,y)$ cipher video. a and b are the number of rows and columns.

- **Root Mean Square Error (RMSE)**

(RMSE) is the square root of the Mean Square Error (MSE). It measures the distortion or difference introduced during the encryption process. A higher RMSE value denotes a larger discrepancy between the original and encrypted frame [28]. A lower RMSE value, on the other hand, denotes greater similarity between the original and encrypted frame. The formula for calculating RMSE is:

$$RMSE = \sqrt{MSE} = \sqrt{\frac{1}{a \times b}\sum_{x=1}^{a}\sum_{y=1}^{b}[(L(x,y) - M(x,y)]^2} \quad (7.9)$$

Here, $L(x, y)$ is the original video pixel value, and $M(x, y)$ is the cipher video pixel value.

- **Peak-Signal-to-Noise Ratio (PSNR)**

PSNR quantifies the amount of distortion introduced during the encryption process. It is defined as the ratio of the video frame's maximum pixel value to the Root Mean Square Error (RMSE). Usually expressed in decibels (dB), a higher PSNR value denotes less distortion. On the other hand, a lower PSNR value signifies stronger encryption.

$$PSNR = 10 \times \log_{10} \frac{MAX^2}{\text{RMSE}^2} \quad (7.10)$$

Here, MAX is the maximum pixel value in the video frame. It is typically 255 for an 8-bit grayscale video.

- **Signal-to-Distortion Ratio (SDR)**

SDR quantifies the degree to which the information in the original video is retained in comparison to the distortions caused by encryption. A higher SNR value means encryption causes less distortion. Conversely, a lower SNR suggests that the encryption has introduced significant changes. The formula to calculate SNR is:

$$SDR = 10 \times \log_{10}\left(\frac{\sum_{i,j} L(i,j)^2}{\sum_{i,j} L(i,j)^2 - M(i,j)^2}\right) \quad (7.11)$$

Here $L(i, j)$ and $M(i, j)$ is the plain and decrypted video frame pixel value.

Applications of Video summarization and Security

The skill of condensing and deriving valuable information from videos at a fast rate has resulted in the creation of many applications in many disciplines:

Surveillance Systems: Hours of footage are also frequently recorded for security and surveillance. The quick review and analysis of critical events is done by using video summarization without viewing the complete video, such as unusual movement or security breaches, etc. By summarizing the occurrences, security personnel can pay attention to possible threats or incidents.

Suggestion and Preview of Contents: Video summarization is applied in the entertainment and media industries to create highlight reels or trailers of movies, television shows, or sports. As an example, websites such as YouTube or Netflix could generate thumbnails or short snippets to provide users with a preview before they decide to watch the content. Because summarization provides short content about the videos, it enhances user interest.

Education and E-Learning: Videos can be summarized to be used in educational settings to break and divide the long lectures or tutorials into smaller and easier-to-understand parts. This enables students to rapidly peruse important concepts or even highlight specific lines of the lecture without necessarily watching the entire thing. In addition, video summarization may assist in producing teaching synoptic or tutorial headings to jump to important information.

Sports Highlights: Sports broadcasters and platforms are able to produce highlight reels of games through video summarization and bring out key moments such as goals, saves, or turning points. The game will enable the fans to quickly follow up on the games without the need to view the whole event. Video summarization in sports not only enhances the viewing experience but also serves as a performance evaluation and analysis tool.

Healthcare and Medical Records: Physicians often deal with the healthcare business. Recording video footage, such as surgical recordings, patient monitoring, and consultations, is important for memorizing significant information, such as major medical events or steps of the procedure. Techniques can be used to reduce the time spent watching these videos. This enables medical education, diagnosis, and treatment planning.

Forensic Investigation and Analysis: To expeditiously scrutinize video material during interviews, crime scenes, or mass surveillance, law enforcement agencies use the method of video summarization. Identifying the summarized videos can be done without having to go through hours of watching videos, identifying, recreating, or providing important evidence. This is particularly useful in surveys with a strict deadline when urgent analysis is necessary.

References

1. Dhingra, D., & Dua, M. (2023). A novel chaotic map-based encryption scheme for surveillance videos. *Physica Scripta, 98*(12). https://doi.org/10.1088/1402-4896/ad0710.
2. Kumari, S., Dua, M., Dua, S., & Dhingra, D. (2024). A novel Cosine-Cosine chaotic map-based video encryption scheme. *Journal of Engineering and Applied Science*, 1–17. https://doi.org/10.1186/s44147-024-00376-z.
3. Hosny, K. M., Zaki, M. A., Lashin, N. A., Fouda, M. M., & Hamza, H. M. (2023). Multimedia security using encryption: A survey. *IEEE Access*, *11*, 63027–63056. https://doi.org/10.1109/ACCESS.2023.3287858.
4. Matta, P., Arora, M., & Sharma, D. (2021). A comparative survey on data encryption techniques: Big data perspective. *Materials Today: Proceedings*, *46*, 11035–11039. https://doi.org/10.1016/j.matpr.2021.02.153.
5. Tabash, F. K., Izharuddin, M., & Tabash, M. I. (2019). Encryption techniques for H.264/AVC videos: A literature review. *Journal of Information Security and Applications*, *45*, 20–34. https://doi.org/10.1016/j.jisa.2019.01.001.
6. Shafiq, S., Hanif, S., Rehman, F. U., Tariq, K., & Nawaz, A. (2019). Video encryption techniques: A review. In *Proceedings of the 2019 International Conference on Digital Landscaping and Artificial Intelligence (ICD 2019)* (pp. 174–177). https://doi.org/10.1109/ICD47981.2019.9105707.

7. Babatunde, A. N., Abikoye, O. C., & Isiaka, B. Y. (2017). Survey of video encryption algorithms. *Covenant Journal of Informatics and Communication Technology, 5*(1), 65–80.
8. Saleh, M. A., Tahir, N. M., Hisham, E., & Hashim, H. (2015). An analysis and comparison for popular video encryption algorithms. In *2015 IEEE Symposium on Computer Applications and Industrial Electronics (ISCAIE 2015)*, pp. 90–94. https://doi.org/10.1109/ISCAIE.2015.7298334.
9. Negi, Y. (2013). A survey on video encryption techniques. *International Journal of Emerging Technology and Advanced Engineering, 4*, 234–237. Available: www.ijetae.com
10. FLiu, F., & Koenig, H. (2010, February 1). A survey of video encryption algorithms. *Computers & Security, 29*(1), 3–15. https://doi.org/10.1016/j.cose.2009.06.004.
11. Zakaria, A. A., Azni, A. H., Ridzuan, F., Zakaria, N. H., & Daud, M. (2023). Systematic literature review: Trend analysis on the design of lightweight block cipher. *Journal of King Saud University - Computer and Information Sciences, 35*(5), 101550. https://doi.org/10.1016/j.jksuci.2023.04.003.
12. Khan, M., & Shah, T. (2014). A literature review on image encryption techniques. *Autoimmune Highlights, 5*(4). https://doi.org/10.1007/s13319-014-0029-0.
13. Pankaj, S., & Dua, M. (2021). A novel ToCC map and two-level scrambling-based medical image encryption technique. *Network Modeling Analysis in Health Informatics and Bioinformatics, 10*(1), 1–19. https://doi.org/10.1007/s13721-021-00324-4.
14. Radwan, A. G., AbdElHaleem, S. H., & Abd-El-Hafiz, S. K. (2016). Symmetric encryption algorithms using chaotic and non-chaotic generators: A review. *Journal of Advanced Research, 7*(2), 193–208. https://doi.org/10.1016/j.jare.2015.07.002.
15. Dua, S., Kumar, A., Dua, M., & Dhingra, D. (2023). ICFCM-MIE: Improved cosine fractional chaotic map based medical image encryption. *Multimedia Tools and Applications*. https://doi.org/10.1007/s11042-023-17438-8.
16. Ghadirli, H. M., Nodehi, A., & Enayatifar, R. (2019). An overview of encryption algorithms in color images. *Signal Processing, 164*, 163–185. https://doi.org/10.1016/j.sigpro.2019.06.010.
17. Kumar, A., & Dua, M. (2023). Image encryption using a novel hybrid chaotic map and dynamic permutation–diffusion. *Multimedia Tools and Applications*. https://doi.org/10.1007/s11042-023-16817-5.
18. Tresor, L. O., & Sumbwanyambe, M. (2019). A selective image encryption scheme based on 2D DWT, Henon map and 4D Qi hyper-chaos. *IEEE Access, 7*, 103463–103472. https://doi.org/10.1109/ACCESS.2019.2929244.
19. Kanwal, S., et al. (2022). An effective color image encryption based on Henon map, Tent chaotic map, and orthogonal matrices. *Sensors, 22*(12). https://doi.org/10.3390/s22124359.

20. Kumar, A., & Dua, M. (2021). Novel pseudo random key & cosine transformed chaotic maps-based satellite image encryption. *Multimedia Tools and Applications, 80*(18), 27785–27805. https://doi.org/10.1007/s11042-021-10970-5.
21. Kumar, A., & Dua, M. (2022). A GRU and chaos-based novel image encryption approach for transport images. *Multimedia Tools and Applications, 82*(12), 18381–18408. https://doi.org/10.1007/s11042-022-13902-z.
22. Hua, Z., Zhou, Y., & Huang, H. (2019). Cosine-transform-based chaotic system for image encryption. *Information Sciences, 480*, 403–419. https://doi.org/10.1016/j.ins.2018.12.048.
23. Dhingra, D., & Dua, M. (2023). A novel Sine–Tangent–Sine chaotic map and dynamic S-box-based video encryption scheme. *Imaging Science Journal*, 1–24. https://doi.org/10.1080/13682199.2023.2187513.
24. Kumar, A., & Dua, M. (2023). Audio encryption using two chaotic map based dynamic diffusion and double DNA encoding. *Applied Acoustics, 203*, 109196. https://doi.org/10.1016/j.apacoust.2022.109196.
25. Kumar, A., & Dua, M. (2022). A novel chaos map based medical image encryption scheme. *Imaging Science Journal, 69*(5–8), 219–238. https://doi.org/10.1080/13682199.2022.2156669.
26. Dua, M., Kumar, A., Garg, A., & Garg, V. (2022). Multiple image encryption approach using non linear chaotic map and cosine transformation. *International Journal of Information Technology, 14*(3), 1627–1641. https://doi.org/10.1007/s41870-022-00885-1.
27. Bisht, A., Dua, M., & Dua, S. (2019). A novel approach to encrypt multiple images using multiple chaotic maps and chaotic discrete fractional random transform. *Journal of Ambient Intelligence and Humanized Computing, 10*(9), 3519–3531. https://doi.org/10.1007/s12652-018-1072-0.
28. Dua, M., Suthar, A., Garg, A., & Garg, V. (2021). An ILM-cosine transform-based improved approach to image encryption. *Complex & Intelligent Systems, 7*(1), 327–343. https://doi.org/10.1007/s40747-020-00201-z.

8

Recent Trends, Challenges, and Open Issues

8.1 Recent Trends in Audio, Video, and Image Security

The convergence of chaos theory and secret sharing schemes as an effective way of cryptographic security is highlighted in recent studies of multimedia security. Chaos theory has been applied in hyperchaotic maps, real-time encryption, and adaptive algorithms to enhance the security of video, audio, and images due to nonlinear complexity and sensitivity to the initial conditions. Conversely, the division of information into several shares enhances the confidentiality of springing secret sharing, which allows reconstruction of the information at a hierarchical and progressive arrangement of information in varied media. A combination of all these methods forms a full multimedia security system that fulfills emerging opportunities in communication systems.

8.1.1 Recent Trends in Audio Security

The rise of new digital audio spreading services like streaming and real-time communication systems is making audio content security increasingly important. Two advanced methods in mathematics have recently been the focus of attention for developing audio security systems; they are chaos theory and secret sharing schemes.

Chaos Theory in Audio Security: Chaos theory is concerned with a class of deterministic systems exhibiting sensitive dependence on initial conditions, or the butterfly effect. Striking and deeply complex

DOI: 10.1201/9781003500841-8

chaotic systems are very suitable for cryptographic purposes, making entertainment and multimedia data protection one of the huge beneficiaries.

High-Dimensional Chaotic Maps: Simple low-dimensional systems, such as the Logistic and Henon map have limited entropy. Newer research has focused on hyperchaotic systems (systems with more than one positive Lyapunov exponent) such as [1]:

- These systems include Lorenz–Chen, Rossler, and 4D Lorenz-Stenflo systems.
- They increase the key space (often over 10^45), making brute-force attacks nearly impossible.
- Due to their sensitivity, small changes in initial parameters produce significant changes in the encryption, which satisfies Shannon's requirements for confusion and diffusion in strong ciphers.

Real-Time Chaos-Based Audio Encryption: New systems engage in streaming audio chaos encryption with pseudorandom key streams generated from chaotic attractors. These keys are shared between the sender and receiver using communal starting values [2]:

- Chaos synchronization enables two chaotic systems to keep in step with each other, which enhances security as decryption can be performed without sharing the full key over public channels.
- More and more parallel computing and FPGA-based architectures are being used to implement chaotic encryption with sub 10 ms latency, which is critical for VoIP and live broadcasts.

Adaptive Chaotic Key Derivation: There are some schemes that now adapt parameters of the chaotic map based on audio features like energy, pitch, or the frequency spectrum. This aids in creating a fluid visualization of the encryption context, enhancing the strength of defense against known plaintext attacks [3]:

- Audio-perception-based encryption aligns chaotic masking with psychoacoustic importance, ensuring stronger protection for parts of the audio most perceptible to human listeners.

- This fusion of signal processing and chaos theory improves both security and computational efficiency.

Secret Sharing Schemes in Audio Security: Based on the secret sharing of Shamir (1979), such schemes split a secret (e.g., an audio file) into n shares so that an arbitrary $k \leq n$ number of shares can be used to recreate the original, but a smaller number of shares (*k*) will give no information. It is based on the finite field integer power secret sharing. The security is guaranteed by the information-theoretic advantages: even a powerful adversary with (infinite) power cannot access any data using fewer than *k* shares [4].

Multichannel and Spatial Audio Sharing: Multichannel audio is the audio system that uses more than two channels. Each channel carries distinct spatial information to create a realistic and immersive listening experience. Spatial audio focuses on the perception of sound in three-dimensional space. It encodes audio signals as well as other information such as direction and movement. Multichannel audio sharing schemes are: Several multichannel forms of secret sharing have also been pioneered. [5]:

- Channel-wise sharing mechanism can be applied to multichannel audio by dividing the audio channel into various shares, and threshold secret sharing can be applied to them. Reconstruction of the audio requires all the channels.
- Cross-channel Sharing is another method in which one channel is diffused across other channels [6]. The security of the system is enhanced in this case as there is no single channel; they are diffused with each other.
- Spatial audio sharing schemes protect audio content and spatial information. Spatial metadata can be divided into shares and then can be protected using secret sharing schemes.

Hybrid Systems and Theoretical Convergence: Secret sharing schemes and chaos theory can be combined to form hybrid systems. These hybrid systems are powerful two-layer security models [7]:

- First, chaotic encryption introduces nonlinear complexity.
- Then, secret sharing disperses the encrypted audio, creating redundancy and resilience.

From a theoretical lens, these systems utilize complementary entropy models: chaos offers high dynamic complexity, while secret sharing ensures information-theoretic secrecy.

Some systems further integrate blockchain for authentication and quantum-resilient lattice cryptography to future-proof against emerging quantum threats.

8.1.2 Recent Trends in Video Security

Deepfakes, rogue access, and stealing of videos have increased the necessity of video security and have brought strong concerns, particularly in the field of telemedicine, surveillance, remote video conferencing, and entertainment. Researchers have placed their emphasis on the development of such advanced techniques based on mathematics and chaos theory, which provide efficient secret sharing schemes aimed at securing video content. Video streams, unlike still photos, are constructed of a great number of individual images, or frames, which are captured at a much faster rate and bear numerous special demands: Real-time data processing capabilities, high frame rates, inter-frame dependencies, large volumes of data, and also high data resolutions. Chaos theory brings a range of encrypted schemes that increase resistance to cryptanalysis through the introduction of nonlinearity and the re-definition of sensitivity to initial conditions.

Spatiotemporal Chaotic Maps for Video: In contrast to a static picture or a sound file, the content in video comprises a sequence of correlated frames with information about space and time. The spatiotemporal chaotic map encryption schemes incorporate an advanced encryption scheme that deals with the spatiotemporal chaotic maps at the same time [8]:

- Pixel-level permutation: Rearranging spatial data based on chaotic orbits.
- Frame-level diffusion: Altering pixel intensities using chaotic functions frame-by-frame.

Recent studies utilize high-dimensional chaotic systems (e.g., 4D Lorenz-Stenflo, Chen-Liu systems) to encrypt:

- RGB channels either individually or interleaved.

- Frame differentials and temporal motion vectors, which guarantee encryption even for an abridged video stream (e.g., H.264, HEVC).

Real-Time Chaos-Based Video Encryption: Live video uses (VoIP, drone surveillance, and CCTV) require the use of a real-time encryption application [9].

- Efficient, GPU-based, and parallel architecture algorithms have made chaos-based encryption on 1080p video have latencies of less than 30 ms.
- Such features as selective encryption: In selective encryption, only motion regions, DCT coefficient, or ROI (regions of interest) are encrypted, leading to less overhead induction but not compromising security.

Adaptive and Content-Driven Chaos Systems: New research incorporates adaptive mechanisms where encryption parameters evolve based on [10]:

- Scene dynamics (e.g., frame change rate, entropy).
- Object recognition feedback (via AI), which increases encryption intensity in sensitive regions.

This creates context-aware chaos encryption, which dynamically changes the key schedule and fortifies the encryption from known plaintext and chosen ciphertext attacks.

Secret Sharing Schemes in Video Security: Secret sharing splits a video stream into a number of components or "shares" so that only a specified quorum (threshold) can be used to reconstruct the original content[11].

Frame-Wise and Block-Based Secret Sharing Recent implementations apply (k, n)-threshold schemes to [12]:

- Individual frames or macroblocks.
- Compressed bitstreams, maintaining format compliance and avoiding data expansion.
- Advanced schemes reduce computational overhead using:
  - Modular polynomial arithmetic.
  - Sparse coefficient interpolation, enabling high-speed processing for high-resolution video.

Spatiotemporal Distribution of Shares: For enhanced security and redundancy, video shares are distributed in space and time:

- Spatial distribution: Distribution of shares on various cloud or edge servers.
- Temporal distribution: Surely, consecutive shares are sent by a path in streaming applications, so MITM attacks cannot receive the whole video.

Progressive Reconstruction in Video: New frameworks for hierarchical reconstruction where [13]:

- Poor quality previews can be constructed with minimal shares.
- Restoration quality of full quality needs all shares.

This is best suited for access-controlled environments, multi-tier video platforms, and pay-per-view.

8.1.3 Recent Trends in Image Security

The swift expansion of digital imaging into areas including healthcare, defense, social media, and surveillance has made image data a critical asset that needs advanced protection. Conventional cryptographic methods are therefore often insufficient because of the large size, redundancy, and structural correlation of the image data. Recent methods in image security are centered around two powerful paradigms: chaos theory and secret sharing schemes. These techniques provide highly secure frameworks that are appropriate for image security.

Chaos theory takes advantage of its unique characteristics of unpredictability and sensitivity to initial conditions. The permutation and diffusion phases are the pillars of chaotic map-based encryption schemes. These properties are very instrumental for image encryption because of the pixel-wise structure and statistical properties of images.

Hyperchaotic Systems: Unlike simple chaotic systems (e.g., the Logistic Map or the Tent Map), hyperchaotic systems have multiple positive Lyapunov exponents, which guarantee more complicated trajectories and improved key space. Key advances include the following [14]:

As an example, the studies include the following topics:

- 2D, 3D, and 4D hyperchaotic maps (e.g., Lorenz, Chen, Rossler, and Lu systems).
- Generation of huge key spaces (often >10^50) to prevent brute-force attacks.
- Application of chaotic scrambling to the pixel positions (permutation) and pixel values (diffusion), often in two stages in order to maximize the entropy.

Pixel-Level and Block-Level Encryption: Chaos-based image encryption techniques often use [15]:

- Pixel permutation: Reordering pixel positions using chaotic sequences.
- Value diffusion: Modifying pixel intensities using XOR operations guided by chaotic sequences.
- Hybrid transformations: Combining chaotic maps with Discrete Wavelet Transform (DWT), Discrete Cosine Transform (DCT), or Singular Value Decomposition (SVD) for frequency-domain security.

Adaptive and Content-Driven Chaos: Advanced encryption schemes dynamically adapt chaotic parameters based on image characteristics [16]:

- Histogram-adaptive systems alter encryption based on brightness distribution.
- Edge-aware models use image features (edges, textures) to prioritize encryption in perceptually significant regions.

These systems ensure not only security but also perceptual robustness and efficient computation.

Secret Sharing Schemes in Image Security: Secret sharing is a technique of partitioning a secret image into n shares such that at least k shares are required for reconstruction. Below k, no information is leaked, which satisfies perfect secrecy conditions [17]. Shamir's Secret Sharing Adaptations Standard (k,n) threshold schemes have been adapted for grayscale and color images using [18]:

- Pixel-wise polynomial encoding using finite fields.
- Matrix-based transformations for multi-layer images.
- Visual cryptography, where shares are noise and do not require any computation to be reconstructed—especially appropriate for biometric and document protection.

Progressive and Region-Based Secret Sharing: Recently, some schemes are available for progressive reconstruction of images, in which the number of shares provides an increasing amount of image quality, which is also useful for tiered or conditional access applications. Moreover [19]:

- ROI-based schemes are focused on Region of Interest (ROI, e.g., faces in medical images) and protecting sensitive parts more heavily.
- Channel-based sharing applies individual schemes to RGB or CMYK channels separately in order to increase the robustness.

Image Authentication and Tamper Detection: Secret sharing is also applied in fragile watermarking, where image integrity can be verified [20]:

- Tamper-evident shares are generated such that any modification leads to incorrect reconstruction.
- Authentication mechanisms using parity checks and redundancy validate the authenticity of reconstructed images.

Hybrid Chaos and Secret Sharing Frameworks: The merging of chaos theory and secret sharing allows defense-in-depth [21]:

- Layered Security: Images are first encrypted with the help of hyper chaotic systems, and then we use secret sharing.
- Hyperchaotic algorithms are used to encrypt the images first and then secret share them.
- Share-Level Chaos: Each share is precipitated separately with the use of chaotic parameters.
- Distributed Recovery: To enable the distributed storage of data in a cloud or to involve multiple parties in accessing by remote collaboration, more than one party needs to contribute to the reconstruction.

8.2 Open Issues and Challenges

The following section is a synthesis and categorization of the substantial open issues and challenges discovered in the recent research publications on audio, video, and image security in dealing with chaos-based encryption and secret sharing schemes.

Audio Security Challenges: The existence of an audio data explosion leads to solving certain cryptographic and implementation issues:

- Efficiency and Complexity: It is not possible to deploy chaos-based audio encryption in real-time applications on the grounds of battling for computational efficiency and complexity and expenditure of resources. Theoretical research about the optimization of chaos and the acceleration of the hardware techniques could defeat this challenge.
- Synchronization Robustness: Reliably synchronizing chaotic systems is one of the major propulsion challenges of noise and network neutral nodes; practical developments of advanced synchronization theory (e.g., adaptive synchronization or noise resilient algorithms) are fundamental for putting theory into real-world use.
- Adaptive Parameter Stability: The utilization of the chaotic feature extraction-based stimulus-based audio parameter modulation poses a menace to the stability of the system, which afterward reduces security and consistency. Further research is required to reduce the domain stability and control strategy, and also the chaotic systems.
- Secure Key Management: Sophisticated sharing and distribution of the parameters for their chaotic encryption for the specific case of distributed playgrounds is still unsolved. Improvements in the theory of cryptographic protocols and secure multiparty computation provide stripe solutions for those cases.
- Scalability of Secret Sharing Schemes: The high-fidelity concepts of secret sharing schemes using heuristic enhancements are hence ineffectively scalable in terms of storage and computational expenditure. Improvement of the theory of polynomial interpolation and optimization of arithmetic in finite fields may provide such edges.

- Quantum Threat Mitigation: When the application of audio encryption is made more difficult due to certain techniques such as lattice-based cryptography that are seen to work in quantum computing due to the efficiency and interoperability of the latter. Research on quantum computing and post-quantum cryptography is required.
- Balancing Security with Audio Quality: Securing Communication Balance between safety and quality of audio, there is an ongoing tension between security concerns for the communication and audio quality concerns.

Video Security Challenges: The huge volume, correlation between pixels, frames, and complex structure of video data makes video encryption a really challenging task. Various challenges involved in video security are as follows:

- Real-Time Processing: The encryption techniques for the high-definition video streams in a real-time environment are very challenging. Parallel processing and optimization algorithms are required in this area to meet these requirements.
- Parameter Control Mechanism: The security of chaotic map-based video encryption schemes directly depends on the initial seed and control parameter. Initialization, selection, and securing those parameters are the key components of chaotic map-based security systems. These tasks need a lot of attention for designing robust mechanisms.
- High-Dimensional Chaotic System Complexity: Although high-dimensional chaotic systems can generate large pseudorandom sequences that are beneficial for encryption, the implementation of high-dimensional chaotic maps is very complex and time-consuming.
- Preserving Video Quality: Video encryption causes jitter, which may degrade the video quality. Preserving the video quality after the encryption and decryption process is also a big challenge in the field.
- Selective Encryption Challenges: In the case of full video encryption, the whole video frame is encrypted; on the other hand, in selective encryption, only the specific parts of the video bitstream are encrypted to achieve a balance between security

and computational efficiency. These specific parts of the bitstream are called syntax elements. Various key syntax elements commonly considered in selective video encryption are motion vectors, transform coefficients, intra prediction mode, slice data, and many more. The selection of these syntax elements for encryption is a challenging task in video encryption.

- Inter-frame Dependency Management: Frames of the video are dependent on each other. Their dependency on each other is encrypted to protect the content from eavesdropping. The research is open in this scenario as very few works have been done in this area.
- Network Robustness: The loss of packets and jitter also compromises the integrity of the video encryption.

Image Security Challenges: The unique structural correlation and redundancy data found within images pose particular difficulties for encryption.

- Image Complexity: It is still quite challenging to keep a high level of encryption and at the same time minimize the necessary computational resources, particularly in the case of high-resolution images. There is a very strong need for research geared toward reducing algorithmic complexity and optimization.
- Control Theory Security: The security breach risks of dynamically adapting chaotic parameters that are founded on the specific image characteristics increase the risk of being exploited. Both adaptive control theory and chaos theory point to directions of exploitation for this issue.
- Vulnerability to Image Processing: There is significant underdevelopment of robust cryptographic algorithms and encryption techniques that are resilient against common image processing and compression methods and can retain their integrity against image concealment.
- Secure Key Management: Distributed environments are a challenge for the management of large keys generated from hyper chaotic systems (more than 10^50 possibilities). Potential improvement can be gained from key distribution theory and secure multiparty computation paradigms.

- ROI Encryption Complexity: The practical challenge of encrypting sensitive metadata without performance degradation, data leakage, or exposure is a big hurdle to overcome. Image processing theories, as well as cryptographic masking methods, can help.
- Visual cryptography Enhancements: Dealing with visual cryptography for color images and complex graphics without dramatically increasing data volume and developing visual cryptographic encoding schemes is an unbiased, unsolved issue that needs further research.
- Tamper Detection and Integrity Verification: Development of delicate but extremely secure tamper-detection strategies that can reliably detect intentional changes over benign ones requires new theories of watermarking and authentication algorithms.

References

1. Babu, S. G., & Ilango, P. (2013, April). Higher dimensional chaos for Audio encryption. In *2013 IEEE Symposium on Computational Intelligence in Cyber Security (CICS)* (pp. 52–58). IEEE.
2. Kafetzis, I., Volos, C., Nistazakis, H. E., Goudos, S., & Bardis, N. G. (2023, June). A real-time chaos-based audio encryption scheme. In *2023 12th International Conference on Modern Circuits and Systems Technologies (MOCAST)* (pp. 1–4). IEEE.
3. Abdelfatah, R. I. (2020). Audio encryption scheme using self-adaptive bit scrambling and two multi chaotic-based dynamic DNA computations. *IEEE Access*, *8*, 69894–69907.
4. Bharti, S. S., Gupta, M., & Agarwal, S. (2018). A novel approach for verifiable (n, n) audio secret sharing scheme. *Multimedia Tools and Applications*, *77*(19), 25629–25657.
5. Disch, S., Ertel, C., Faller, C., Herre, J., Hilpert, J., Hoelzer, A., ... Spenger, C. (2004, October). Spatial audio coding: Next-generation efficient and compatible coding of multi-channel audio. In *Audio Engineering Society Convention* (p. 117). Audio Engineering Society.
6. Liu, F., Zhu, X., Feng, P., & Zeng, L. (2023). Anomaly detection via progressive reconstruction and hierarchical feature fusion. *Sensors*, *23*(21), 8750.
7. Niu, F., & Nian, X. (2025). Predefined-time convergence strategies for multi-cluster games in hybrid heterogeneous systems. *Nonlinear Analysis: Hybrid Systems*, *55*, 101537.

8. Al-Saeed, S. J., & Mahmood, A. S. (2025, April). Securing videos using chaotic maps in a parallel processing environment. In *AIP Conference Proceedings* (Vol. 3282, No. 1, p. 030010). AIP Publishing LLC.
9. Bajaj, H., Das, P., & Mandal, S. (2025). Chaos based novel video encryption scheme to secure video/image information from any AI-generated attacks. *Methods*, *50*(1), 1–20.
10. Sangwan, N., & Bhatnagar, V. (2025). Multi-branch LSTM encoded latent features with CNN-LSTM for Youtube popularity prediction. *Scientific Reports*, *15*(1), 2508.
11. Jabbari, A., & Fung, C. (2025). A privacy-preserving surveillance video sharing scheme: Storage, authentication, and joint retrieval. *Journal of Network and Systems Management*, *33*(1), 7.
12. Sadek, M. M., Khalifa, A. S., & Mostafa, M. G. (2015). Video steganography: A comprehensive review. *Multimedia tools and applications*, *74*, 7063–7094.
13. Zheng, Z., Zhong, H., Hu, Q., Zhang, X., Song, L., Zhang, Y., & Wang, Y. (2024, October). HPC: Hierarchical progressive coding framework for volumetric video. In *Proceedings of the 32nd ACM International Conference on Multimedia* (pp. 7937–7946). ACM.
14. Wang, Y., & Yang, F. (2021). A fractional-order CNN hyperchaotic system for image encryption algorithm. *Physica Scripta*, *96*(3), 035209.
15. Hanif, M., Iqbal, N., Ur Rahman, F., Khan, M. A., Ghazal, T. M., Abbas, S., ... Yeun, C. Y. (2022). A novel grayscale image encryption scheme based on the block-level swapping of pixels and the chaotic system. *Sensors*, *22*(16), 6243.
16. Zhang, L. X., & Leung, B. W. (2023). Context matters: Adaptation of student-centred education in China school music classrooms. *Music Education Research*, *25*(4), 418–434.
17. Zhao, R., Zhao, J. J., Dai, F., & Zhao, F. Q. (2009). A new image secret sharing scheme to identify cheaters. *Computer Standards & Interfaces*, *31*(1), 252–257.
18. Ulutas, M., Ulutas, G., & Nabiyev, V. V. (2011). Medical image security and EPR hiding using Shamir's secret sharing scheme. *Journal of Systems and Software*, *84*(3), 341–353.
19. Liu, Y., Sun, Q., Yang, Z., Zhou, Y., Zhao, W., & Shi, D. (2024). Progressive reconstruction on region-based secret image sharing. *Electronics*, *13*(8), 1529.
20. Chennamma, H. R., & Madhushree, B. (2023). A comprehensive survey on image authentication for tamper detection with localization. *Multimedia Tools and Applications*, *82*(2), 1873–1904.
21. Umar, T., Nadeem, M., & Anwer, F. (2024). Chaos based image encryption scheme to secure sensitive multimedia content in cloud storage. *Expert Systems with Applications*, *257*, 125050.

9 IMPLEMENTATION AND ADOPTABILITY OF THE MULTIMEDIA ENCRYPTION STRATEGIES USING PYTHON

9.1 Platforms Supporting Implementation

9.1.1 Python

The foundation of this implementation is Python because it has a huge ecosystem and support. To do numerical calculations, image/audio/video processing, and encryption algorithms, the best version is Python 3.9 or above, as it is compatible with most of the libraries.

9.1.2 Anaconda

Anaconda is a user-friendly and simple environment that works efficiently. It includes popular data science libraries by default and integrates smoothly with Jupyter Notebook, making it ideal for developing and testing encryption algorithms.

9.1.3 Jupyter Notebook

Jupyter Notebook enhances the development experience by allowing code execution, visualization, and documentation in a single interface. It is especially useful for demonstrating the step-by-step execution of encryption algorithms and for visualizing multimedia data.

DOI: 10.1201/9781003500841-9

9.2 Python Libraries for Chaotic Map-Based Encryption

Python provides a rich ecosystem for image, audio, and video processing for chaotic map-based encryption schemes; some of the libraries are presented in Table 9.1.

9.3 Installation of Libraries

To set up the development environment, install the necessary packages with the following commands:

```
pip install numpy matplotlib opencv-python pydub moviepy cryptography sympy scipy pillow scikit-image soundfile for audio and video processing, ensure that FFmpeg is installed
```

Table 9.1 Python Libraries for Image, Audio, and Video Processing

LIBRARY	PURPOSE
NumPy	Supports numerical computations and matrix operations required in chaotic systems.
Matplotlib	Visualizes encryption effects on data, such as histograms or encrypted image outputs.
OpenCV-Python	Handles image and video preprocessing and pixel-level encryption.
PyDub	Used for audio file manipulation and transformation in encryption workflows.
MoviePy	Enables video editing and per-frame processing for encryption.
Cryptography	Implements standard encryption functions, often combined with chaotic techniques
SymPy	Assists in symbolic calculations, useful for chaos system formulations.
SciPy	Offers signal processing and interpolation tools crucial for multimedia encryption
PIL/Pillow	Simplifies image loading and pixel manipulation needed before and after encryption.
Scikit-image	Facilitates advanced image processing techniques.
Wave	Provides tools to read/write .wav audio files for encryption at the byte level.
SoundFile	Enables efficient I/O for audio files, especially useful for time-domain encryption.
FFmpeg	Processes multimedia streams, used indirectly via wrapper libraries.
ChaosLib	Implements different chaotic maps (e.g., Logistic, Henon, Lorenz) for use in encryption
PyChaotic	Python library for generating chaotic sequences essential in encryption algorithms.

For audio/video processing, install FFmpeg:
Linux/macOS: sudo apt install ffmpeg
Windows: Download from ffmpeg.org and add to PATH.

For chaos-specific packages:

```
pip install chaospy pychaotic
```

9.3.1 Environment Setup with Anaconda

Step 1: Install Anaconda

- Download and install Anaconda from the official website.
- Verify with: conda—version

Step 2: Launch Jupyter Notebook

```
jupyter notebook
```

Step 3: Create Virtual Environment

```
conda create --name chaos_env python=3.9
conda activate chaos_env
pip install numpy matplotlib opencv-python pydub moviepy cryptog-
raphy sympy scipy pillow scikit-image soundfile chaospy pychaotic
jupyter notebook
```

This environment is optimized for implementing chaotic map-based encryption across image, audio, and video data.

9.4 Python Implementation Code

The application of encryption techniques using chaotic maps is demonstrated in this section and how these systems can be applied to carry out secure multimedia processing. It discusses how to create chaotic sequences, draw them, code them, and share secrets with the help of Python and its companion modules. We have developed powerful and effective encryption codes through chaos theory.

9.4.1 Creating Chaotic Sequence

The logistic map is the discrete map which is simple to implement. The logistic map is iterated in function 1 to generate a chaotic sequence. This sequence can be used as a pseudorandom key that can be used to encrypt images, audio, video, etc.

Function 1 : *Creating Logistic Map Chaotic Sequence*
Input : r, x, n
$sequence = [\ ]$ $for\_in range(n):$ $x = r * x * (1 - x)$ $sequence.append(x)$ $return\ sequence$
Output : $sequence$

The logistic function's control parameter r shows chaos, in between [3.5, 4.0]. The initial seed satisfies the condition $0 < x < 1$. The logistic map Equation (9.1) is iterated n times to produce a chaotic sequence of length n. With the help of the logistic map, the function creates a list with n chaotic values.

$$x = r * x * (1 - x) \tag{9.1}$$

Our values are $r = 3.99$, $x_0 = 0.5$, and $n = 1000$. The map generates an unpredictable and random sequence that changes drastically as we vary the initial conditions. This sequence can be used in the permutation and diffusion processes of encryption algorithms to protect the data [1, 2]. These chaotic sequences can be used as secret keys; in others, they can be used as S-boxes or as chaotic matrices that help to produce robust algorithms.

9.4.2 Analyzing Chaotic maps

The analysis of chaotic maps is a must before using them in an algorithm. The randomness and unpredictable nature of the chaotic maps guarantee the security of the algorithm in which they are applied. Bifurcation diagram and Lyapunov exponent are used in this section to analyze characteristics of the chaotic map.

Bifurcation diagrams show the variation of chaotic values produced by the map with respect to the control settings. Lyapunov exponents measure the rate at which two near trajectories separate from each other [2, 3].

By using these parameters, we can confirm that the chaotic values produced by the map produce a safe encryption algorithm. Implementations and explanations of these evaluation parameters are provided in this section.

- **Analysis of Bifurcation Diagrams:**

An effective visual aid for analyzing the dynamics of a chaotic system as its control parameter changes is given by the bifurcation diagram. The bifurcation diagram for the logistic map illustrates its long-term behavior, which changes from stable, predictable behavior to complex, chaotic dynamics. The construction of the bifurcation diagram involves a horizontal axis that represents value of r from 0 to 4. To analyze the long-term behavior of the map, the first 100 iterations are discarded to pass the transient behavior. The value of x is plotted on the vertical axis. In the range $0 < r < 1$ the population approaches 0, there is a single line along the x-axis. In the range $1 < r < 3$ the population produces a stable fixed point. For $3 < r \approx 3.57$ first bifurcation occurs at $r = 3$ the single stable point becomes unstable and the system oscillates between two distinct values. This is known as period doubling. As we further increase r, it splits into four values. For $r \approx 3.57$ the system shows a chaotic nature. We can see an infinite number of non-repeating values within a certain range [4, 5]. The pseudocode to visualize the bifurcation diagram is given in Function 2.

Function 2 : *Draw Bifurcation Diagram*

Input : x, r

```
import matplotlib.pyplot as plt
r_values = np.linspace(2.5,4.0,10000)
x = 1e − 5
iterations = 1000
last = 100
rs, xs = [],[]
for r in r_values :
 x = 1e − 5
 for i in range(iterations) :
  x = r * x * (1 − x)
  if i ≥ (iterations − last) :
    rs.append(r)
    xs.append(x)
plt.figure(figsize = (10,7))
plt.plot(rs, xs,',k', alpha = 0.25)
plt.title("Bifurcation diagram")
plt.xlabel("r")
plt.ylabel("x")
plt.show()
```

Output : *Bifurcation Diagram*

r_values generates a range of values for the control parameter *r* from 2.5 to 4.0. It is the initial condition of the logistic map. *Iterations* represent total iterations to evolve the map for each *r*. *Values* is the number of iterations considered for plotting (to ignore transients). *rs*, *xs* are lists to store control parameters and corresponding output values. The nested loop runs the logistic map for each r and stores the last 100 values. The plot function visualizes the result. The bifurcation diagram illustrates how the behavior of the logistic map changes with r. The presence of a chaotic regime (irregular, dense points) versus periodic regions (discrete bands) helps verify suitable r values for secure chaotic encryption.

This analysis ensures the chosen control parameter leads to a strong chaotic behavior suitable for cryptographic use.

- **Lyapunov Exponent Analysis**

The Lyapunov exponent is a key statistic used in the study of nonlinear dynamical systems to describe how sensitive a system is to initial conditions. A characteristic of chaos is a positive Lyapunov exponent, which means that adjacent paths in the phase space diverge exponentially with time [6, 7]. Function 3 examines the underlying mathematical ideas and provides a Python implementation of the Lyapunov exponent.

Function3 : *lyapunov_exponent*
Input : r, x_0, n

$x = x_0$
$lyap = 0$
$for\, i\, in\, range(n):$
    $x = r * x * (1 - x)$
    $lyap += np.log(abs(r * (1 - 2 * x)))$
$return\, lyap / n$
$\#Example$
$r\_val = 3.99$
$x\_init = 0.4$
$n\_iter = 1000$

Output : *lyapunov_exponent*

This derivative quantifies how a small change in the current value of x affects the next value in the sequence. The Lyapunov exponent is a numerical indication of the stability or chaotic behavior of the system when averaged across a large number of repetitions.

9.4.3 Image Encryption Using Chaotic Map

Chaos-based systems have drawn a lot of interest in the field of picture encryption because of their intrinsic qualities, which include ergodicity, pseudorandom behavior, and sensitivity to initial conditions. Function 4 presents pseudocode of an image algorithm that is based on the logistic map.

***Function* 4** : *Image Encryption using Logistic map*

Input : *image*

```
import cv2
import numpy as np
#Load grayscale image
image = cv2.imread('input.jpg', cv2.IMREAD_GRAYSCALE)
rows, cols = image.shape
size = rows * cols
#Flatten image
flat_img = image.flatten()
#Generate logistic map sequence
r = 3.99
x0 = 0.5
sequence = logistic_map(r, x0, size)
indices = np.argsort(sequence)
# Permutation process
permuted_img = flat_img[indices]
#Diffusion process
key_stream = np.floor

    (255 * np.array(logistic_map(r, 0.7, size))).astype(np.uint8)
diffused_img = np.bitwise_xor(permuted_img, key_stream)
# Reshape and save
encrypted_image = diffused_img.reshape((rows, cols))
cv2.imwrite('encrypted_image_perm_diff.jpg', encrypted_image)
```

Output : *encrypted image*

- The image is first compressed into a one-dimensional array. By treating pixel values as a linear series, this transformation streamlines the encryption process.

The permutation and diffusion processes are based on a chaotic sequence that is created using a logistic map. The logistic map is iterated using parameter $r = 3.9$, $x_0 = 0.5$.

- Permutation Phase: Using the sorted indices from the chaotic sequence, the pixels of the flattened image are rearranged in this step [8, 9]. A crucial stage in hiding visual information is the disruption of the spatial connection between neighboring pixels.
- Diffusion Phase: Starting with another beginning condition and another chaotic sequence, this phase involves the creation of a key stream. In order to accommodate the number of pixel values, this stream is represented and converted into 8-bit unsigned integers. To change pixel intensity values pseudorandomly, the XOR operation is done between the key stream and the permuted image. This move will enhance its statistical properties, increasing the resistance of the encrypted image against differential attacks and statistical attacks.
- The final encrypted image is reshaped back to its original two-dimensional format and saved to disk.

9.4.4 Video Encryption Using Chaotic map

The nature of video encryption has made it a very critical component of secure communication systems due to the increase in multimedia information. In this part, there is a frame-by-frame chaotic system encryption scheme. The methodology particularly involves the utilization of the logistic map to generate frame-dependent pseudorandom keys, which ensures cryptographic strength and time fluctuation [10, 11]. Function 5 provides the pseudocode for encrypting video with the help of a logistic map.

Function 5 : *Image Encryption using Logistic map*
Input : *image*

```
import cv2
import numpy as np
cap = cv2.VideoCapture('input_video.mp4')
fourcc = cv2.VideoWriter_fourcc(*'mp4v')
out = cv2.VideoWriter
('encrypted_video.mp4', fourcc, 20.0, (int(cap.get(3)), int(cap.get(4))))
frame_count = 0 while cap.isOpened():
  ret, frame = cap.read()
  if not ret:
    break
  gray = cv2.cvtColor(frame, cv2.COLOR_BGR2GRAY)
  rows, cols = gray.shape
  flat = gray.flatten()
  key = logistic_map(3.99, 0.5 + 0.01 * frame_count, rows * cols)
  key_scaled = np.floor(255 * np.array(key)).astype(np.uint8)
  encrypted = np.bitwise_xor(flat, key_scaled).reshape(rows, cols)
  encrypted_bgr = cv2.cvtColor(encrypted, cv2.COLOR_GRAY2BGR)
  out.write(encrypted_bgr)
  frame_count += 1
cap.release()
out.release()
```

- Initialization and Video I/O Configuration: Video input and output streams are prepared in advance of the encryption process. In order to load the input video file, one must use cv2. VideoCapture(). VideoWriter_fourcc makes the codec MP4V compatible. VideoWriter() sets the video writer with the original size of the frame and a frame rate of 20 FPS.
- Logistic Map-Based Key Generation: A key sequence is generated using a one-dimensional logistic map, where r is set to 3.99 for chaotic behavior, and the initial condition varies with the frame count to ensure temporal uniqueness:

- XOR-Based Diffusion Encryption: Pixel-wise XOR is performed between the flattened grayscale video frame and the generated key stream.
- This diffusion process obfuscates pixel values in a nonlinear and highly sensitive manner, effectively removing visual coherence in the encrypted frame.

9.4.5 Audio Encryption Using Chaotic Map

Numerous algorithms have been developed to encrypt audio files with chaotic systems like [12]. The section implements audio encryption using a chaotic sequence derived from the logistic map. The key steps are as follows:

1. **Audio File Loading**:

The code takes an input .wav file (input_audio.wav) as input. It extracts all the audio parameters and frame data and stores them to be used later during the encryption process and writing the output.

2. **Data Conversion**:

The raw audio frames are converted into a NumPy array of 16-bit signed integers (int16) to facilitate numerical manipulation.

3. **Chaotic Key Generation**:

A chaotic sequence is generated using the logistic map—a well-known chaotic function defined as $x\left[n+1\right]=r^{*}x\left[n\right]^{*}\left(1-x\left[n\right]\right)$, where $r=3.99$ and $x\left[0\right]=0.5$ [13]. The sequence is scaled to the range of 16-bit integers to match the audio sample data.

4. **Encryption via XOR Operation**:

A sample-wise bitwise XOR operation is performed between the original audio samples and the scaled chaotic key sequence. This effectively masks the original signal, producing an encrypted version.

5. **Saving the Encrypted Audio**:

The encrypted sample array is then written to a new .wav file (encrypted _audio.wav), preserving the original audio format parameters.

Function 6 presents the pseudocode of the encryption algorithms that use the logistic map to encrypt the audio file.

Function 6 : Audio encryption using chaotic map
Input : *A* udio file

import wave
import numpy as np
import struct
# Load audio file 	
with wave.open('input_audio.wav','rb') as wf :
  params = wf.getparams()
  frames = wf.readframes(params.nframes)
#Convert audio frames to numpy array
samples = np.frombuffer(frames, dtype = np.int16)
#Generate chaotic sequence
key = logistic_map(3.99,0.5, len(samples))
*key_scaled = np.floor(32767 * np.array(key)).astype(np.int16)*
#XOR encryption
encrypted_samples = np.bitwise_xor(samples, key_scaled)
#Save encrypted audio
with wave.open('encrypted_audio.wav','wb') as wf :
  wf.setparams(params)
  *wf.writeframes(encrypted_samples.**tobytes**())*

Output : *encrypted_audio*

9.4.6 Secret Sharing Scheme Using Logistic Chaotic Map

In the implementation of the secret sharing scheme, a secret (e.g., a pixel value or key) is split into multiple shares using a chaotic map-based approach. The idea is to create pseudorandom values influenced by chaotic behavior and distribute parts of the secret in a way that only a certain number of shares (threshold) can reconstruct it.

A chaotic map generates random sequences. These sequences modify the secret and produce different shares. Shares are distributed to participants. Reconstruction is only possible if the threshold number of shares is available.

```
import numpy as np
#Logistic map function
def logistic_map(r, x, n):
  seq = []
  for _ in range(n):
    x = r * x * (1 - x)
    seq.append(x)
  return seq
#Split secret into shares
def chaotic_secret_sharing

  (secret, n_shares = 5, threshold = 3, r = 3.99, x0 = 0.4):
chaotic_seq = logistic_map(r, x0, n_shares)
shares = []
random_parts = np.random.randint(0, 256, threshold - 1)
final_part = secret
for part in random_parts:
  final_part ^= part
for i in range(threshold - 1):
  shares.append((i + 1, random_parts[i]))
shares.append((threshold, final_part))
return shares
#Reconstruct secret from shares
def reconstruct_secret(shares):
  secret = 0
  for _, val in shares:
    secret ^= val
  return secret
#Example usage
original_secret = 123
shares = chaotic_secret_sharing(original_secret)
print("Shares:", shares)
# Assume we collect threshold shares
selected_shares = shares[:3]
recovered_secret = reconstruct_secret(selected_shares)
print("Recovered Secret:", recovered_secret)
```

The chaotic_secret_sharing function uses XOR-based secret splitting. It ensures the secret is recoverable only when the minimum required number of shares (threshold) is available. The chaotic logistic map contributes randomness for variability and security.

References

1. Hua, Z., Zhou, Y., & Huang, H. (2019). Cosine-transform-based chaotic system for image encryption. *Information Sciences*, *480*, 403–419. https://doi.org/10.1016/j.ins.2018.12.048.
2. Dhingra, D., & Dua, M. (2023). A novel chaotic map-based encryption scheme for surveillance videos. *Physica Scripta*, *98*(12). https://doi.org/10.1088/1402-4896/ad0710.
3. Sharma, M. (2020). Image encryption based on a new 2D logistic adjusted logistic map. *Multimedia Tools and Applications*, *79*, 355–374. https://doi.org/10.1007/s11042-019-08079-x.
4. Naim, M., & Ali Pacha, A. (2023). New chaotic satellite image encryption by using some or all the rounds of the AES algorithm. *Information Security Journal*, *32*(3), 187–211. https://doi.org/10.1080/19393555.2021.1982082.
5. Bisht, A., Dua, M., & Dua, S. (2018). A novel approach to encrypt multiple images using multiple chaotic maps and chaotic discrete fractional random transform. *Journal of Ambient Intelligence and Humanized Computing*, *10*, 3519–3531. https://doi.org/10.1007/s12652-018-1072-0.
6. Dua, M., Suthar, A., Garg, A., & Garg, V. (2021). An ILM-cosine transform-based improved approach to image encryption. *Complex & Intelligent Systems*, 7(1), 327–343. https://doi.org/10.1007/s40747-020-00201-z.
7. Dua, S., Kumar, A., Dua, M., & Dhingra, D. (2024). ICFCM-MIE: Improved Cosine Fractional Chaotic Map based Medical Image Encryption. *Multimedia Tools and Applications*. https://doi.org/10.1007/s11042-023-17438-8.
8. Masood, F., et al. (2021). A lightweight chaos-based medical image encryption scheme using random shuffling and XOR operations. *Wireless Personal Communications*. https://doi.org/10.1007/s11277-021-08584-z.
9. Dhingra, D., & Dua, M. (2024). A novel video encryption scheme using chaotic map based simultaneous permutation-diffusion. In *2024 International Conference on Computing, Electronics & Electrical Engineering and Their Applications (IC2E3 2024)* (pp. 1–5). IEEE. https://doi.org/10.1109/IC2E362166.2024.10826646.
10. Hua, Z., Jin, F., Xu, B., & Huang, H. (2018). 2D Logistic-Sine-coupling map for image encryption. *Signal Processing*, *149*, 148–161. https://doi.org/10.1016/j.sigpro.2018.03.010.

11. Dua, M., Kumar, R., Dua, S., & Chakravarty, N. (2025). A novel one-dimensional chaotic map, novel diffusion and DNA encoding-based image encryption scheme. *International Journal of Dynamics and Control, 13*(5). https://doi.org/10.1007/s40435-025-01653-2.
12. Kumar, A., & Dua, M. (2023). Audio encryption using two chaotic map based dynamic diffusion and double DNA encoding. *Applied Acoustics, 203*, 109196. https://doi.org/10.1016/j.apacoust.2022.109196.
13. Kumar, A., & Dua, M. (2022). A GRU and chaos-based novel image encryption approach for transport images. *Multimedia Tools and Applications*, 18381–18408. https://doi.org/10.1007/s11042-022-13902-z.

For Product Safety Concerns and Information please contact our EU representative GPSR@taylorandfrancis.com
Taylor & Francis Verlag GmbH, Kaufingerstraße 24, 80331 München, Germany

www.ingramcontent.com/pod-product-compliance
Ingram Content Group UK Ltd.
Pitfield, Milton Keynes, MK11 3LW, UK
UKHW020202200926
475702UK00004B/583